Flutie

Flutie

By Doug Flutie
with Perry Lefko

SPORTS PUBLISHING INC.
A **SPORTS**MASTERS Book

© 1999 Revised Edition
© 1998 Douglas Flutie & Perry Lefko

ISBN 1-58382-021-3
Library of Congress Catalog Card # 99-60246

SPORTS PUBLISHING INC.
A **SPORTS**MASTERS Book

www.SportsPublishingInc.com

First published by:
Warwick Publishing Inc.
• 162 John Street, Third Floor, Toronto, ON M5V 2E5
• 1300 North Alexandria Avenue, Los Angeles, CA 90027

Distributed in Canada by:
Firefly Books Ltd.
3680 Victoria Park Avenue, Willowdale, Canada, M2H 3K1

Jacket Design: Kimberley Young, mercer digital design, Toronto
Front Cover Photograph: Jack Boland, Toronto Sun
Back Cover Photo: Jack Boland, Toronto Sun

Printed and bound in Canada by Webcom Ltd., Toronto

To Laurie, for being there from the start and supporting me in good times and bad, and to my children, Alexa and Dougie, who mean the world to me.
— *Doug Flutie*

To my wife Jane, the MVP — Most Valuable Person — in my life, and our two children — Ben and Shayna, and the 1971 Toronto Argonauts. The greatest team that didn't win a Grey Cup.
— *Perry Lefko*

Acknowledgements

When I first approached Doug Flutie about writing this book he had lukewarm interest. "I don't think my life's that interesting," he said matter-of-factly.

Imagine someone who has met Ronald Reagan and George Bush and talked football with them, had Donald Trump pursue him with a record $8.3 million contract, played drums with Jon Bon Jovi, had *Saturday Night Live* parody him, and captured the attention of an entire continent of sports fans with a single play, saying he didn't have an interesting life! But that is Doug Flutie, who can best be described as a tremendous athlete with a modest ego.

Doug Flutie's accomplishments — beginning with his exploits in college, in which he transformed an unranked school into a national contender, then continuing into a record-setting pro career — have made him one of the all-time greats in football history. Flutie is so respected, both as an individual and an athlete, that the likes of Donald Trump, Mike Ditka and Tom Coughlin generously gave of their time to be interviewed for this book. In particular, Tom Coughlin (head coach of the NFL's Jacksonville Jaguars), was effusive in his praise of Doug and added: "Don't hesitate to call if you need anything else." As a sports journalist I can attest that this kind response to an interview is very rare.

Doug Flutie may be modest about himself and what he has done in his life, but there are enough people who are willing to trumpet his accomplishments. Ultimately, however, this book would not have happened without Doug's willingness and cooperation. For that I am grateful.

Thanks to Jim Williamson and Nick Pitt of Warwick Publishing, who supported it from the outset, and Kristen Kuliga of Woolf Associates, who coordinated the efforts of both authors.

In addition special thanks to *Toronto Sun* sports editor Scott Morrison and the entire sports department.

Thanks to the *Sun* computer department, particularly Jeff Rickard for technical advice.

Thanks to the library staffs of the *Toronto Sun*, particularly Julie Kirsh and Jillian Goddard, the *Calgary Sun, Edmonton Sun, Boston Globe, Buffalo News, Chicago Tribune, Newark Star-Ledger, Vancouver Province* and *Orlando Sun-Times.*

Thanks to the *Toronto Sun* photo department, particularly Wanda Goodwin, Dania Santos and Mel Clarke. Also Mark Murphy of the *Middlesex News* in Massachusetts for supplying photos of Doug's early life.

Thanks, in particular to publicists Reid Oslin, Gary Croke, Roger Kelly, Ron Rooke, Dave Watkins and Gary Lawless for background information.

A special thank you to the Jacksonville Jaguars media relations department for setting up the interview with Tom Coughlin, and to the Trump organization, which set up the interview with Donald Trump.

And thanks to the numerous writers such as Kent Spencer, Kent Gilchrist, Eric Francis, Don Pierson and Chris Thorne, who offered their insights.

And thanks to the organizations of the Toronto Argonauts, Calgary Stampeders, B.C. Lions, New England Patriots, Chicago Bears, New York Cityhawks and New Jersey Generals for all their help — even if the Generals are alive only in spirit.

And to all those who were interviewed and offered their insights, recollections and assistance, a special thank you.

Thanks to the Buffalo News' Bob Summers (Happy Handicapper) for all of his help in providing material about Doug's Buffalo year for this book.

Last but not least, a personal thank you to my brother Elliott for his expert editing and advice.

Perry Lefko,
Toronto, Canada

Table of Contents

"Without the Hail Mary, I think I would have been easily forgotten. Fame is fleeting, especially for college athletes. I'd probably be just another guy who won the Heisman Trophy. But that play has given me a mystique or an aura. Everybody believes now that there is no situation that is out of the question for me. If anybody's gonna do it, I'm gonna do it."

—Doug Flutie, November 1985, *USA Today*

Introduction

Sometimes I can't believe what's happened to me. I made a name for myself in sports history throwing a pass that everyone remembers, which isn't necessarily a bad thing. I'm often reminded of the Hail Mary when I make a similar type of play.

So much has happened since that game in Miami. I've won the Heisman Trophy, played in three professional leagues — the United States Football League, the National Football League, and the Canadian Football League — signed record contracts, won championship games and most valuable player awards and suffered through a contract squabble I hope to never go through again.

I've had so many things happen to me — good and bad — because of football and yet I still love the game and want to keep playing as long as I'm healthy and can make a contribution. I never expected any of this. I just played football because it was fun.

The thing that really amazes me looking back is that I felt I was very fortunate to play major college football because of my size: 5 foot 10, 175 pounds. I'm in my 14th year of professional football and that amazes me more than anything. It doesn't feel to me like I've been playing pro ball for that long, but to look back on it and to say I played a year in the USFL, four years in the NFL, seven years in the CFL, and now I'm back in the NFL — well, that amazes me more than anything else.

I've always said football chose me, I didn't choose it. I loved playing all sports. I loved playing basketball — it's always been my first love — and I loved playing baseball, but it became evident to me in high school that the attention and the college scholarship opportunities were coming from football, so that was the direction I went. I thought I was equally as good at all three sports in high school, and I didn't really have a game of preference — except basketball was the most fun to play.

Growing up I definitely didn't dream of playing in the CFL. If you're talking about aspirations, yes, it was the NFL, but I wasn't looking that far ahead. I was just trying to look at the next couple of years or the next level. The first time I'd ever heard of or seen the CFL was on TV when I was 11 or 12. I didn't watch a lot of it — maybe a handful of games — but I loved football regardless and I would have watched any football growing up. If there had been flag football on TV, I would have watched that. If there was arena football or whatever, I would have watched that.

My wife, Laurie, has always supported me in everything I've done and has always been there. I'm sure she didn't like having to go to Vancouver or to travel as much as we have. When I played in New England it was the easiest of all. All the traveling has made it hard on the family, but this is the lifestyle. Every chance I've had to come home during the season, I've done it to be with Laurie and the kids.

I have a daughter, Alexa, who was born in 1988, and a son, Dougie, who was born in 1991. Alexa is a good athlete and loves to play soccer. Dougie developed a form of autism when he turned three and while it has not impacted on my career, it has made a huge impact on my life. I wouldn't trade him for anyone in the world. He's the happiest kid I've ever seen. He's always smiling, he never cries and his face lights up when I walk into the room — that makes your day. Yeah, he struggles and doesn't speak and we're working with him on his education. But if anything it makes you stop taking things for granted. It makes me appreciate the fact I have a hundred percent healthy daughter and maybe I never appreciated that fact before.

Dougie is my son and I'm very proud of him and the things he does. I thoroughly enjoy being around him. It is a strain sometimes and a lot of work, but Laurie is unbelievable with Dougie. She spends so much time and gives so much effort. We have private tutors for him after school and there's a one-to-one tutor with him throughout a six-hour day of school. Just to feed him is a chore. It's a step-by-step procedure trying to get him to understand how to use a fork or how to drink from a glass. Every little thing is a major, major step for him. It's just a lot of work and takes a lot of patience but it puts everything else in perspective. It tells you how insignificant football really is.

When I'm not playing football, I like to relax by playing drums. Music was never a huge part of our lives — my father played in a dance band in the late 60s and early 70s in the Baltimore area — but there was always a keyboard in the house or something to mess around on. While we were never musicians growing up — I took trumpet lessons in junior high school — I'd always wanted to play the drums, and Laurie bought me a drum kit for Christmas the first year of our marriage. I was 22 and just fooled around in the basement. My brother Darren started learning to play guitar about the same time. It was never a big deal to us; we were just fooling around having fun. That's the way it's always been and that's the way it is now.

We started getting together with guys — just jamming and having fun in the basement — and it started sounding pretty good. The guys in the band said we sounded better than a lot of bands they played with, so we scheduled a few gigs. Originally we called ourselves Catch This, but the group is now known as the Flutie Brothers. It isn't to make money — that's for darn sure — more than anything it's to have fun. We'd been doing it for four years when we recorded an album with Danger Records in Toronto in 1995. I don't see the thing going much further than it has, although we've had some opportunities to play some pretty good-sized shows and have a lot of fun with it. And that's all it's about, having some fun. If we make a couple bucks on the side, that's fine, but we've probably spent more money than we've made paying for equipment. Like I said, it's just fun. I have no intentions of quitting football to become a full-time musician.

I don't really think about what's going on at the moment so

much. It's more year by year, game by game, week by week or day by day. At the end of each season, you get to look back and be proud of what you've accomplished. Everybody strives to be remembered. A buddy of mine, Scott McGhee, used to say, "I strive to have been a has-been." It's like you want to have made your mark in one way or another. It's very important for me to win MVP honors. If I could win a sixth that would make it that much more special. I'd love to try and get an undefeated season one year. Those are things that people are going to remember. They're going to remember the pass out of Miami. They're going to remember the Heisman Trophy. They're going to remember that I've won all those MVPs and those types of things. That's how an athlete lives on, especially because your career is so short. I've been very fortunate to play as long as I have. A lot of guys play four or five years and that's it; sometimes even less.

The part of it that the average person might not understand is that I don't feel like I'm doing anything special. I'm doing what I enjoy doing, but I'm just fighting to survive year after year. Every year that you go back to play, there is a little bit of doubt. It's kind of scary that you want to be successful and you think to yourself, "was I a little bit lucky last year? Did things just happen to fall into place?" If you don't stay on edge like that and you don't keep focusing on what you're doing, you have a tendency to become complacent.

I look around me and see the things that people do better than me and that keeps me on edge. I don't know what I'm trying to say, but you don't have a lot of time to stop and smell the roses along the way. You wind up just fighting to make it each year and to survive and keep playing. Then after it's all said and done, you have time to sit back and reflect on it.

Growing Up

I was born in Baltimore and grew up in the inner city in Catonsville, where we rented a small place in a district with brick houses all interconnected. It was anything but high rent. I remember playing football in the side yard with my sister Denise, who is two years older and my brother Bill, who is a year older. Darren is four years younger than me. We hated it when Denise played because she was always bigger and we couldn't tackle her. Those are my only sports memories from that time.

When I was three or four we moved out to Manchester, primarily for money reasons, and lived with my mom's parents, William and Thelma Rhodes, for a couple of years. My dad — Richard — worked for Black & Decker in research and development.

I grew up an Orioles fan and I have these visions of my grandfather sitting there drinking his beer and watching the Orioles play all the time. Jim Palmer was my favorite pitcher and the first player I really looked up to who wore number 22, which became my favorite jersey number, although I haven't always been able to wear it. Sometimes it's been because of the rules — in the National Football League quarterbacks are only allowed to have numbers from one to 19 — other times it's because the number belonged to another player on the team or was already retired. I've always tried to have 2 as part of the jersey number wherever I've played.

I remember watching a Baltimore Colts game and going to Memorial Stadium. It was kind of neat almost 30 years later playing for Calgary at Memorial Stadium against Baltimore when it entered the CFL in 1994. I had gone to many Orioles games at Memorial Stadium in between that time frame, but it just brought back memories of being there as a young kid watching the Colts play.

Each year we would vacation at Ocean City, Maryland, and stay at a beach house. It was just a big group of people that always went — my cousins and everyone. But I remember a picture of me, probably at age four, lying on the floor, falling asleep with a football in my arms. If there was any foreshadowing, that was it.

We moved down to Florida when I was six and I attended Gemini Elementary School. We started out in athletics when Bill registered for Farm League baseball at the age of eight. We went to some of his games and my dad became all frustrated that the guy coaching Bill didn't know what he was doing. Bill was a decent athlete, but he wasn't getting any good coaching. Neither my mom — Joan — nor my dad were really true athletes. My dad played a little junior varsity basketball, while my mom played basketball in high school. Once my dad saw Bill's interest in sports and athletics, he took a definite interest. He started checking out books from the libraries, reading up on coaching, figuring out what is the correct way to do things. He started coaching Bill the next year in Little League. My mom coached my sister and ran the concession stands at the Little League field. We practically lived at the ball field. Dinner was a hot dog at the concession stand. My mom would get there early and open it up.

Even though I was only a year younger than Bill, by Little League standards I was only seven and my dad put me into the Farm League a year early. I was one of those kids who stood there with the bat on his shoulder, didn't swing at the ball and wanted to get his walk. The whole situation kind of intimidated me. I came back the next year and all of a sudden, I was pitching, playing shortstop, hitting the ball and becoming frustrated with the kids around me because they didn't know what they were doing.

It was that year my dad built a little pitcher's mound and

home plate in the backyard. I pitched at a contraption that was like two volleyball poles with a net across it and a hole in the middle that was the strike zone. My brother and I would play games where the idea was just to throw strikes. You walked batters or struck them out. At that age it was very difficult to be consistent enough to throw strikes, and the idea was to try not to walk in a run or walk four guys before you strike out three. Obviously at that time we'd pick up a little football and throw that around in the backyard as well.

Across the road from the house we rented lived an elderly couple who had a basketball net on a pole cemented into the ground. All the kids in the neighborhood went over there to play, and the couple never minded. They never used the basket anyway, so one day we dug it all up, put a chain around it and dragged it across the street with the car and set the hoop up in our driveway. Then all the kids were playing at our house.

It was always that way for us. My dad always went out of his way to do things for us. We didn't have a lot of money at the time. We were always making it paycheck to paycheck. There were times when the hot water was turned off or you'd have to boil the water on the stove and heat the tub that way. We always knew when the paycheck was coming and we'd stop off at McDonald's on the way home or go out to dinner. I always just assumed everybody didn't have things.

The good part was that when my dad decided to coach, he always had the Little League equipment or the basketballs for the recreational teams. And that was a big deal. We always had decent equipment to play our pickup games and throw the ball around in the backyard. We always had all the kids at our house playing basketball or going to Farm League practice. My dad or mom would pick everybody up and drive them to the field. From age eight to twelve, while my parents were busy coaching and coordinating games, we'd go to Hoover Junior High School on Saturday morning at eight and come home at six in the evening.

Bill and I played together in Little League and then in football. We began with flag football and then turned to tackle. Bill was always a good athlete, but I did things with a bit of a flair.

Darren was always the little rug rat that ran around. I started out the first year of tackle football at age nine sitting on the bench, getting in three or four plays a game on the kickoff or kickoff return team. I weighed about 63 pounds and I really wasn't heavy enough to make the minimum limit, which was about 68 pounds. They kept pushing me to the side, not letting me play, but about midway through the year I had a chance to get in late in the game as a free safety. Teams rarely threw the ball, but I almost intercepted two passes and because of my aggressiveness they decided to let me play the following week. I made an interception and some tackles and you could see some of my athletic ability starting to come through— this was with an age group ranging from nine to twelve.

Bill was always the quarterback. At 10 I moved over to offense, started playing running back and other things, and made the all-star team. Bill made the all-star team at 12. We had some undefeated teams in baseball and basketball and won some championships, but our football teams never did well. I think 3-7 was our best season. We lived in the South Beaches area in Melbourne. We had a lot of surfers in the area who were not into organized team sports.

I played quarterback in flag football — Bill and I both bounced between quarterback and receiver — and beginning at age 11 in tackle football also. I was bored because all I did was hand off, so the following year I asked to play running back. I enjoyed that a lot more and my running skills really came through.

When I was 12 we played in the Pop Warner League. The all-star team was always a big deal at the end of the year because you went into tournaments. I was hoping to make the all-star team and did, but not at running back because I injured myself messing around in the front yard with Darren. He was eight at the time, and I pretended to run and let him tackle me. I gave him a little fake and sort of fell into him. I broke my left foot, cracking the fifth metatarsal bone on the outside. I don't know how it happened. I guess I planted my foot the wrong way. I wasn't wearing any shoes because you never wore shoes in

Florida. You just rolled out of bed and threw on a pair of shorts. Anyway, I just limped back in the house and kind of crawled on the floor. My mom realized something was wrong. I ignored it for a day, but finally the pain was so bad I had to go to the hospital. They determined it was broken and put me in a walking cast for what was supposed to be four weeks.

At the end of the first week it felt fine to me. It felt like I could move around really well and I became really frustrated, so I made the doctors remove the cast. The following week I played on the all-star team as a defensive lineman and had a couple sacks. It was fun for me to be a part of it because I thought I wasn't going to get a chance to play at all after the injury.

That wasn't my first injury. Two years before, I broke a finger wrestling a kid named Timmy Burklew on my Little League team. I played basketball for a couple weeks with a splint on my right hand, so I tried playing left-handed. I scored just a couple points, but I had a chance to play and that was a big deal.

It seemed like I had all-around bad luck with Timmy. He was pitching in Little League and walked a batter and threw the ball to the ground in disgust, and the kid he walked ran to second. I was covering second and Timmy wheeled and gunned it. The ball hit me smack in the nose and I dropped like a ton of bricks. The kid took off for third and I scooped up the ball and threw him out. The next thing I knew there was blood all over the place and I got light headed and dizzy. They had to take me to the hospital where it was determined I had broken my nose.

We moved to Natick, about 17 miles west of Boston, when I was 13. I was finishing up eighth grade in the spring, but I was put in seventh grade because I was so much younger than most of the kids in the eighth at that time. It put me an extra year behind Bill, but it also gave me an extra year to mature as an athlete.

We used to play sandlot baseball on a piece of land that was part of an estate. There was a stone wall for a fence and it was a pretty nice setup. We used to take our own lawn mowers up there to cut the field. We would line it and dig out areas for the bases and really make it look like a baseball field. We used to play there all the time. We used to play street hockey out front. We'd turn the patio area into a little baseball diamond and play what we'd call cupball. You'd take two paper cups and put one inside the other and pitch it and hit it with your hand. You could throw the ball at the runner, things like that. We just made up our own games, made up our own fields. It was what we did. It was our life. After school we'd spend every night just playing.

They didn't have a Pop Warner program, so my father got involved with the people in the town and got a league started. It was basically just my age bracket. The coaches always loved my instincts on the field, so they let me call my own plays. I could run a no-huddle situation. I was one of those kids who watched the NFL and guys like Terry Bradshaw, Roger Staubach, Bert Jones — who was a favorite of mine — and Fran Tarkenton. I always used to criticize the quarterbacks because of the way they used their timeouts. Why didn't they call it here? Why didn't they call it there? They wasted twenty seconds or wasted five seconds on the clock. They could have done it differently. I always looked at the game from that perspective.

That was the first time I was on a winning football team. We went something like 8-2. At the same time, my dad took Darren to the next town over, Wellesley, so he could start playing tackle football. He played for a year and then came back to Natick. By that time they had established a decent program for all age brackets. Denise started running the cheerleading squads and my mom became involved as well.

After Pop Warner, I started playing junior high school football. I had a coach named Kirk Buschenfeldt, who was probably one of the first people to realize I was thinking ahead of the other guys. He made me memorize all the plays and the formations that go with them so I could call my own plays. Here I was at age 14, in ninth grade at junior high school, calling my own plays and running my own show. It always made me try to think ahead.

KIRK BUSCHENFELDT:

He was the quarterback right away. We had another kid who was probably as good, if not a better athlete than Doug was, that played tailback. Unfortunately, he was quite the opposite of what Doug was and ended up in prison and what have you and never finished his school career.

But Doug was the smartest one. Not only was he a tremendous athlete, but he had the brains to go along with it. That's where he stood out. Looking at the way Larry Bird was with the Celtics, he always seemed to be two plays ahead of everybody. Doug's the same way. He still is. He's always anticipating and thinking ahead. Instead of always reacting to situations, he was always anticipating situations, and his reactions were so much more on the mark because of that.

Even at that young age he had that knack of being able to think ahead and anticipate. We called plays from the sidelines, but there were situations where we just let him go because he had such a feel for the game. He was such an intelligent player. That was certainly unusual, letting him call plays. There was no other quarterback we allowed to do that.

Kirk Buschenfeldt told my high-school coaches that he thought there was something special about me, and to give me a look and not let me get lost in the shuffle. Kirk told them he thought I had the best hand-eye coordination of any athlete he had ever seen. The first day the high school coaches made me practice with all the sophomores at the other field. I did very well, but I was just working my butt off because it was the first day I had ever heard of practising twice a day. The second day they brought me up to the varsity for the afternoon practice and let me play with them.

Within a couple days they just kept me with the varsity and I started rotating in at free safety and wide receiver — but they knew I was a quarterback.

We started out 3-0, but we struggled offensively. The fourth game we played Wellesley, a team we should have beaten, but lost 8-6. Our coach, Tom Lamb, was really upset about it. The next day, for the junior varsity game against Wellesley, I was at quarterback with all these guys that were pretty damn good. They were basically your starters for the varsity. Anybody that was an underclassman could play. We scored 52 points. I guess that was my testing ground, because the next week against Milton, I started at quarterback and Bill was moved to receiver. Now, both of us never left the field.

TOM LAMB:

Coming out of that previous game, the coaching staff met and made the decision Billy would go to wide receiver and Doug would go to quarterback. That JV game was a good way to give him an extra game, too, with a little bit lesser competition to work with those kids. So we turned it up and let him throw a lot and really turn it loose. When you score a lot of points in a JV game you say, "That's good, looks like we made the right move, it looks like he's ready."

The thing that I remember the most is probably one of the bigger problems you would have in making that move in starting a sophomore quarterback is both the reaction of the player and the parents of the quarterback you're displacing. In this particular case it wasn't too much of a problem. They were the same parents, so we were replacing Billy with Doug and it seemed to be a pretty natural one.

In the first half against Milton I threw four interceptions. The coaches were kind of second-guessing themselves, but in the second half I threw three touchdowns to Bill. We scored a mess of points and won the game. We took off and started winning games. Bill and I never left the field. We returned kicks and punts. I was the field goal kicker and kickoff guy, and Bill was the punter. I hadn't even thought about trying out as a kicker for the varsity, but Bill said to the coach, "Bring Doug over here and let him show you how he kicks the ball." I walked over and Bill said, "Just tee one up and kick it." I stood there, put the ball on the tee, took my shoe off, took a step-and-a-half back and kicked the ball about 50 yards. The coach was pretty amazed that, number one, I kicked it as far as I did, and number two, I kicked it barefoot with the toe.

As I said before, we never wore shoes in Florida, and I kicked field goals with my friend Mark McLean, who always hung around with Bill and me. I didn't know Mark kicked soccer-style, so I learned to kick the darn thing with my toe straight on. I did that for the first few weeks of the year and then they bought me a square toe shoe, which I used as the year went on. It turned out to be a useful piece of equipment — sort of. In the final game of my sophomore year against Braintree, the opposition scored late in the final minute of the game to lead 25-24. We took possession with 19 seconds left and I threw three straight balls to Bill, who fell down to his knees on the final catch at the 21-yard line with three seconds left on the clock. I had kicked extra points but never any field goals, and this was a 38-yarder.

I went to the sidelines to put the square toe shoe on, but I couldn't get my regular shoe off. The coaches had to rip it off my foot. When I tried to tie the square toe shoe on, the shoelace broke, so I tied that off half way down. While I was rushing to do this, I didn't have any time to become nervous about the kick. I just ran out, lined up — Bill was the holder — and I pumped the thing through. I probably hit the best ball of my life.

TOM LAMB:

It was one of those things where there weren't a lot of decisions to make. We had a chance at a field goal, and he hadn't kicked a field goal in a game, but we knew his range pretty well. We gave it a shot and he was amazing.

BILL FLUTIE:

It was a shocker. I don't think the Braintree guys thought it was a realistic thing and they kind of didn't even rush. They stood there, and Doug just pumped that thing. It sailed way over the goalpost. It would have made it from 50 yards out. No question. He just bombed it straight through down the middle.

During that year I was seeing a girl named Mary Kushmerick. She came to all my games and I watched her ride her horses at her shows. After the Braintree game, my wife-to-be, Laurie Fortier, came up and congratulated me. We sat next to each other in home room. She was really a sports nut and Mary never really was. I don't even know if she was at that game. The week before, against Wellesley, Laurie and a friend were driven to the game. They walked home probably five or six miles because they didn't have a ride back.

Laurie still tells the story of the first day of school in our sophomore year. We sat in home room and went together through orientation. I held the door open for her. She told her friends at lunch she found the guy she wanted to marry and then went home and told her mom. We started dating at the end of that sophomore year.

All through high school I was always a real quiet kid. I kept my mouth shut, kept my nose clean. Never drank. Never smoked. Said "Yes sir", "No sir." Never swore. I got very good grades. I was on the honor society in my senior year with straight As, but my whole life revolved around sports. School was a necessary evil. I went to my classes. I studied for tests because it was a challenge trying to get a good mark, but I wasn't gung-ho on getting the grades to get to a good school.

Basketball was always my first love. I made the varsity as a sophomore, played point guard, and was a co-captain. I quit baseball in my sophomore year to work at an ice cream stand because we had the telephone turned off and my dad couldn't pay the bills. I worked for about two months and made enough to pay the phone bills. I got the phone re-connected so I could call Laurie, whom I had just started dating.

My three sports were basically baseball, basketball and football, but it was always evident the opportunities were going to come in football. We had some great finishes. I had a bunch of last-second victories going back to junior high. The coaches trusted my decision making. I would audible things off and just look at the defensive fronts and make the calls, mostly within the running game. I got a feel for using audibles and doing things at the line of scrimmage. I was getting really good at running no-huddle offenses and two-minute offenses throughout high school. I was all-state in football, but never made it to that level in baseball and basketball, in which I was all-league.

I started getting recruited in my senior year by all the major universities. Everybody started sending me letters and was talking to me. The only schools willing to give me scholarships were Division 1-AA schools, such as Holy Cross, Boston University and University of New Hampshire. I really liked my visit at UNH, but none of the Division 1 schools were going to offer me a scholarship because of my size, and that became frustrating for me.

I remember a guy from Ohio State coming to the school to recruit me. The first thing he asked was if I could dunk a basketball. Of course I couldn't. I was basically 5'-9". I could get up around the rim, but I couldn't dunk the ball. He said, "Let's face it, you're not going to be a quarterback at the Division 1 level. You're a good athlete. You might be a defensive back; you might be a wide receiver." That kind of stuck in my craw. I didn't like being told I wasn't good at something. I had had a handful of coaches hint to me I wouldn't make it as a quarterback, but no one really came out and said it.

I wanted to go to Harvard because of the prestige. Harvard played Yale every year, and ABC televised it. I knew that I could play at that level, and to be on TV would have been a big deal. That would have been a nationally televised thing. When it came down to it, Boston College played a big-time schedule. They played Alabama, Clemson, Penn State. Even though it wasn't a really established school at that time, I realized that was what I wanted. But I wasn't getting the offer from Boston College yet, and it was getting frustrating.

If I was going to take a scholarship, it was going to be University of New Hampshire because I really enjoyed my visit there. It was either that or go to a place like Harvard, but then we would have had problems with finances. We didn't have a lot of money. I would have had all the loans to pay off and it just wouldn't have been a good situation. But a series of coincidences — call it luck or fortune smiling my way — gave me my big break.

Ed Chlebek, the head coach from Boston College, resigned and Jack Bicknell, a guy from Maine who had been recruiting me at one time, took over. Now they were scrambling around trying to sign athletes, and it was late in the recruiting season. One of the quarterbacks BC wanted, Pete Muldoon, signed with Holy Cross. Steve Peach, who they also really wanted, went to Syracuse. So, Boston College didn't get the top two quarterbacks it wanted. Then it offered me a scholarship. It's been written in articles about me that I was given the last scholarship offered by BC that year, but it was one of the last three or four. At that point, Boston College was just bringing in athletes. The coaching staff knew that even if I wasn't going to be a quarterback, I was a decent athlete regardless and maybe I could help out at another position.

Tom Lamb and Barry Gallup (who was the recruiting coordinator at Boston College, the receivers' coach and probably my best friend during my college years) knew one another for a long time. They had played opposite one another in college when Tom was at Holy Cross and Barry was at Boston College. Tom first spoke to Barry about me during my junior year, telling him I was a special athlete.

TOM LAMB:

We felt from day one that he was special. A lot of people have asked me, "Did you know he would be a Heisman Trophy winner?" I don't think anybody knows that, but you knew from the things like the field goal in the sophomore year and other kinds of things there was something special here. After working with him for a couple of years, you knew this was special and this kind of athlete doesn't come along every day.

That's the kind of thing we tried to communicate to Barry and to Jack Bicknell and other people, too. Jack and Barry were the two who spent time really researching it and in the end ended up agreeing with us. The one thing I can still remember saying to Barry and to Jack was that he's special. They wanted him at least as an athlete and I can remember saying, "If you put him in at quarterback he'll never get out of there so you'd better not put him in unless you're serious about it."

BARRY GALLUP:

I said, "Tom, he's a great athlete, but he's not really big — where's he going to play? He can't really be a quarterback?" In Doug's senior year, Tom said, "Barry, you've got to look at him again. He does too many things too well. He's just a winner." After the season we looked at him and I said to Tom, "We'll keep him in mind. He's not someone we're going to offer a scholarship to right now, but keep in touch."

Tom called me in late January and I said, "Bring in some film and we'll look at him." He brought in four game films. I'll always remember it. In one of them Doug kicked the winning field goal with no time left on the clock, and he had never kicked a high-school field goal before. The other game film he had three interceptions as a defensive back. He really looked athletic. The third film he scrambled all over the place. The fourth film he threw the ball really well. Late in the recruiting process we had some scholarships left. Doug was a local player with a good reputation and good grades and we thought he would play some place for us.

I'll always remember going to his house and his dad had a lot of questions about academics because Doug's older brother Billy was at Brown. His dad kept talking about the computers. He wanted computer science for Doug. He said Harvard had a great program there and wondered how good was BC's. We told him it was good but that he'd have to investigate that more fully. I still have a picture at my house of Doug signing the national letter of intent. I'll always remember walking out the door and the last thing his dad said to me was, "I don't think you know what you're getting." He always told me that later. He said, "Barry, I told you you were getting something special."

My big break came that summer when I played in the Massachusetts Shriners high school all-star game at Boston College. The coaching staff was around and there were all these high-profile guys from the area. Steve Peach quarterbacked the North team, which also had Mark Bavarro who played tight end as a professional for the New York Giants. I was the only Division 1 scholarship guy that was playing for my side and we were heavy underdogs. I threw a couple touchdown passes, did a lot of running around and we won the game in an upset. I won the MVP award and I think I made my mark as a quarterback in that game. I kind of opened the eyes of the coaching staff — I did have a good arm and could do other things. I think that gave me the opportunity to play quarterback at Boston College.

The Road to the Heisman

When I got to Boston College I was probably about eighth on the depth chart. All these upperclassmen were ahead of me and within the first couple weeks it became really frustrating. My first freshman roommate, Gerard Phelan, who caught the famous Hail Mary pass I threw, looked like he was going to get some playing time as a wide receiver — even though he was recruited as a running back — and I felt I was as good an athlete as he was. Yet, here I was, buried on the depth chart and not anywhere close to playing. I contemplated asking them to move me to a different position where I could have a better chance to play.

I was about fourth-string on the depth chart by the end of training camp. The first-string quarterback, John Loughery, who was a junior, tore a ligament in his thumb, and the second and third-string guys, Doug Guyer and Dennis Scala, who were also juniors, played the first three games. They couldn't do the job. We were getting blown out. John Loughery played the fourth game against Penn State and he completed only one of 15 passes for two yards. At halftime, Barry Gallup told me to loosen up because I might get a chance to play. I thought, "Yeah, right." Here we are at Penn State. There's 85,000 fans in the seats. I just shook my head at Barry.

JACK BICKNELL:

When we recruited him we promised him the opportunity to play quarterback and we were committed to him, certainly for that first

*year. We had no idea whether he could do it or not. I had seen every-
body else in live play. We had three older quarterbacks that I had
basically inherited because it was my first year at BC and I hadn't
seen anything that really excited me. I just wanted to make sure I
saw everybody.*

Around the start of the fourth quarter they told me to start
warming up. We were losing 38-0. I remember walking onto the
field, with the sun shining brightly. I thought this was something I could tell my kids or grandkids about some day. I figured it was probably a one-time shot, that I'd go out and mess
around and play the last few series.

We had the ball on the 22-yard line, and the coaches called
the plays. On the third down of my first series, I sprinted out
and completed a 15-yard pass to Brian Brennan. Three plays later,
it was another third-down situation and Howie Brown ran the
draw for 18 yards. The next play I threw 20 yards to Kevin Ben-
jamin to make it to Penn State's 23. On the next play I hit tight
end Scott Nizolek on a 23-yard touchdown. Three passes, three
completions, 58 yards. It was easy. Just take your read, throw
the ball and hit the guy who was open. The protection was good
and I was relaxed in the game situation. I think that's what
amazed the coaches.

We had one more possession and marched the length of the
field. I talked the coaches into changing the play near the goal
line and we didn't get it into the end zone. I was intercepted at
the two-yard line. Coach Bicknell came up to me afterward and
gave me an earful about me being young and talking him into
doing something he didn't want. That was the last time it would
happen. I felt kind of stupid at the time, because here I was going from not expecting to go out on to the field to telling the
head coach what I wanted to run.

I completed 8 of 18 passes for 135 yards and had one interception and one touchdown.

Not bad for a debut.

JACK BICKNELL:

It was just like somebody turned a switch and all of a sudden, everything was going at a faster pace. Instead of just being out there, we're moving up and down the field, and it became obvious in a very short period of time that this guy was special. He was never really special in practice. He was okay, but he wasn't getting much opportunity to show what he could do because we had other guys that were ahead of him. But, from that point on, there was never any doubt that this guy was special, and he started every game after that for his entire career.

It wasn't like we had to rethink and say, "Well, we'll start the seniors and let this kid see what he can do." From that time on it was obvious to me, as the head coach, that this was the guy we were going to play at quarterback. As it turned out, he just kept getting better and better and he made everybody around him play better and better. As a result we were a better team. We didn't have really great talent at the time. We had a very young team. We had mostly kids in his class that were the keys to the future, but he just made everyone around him play better and it was obvious he was the guy.

The following week I started against Navy and had a mediocre game. We lost 25-10, but the coaching staff stuck with me for the next game against Army. I lit it up, completing 15 of 21 passes for 244 yards and 3 touchdowns. We won 41-6 and that got my confidence going.

Then we played Pittsburgh, ranked No. 2 in the country with the No. 1 defense. The Panthers were quarterbacked by Dan Marino. We made all kinds of mistakes in the first half, and Pittsburgh led 29-10. But I realized, just like in the Penn State game, as long as I took my reads and threw the ball, people were open. We were moving the ball and narrowed the lead to 29-24. It was the first game I did some fancy things, like falling down and shoveling the ball, throwing left-handed. A lot of those instinctive plays were coming out. We had a chance to win the game when Todd Russell intercepted a pass and was tackled by Marino at Pitt's eight-yard line. We ran the option the next play and I pitched the ball to Geoff Townsend, who later played pro with the Argos. He got hit and fumbled. With four and a half minutes left, we made it to Pitt's nine-yard line. But we were pushed back to the 23 on a penalty and a sack. Then John Cooper missed a field goal.

I completed 23 of 42 for 347 yards and had two touchdown passes and two interceptions. That was the first time people started noticing the things I could do. We played four more games that year and won three. I finished among the top 10 in the country in quarterback efficiency ratings, with 105 completions in 192 attempts for a 54.9 percentage. I had 1,652 yards, nine touchdowns and eight interceptions.

I went into my sophomore year and we had a great opener on the road, beating Texas A&M 38-16. They were ranked in the top 20 and were favored by 15. Jackie Sherrill, the former University of Pittsburgh coach, had signed a six-year, $1.7 million contract in the off-season to coach the Aggies. It was a big deal for them and they were hoping to blow us out. I had a hell of a game, ripping them apart with 18 completions in 26 attempts for 356 yards and three TDs. The game was televised on ESPN and it received a lot of attention nationally. That was the day we realized that all of a sudden we were competing against the best teams in the country.

The following week we played at Clemson, the defending national champion, and the game was televised on CBS. We were 12-point underdogs. We were down 14-0 at halftime and I had thrown two interceptions and fumbled once on their 11-yard line. On our first series in the third quarter, we drove 72 yards for a touchdown, running the ball almost exclusively. In the fourth quarter, I directed a 4-play, 61-yard touchdown drive, including a 36-yard pass to Scott Nizolek on third and short. Both teams added field goals, although Clemson missed a chance to win it when Donald Igwebuike missed a 43-yard attempt with eight seconds to go.

All of a sudden we received a lot of national recognition and I was being interviewed by newspaper and TV reporters. We cruised through our schedule, winning seven of the remaining nine games, beating the teams we were supposed to and cracking the top-20 polls at times.

One of the two losses was to West Virginia, who beat us 20-13. We never beat West Virginia in four years. They always played us tough. I threw four interceptions in that game and fumbled once. One of my roommates, George Radachowsky, fumbled a ball on a punt return late in the game and the Mountaineers, who were quarterbacked by Jeff Hostetler, took it in for the touchdown four plays later. The local newspaper had head shots of us, and underneath them it said, "Doug Flutie, four interceptions," "George Radachowsky, costly fumble." The guys in our apartment unit cut those pictures out of the paper and put them up on the dartboard. They stayed on it all week.

We lost 52-17 at home against Penn State in front of a record crowd of 33,205 at Alumni Stadium. I completed 26 of 44 passes for 520 yards, which was the best in the nation that year and the 10th best in NCAA history. Overall, we had 656 yards, but Penn State had 618 and we committed 6 turnovers.

Syracuse also played us tough. We beat them twice at home, and they beat us twice at their stadium in my four years. We won 20-13 in the second-last game of my sophomore year when I called an audible near the end and threw a 29-yard touchdown pass to Gerard Phelan. That won us an invitation to play in the Tangerine Bowl against Auburn.

It was Boston College's first Bowl appearance in more than 40 years, and that was pretty exciting for us. We spent a week in Orlando and went to Disney World. We stayed on the main strip — International Drive — and every night the guys go-karted on a slick track at Fun and Wheels. It was a great week. John Loughery, who came back for his fifth year even though he knew I was going to be the starter, came up to me and thanked me for getting him there and making it the highlight of his career.

That was a special moment for me. I remember coming in as a freshman, thinking I was kind of outclassed by all these guys.

I didn't think I belonged in a Division 1 school. I looked at John, he was a 6-foot-2 kid who threw the ball really well, and to have him come back to me two years later and thank me for getting him to that point made me feel really good. It proved to me that although I really didn't think I could do it — that I'd thought I was in over my head and was maybe taking advantage of Boston College for this scholarship — I was actually doing something special.

We lost 33-26 to Auburn but we scored a touchdown on the last play of the game. I spiked the ball in the end zone on the two-point conversion. They had Bo Jackson and we were totally outclassed, but we went down fighting.

I didn't know what I wanted as far as my education was concerned. I always had a strong math background and my dad directed me to computer science. In my first two years of school I received good grades, but by my second semester in my sophomore year I stopped going to classes a little bit, became really lazy, and had to withdraw from one course. My grades slipped.

Tom Coughlin, who was the quarterback coach and later became head coach of Boston College and is now the head coach of the NFL's Jacksonville Jaguars, straightened me out. He was a disciplinarian. He'd get more out of you than you knew you had. He just had a knack for it. He didn't let you become lazy. We had the longest meetings and watched more film than you can imagine. This is where I think I built a work ethic. He got on me about my grades and made sure I paid attention to what the heck I was doing. He kept me in line. Working with him has made everything else 10 times easier because he was so demanding of your time and your effort from every snap in practice to everything else.

TOM COUGHLIN:

He's always referred to me in a more casual light as Technical Tom. I think I was probably the first guy to take his athletic ability and to kind of put him in a more productive schedule and demand that he perform the numerous functions and tasks of a quarterback in a specific way. I can remember Jack Bicknell coming to me and being concerned that we allow this young quarterback to grow and develop because he had natural instincts and natural ability and we didn't want to make him a robot. Jack was concerned about that and I assured him that was not going to be the case, that we wanted him to perform above the Xs and Os and be the great winner and leader that he was and is.

Boston College was blessed at that time with many outstanding football players, but I think the greatest compliment you can pay anyone is that he played the game at such a level it was contagious and those around him knew they had to play to the best of their ability in order to remain on the same field with this guy.

Doug had the great gleam in his eye. He loved to play the game and had a tremendous hunger and thirst for more information about the game. He loved to sense the motivation behind being prepared and had a unique ability to take the play from the classroom to the field and then exhibit a great ability to master the Xs and Os and play above the Xs and Os.

Coach Bicknell was more like a friend. It was great because in practices you'd have Tom Coughlin constantly in your ear all the time and you had to stay disciplined and focused, but come game day he was upstairs calling the plays and Jack was on the sideline signaling things in to me. On game day all I had to do was deal with Coach Bicknell and it made things a lot easier. It was a lot more fun and the pressure was off. It made the games feel like they were so easy compared to practices. I always looked up to Coach Bick like a father figure. He was always a close friend. He was a fun guy to play for. When he was loose and relaxed, it was always Tom Coughlin who kept you working.

During the off-season before my junior year we replaced the turf at Alumni Stadium with Super Turf. They offered the job to some of the football players, and I figured it would be decent-paying. But it was really back-breaking. We were scraping the old pad off the cement. The group of us lasted a week and a half before we said, "To heck with this." We made about $10 an hour, but it really wasn't worth it. It was awful work. Once we got the pad up and the old stuff off, they were ready to roll the new one down. We said, "Okay, you guys are on your own," and let them deal with it.

I changed my major going into my junior year to speech communications because I realized football was basically taking off for me. When I was doing the computer thing, I'd stay up on a Thursday night trying to get various programs to run for a Friday class, even though we had the game on Saturday. They say two days before a game is your most important night of sleep. I'd be up to five, six in the morning trying to get the darn programs to run, so I basically switched my major and went into more of a broadcast-type field where I did some radio and TV classes.

Interest was high in the team, both locally and nationally. Season tickets doubled to 10,000, opposing coaches attended our spring practices to study our passing game, and CBS offered to pay our school $600,000 to switch our game against Alabama to later in the season so it could be televised nationally. Athletic director Bill Flynn obliged, although it left us with a two-week gap in the middle of the schedule.

I broke Frank Harris's BC passing record of 4,555 career passing yards in the home opener against Division 2 Morgan State, which lost 45-12. We beat Clemson 31-16 next and I was named NBC's Sportsman of the Week and was interviewed on the *Today Show*. ABC and CBS scheduled interviews for our following game against Rutgers at Giants Stadium, where I never lost a game in college and at the professional level with New Jersey. We beat Rutgers 42-22, but I only played briefly after suffering a concussion early in the second quarter.

Sports Illustrated did a cover story on me headlined, "A Little Man On Campus." It was the first time in the history of BC one of its athletes appeared on the cover, which had a picture of me standing on a chair throwing over the offensive line. The story detailed how we climbed up to No. 12 in the nation in *SI*'s poll, how the season-ticket sales jumped considerably and how some of our games were being moved from Alumni Stadium to Sullivan Stadium where the Patriots played and had a seating of more than 60,000. That was about double the size of the capacity at Alumni Stadium. The story also indicated how we were gaining more TV exposure and how the school was profiting from it.

We lost our next game 27-17 to West Virginia but beat Temple and Yale in our next two. Then we waited two weeks to play Penn State, which lost its first three and then won five straight. The game was played at Sullivan Stadium and attracted a crowd of 56,188 and a national TV audience. We led 7-0 on an 80-yard drive to start the game and upped the score to 14-0 on a fluke play. I threw a 25-yard pass to Brian Brennan, but the ball was a little high and he got drilled. The ball deflected to Troy Stradford and he took it 34 yards for a touchdown. We wound up winning 27-17. We just jumped all over them and then just hung on for dear life the rest of the game. Late in the game, I audibled and threw a long ball to Gerard Phelan down the left sideline. It was kind of ironic that he caught the ball to give us a first down. He dove and laid out parallel to the ground right in front of Penn State head coach Joe Paterno and it was like *the* play of the game. Gerard had a knack for coming up with those big plays at the big times. That catch let us work more time off the clock and got us in range to kick a 40-yard, game-clinching field goal by Kevin Snow.

We cracked the top 20 in the rankings, but Penn State was still ahead of us. We beat Army the next week and moved up to No. 13 in the rankings. Suddenly we were being considered for all kinds of Bowls. We then lost 21-10 to Syracuse in which I was good on only 12 of 36 and had three interceptions and only 114 yards. Coach Bicknell was quoted as saying: "I have to keep telling people the kid is just a kid." The next day we were granted an invitation to play Notre Dame in the Liberty Bowl. We beat Holy Cross 47-7 after the Syracuse loss and accepted the Bowl invitation. That led to our final regular-season game against 13th-ranked Alabama at Sullivan Stadium. It was another nationally televised game. Alabama came up and expected to kick the crap out of us. We won the game 20-13 with a late drive, sticking it in the end zone with just a short running play. Brian Brennan made a great catch over the middle in the series.

But that isn't my greatest memory of that game. It was the

weather and the blackout. It was a sleety, rainy, snowy, cold day with the wind blowing, and it was like a war of attrition. You just tried to get through it. Until I learned to play in Canada, it was the most miserable weather I'd ever played in. At halftime I went into the locker room, and I was freezing cold. It was ridiculous. You were soaked through. I stripped down in the bathroom area underneath one of the hand warmers and suddenly while trying to get warm, the power went out. A tree fell about three miles from the stadium and landed on a transformer feeder and knocked out all the power. We all dressed in the dark to go back on the field. It was still daylight out but with no power in what became known as the Blackout Bowl. Alabama blocked a punt and scored to lead 13-6, but no one saw it on TV. The officials were going to call the game because of darkness, but 43 minutes after the lights went out, power was restored.

I was one of the Heisman Trophy finalists that year, which was won by Nebraska's Mike Rozier. Brigham Young's Steve Young was the runner-up and I finished third. All three of us played in the USFL, which was trying to sign big-name players to build up the credibility of the league. I thought it was great to be a finalist. Steve Young and I spent some time together and played some basketball at the Downtown Athletic Club, where they announce the Heisman winner. We both knew Mike Rozier was going to win it. That was my introduction to the elite of college football. I really admired Steve Young. We had similar styles coming out of college, and we really got along great those few days.

The whole week in Memphis for the Liberty Bowl was terrible. It was so cold that pipes were bursting in the hotel, which was going to be shut down right after we left. They just kept it open the extra couple of weeks because they knew we were coming. It was the first time I spent Christmas on the road in a hotel room. Gerard Phelan and I stole two Christmas trees from meeting rooms, and we put them in our room. We had brought along some decorations to our room and covered it from head to toe. I thought it was pretty cool. We enjoyed it, but otherwise it was kind of a miserable week.

Gerry Faust was the head coach of Notre Dame, which was 6-5 and unranked. We were 9-2 and ranked 13th in the nation. We lost 19-18. They were definitely more physical and they ran the ball down our throats, which is why we lost the game. The first drive of the game, we marched the ball right down the field and I threw a touchdown pass to Brian Brennan. As the game progressed the whole field was a sheet of ice. Both teams scored three touchdowns, but only one extra point was scored the whole game — by them on their first major — because the out kickers were slipping on the icy turf. We tried a play-action pass on the two-point conversion after our final touchdown. I threw it right in the hands of our tight end, Scott Gieselman, and he dropped it. It was so cold, he just couldn't clutch the ball. (Scott caught the touchdown setting up the two-point attempt.)

Darren joined me at Boston College in my senior year after he graduated from high school. He had some great games. He was just unbelievable. He led Natick High to back-to-back State championships by rushing for a total of 2,150 yards and intercepting 12 passes. Athletically and physically he was ahead of the other guys his age.

Darren and I didn't get along great at that point. I loved the heck out of Darren and I loved going to his games and watching him play. I was very proud of him. He kind of had this chip on his shoulder, maybe because of the things I was doing in college, but he was achieving things in high school that I never came near. The championship game against Melrose in his junior year was more amazing than his senior year. Darren ran in the touchdown and the two-point conversion to win the game by a point with 12 seconds left. The other team was leading by one and running out the clock with a minute to go. They scored another first down near the five-yard line and Darren stepped into the huddle and told the guys, "Hey, we've got to let them score so we can get the ball back."

Darren and I had talked about this scenario countless times — letting the other team score when you're down by one and the clock's running out. You're down by eight if they score the extra point, but either way you get the ball back and have a chance to tie it. If Natick stops Melrose for a couple of plays, the clock could run out. At least this way Natick gets the ball back for one more chance. Natick had a chance to win when Melrose missed the extra point after hitting the upright. Natick had a quarterback named Paul Ghilani, who is a real close friend of mine now, and he completed a few passes and got the team down close to the goal area. Then Darren won the game.

Darren was highly recruited and I was very excited when he decided to come to Boston College. I was afraid he was out to prove his own point and didn't want to have anything to do with me at that time. When he made his decision to go to Boston College, it really brought us closer together. I won the Heisman and did all the things I wanted to do that year, but Darren was a part of it because he had a chance to start playing. I remember thinking when he signed his scholarship offer that I just wanted him to get in a game so I could throw one pass to him for a completion. He caught a mess of catches that year and two touchdowns in the final against Holy Cross. He was a big part of the team and it really made me feel a lot better.

It was an active off-season for the team and myself. Coach Bick declined an invitation to interview for the head coaching job of the Miami Hurricanes and Tom Coughlin resigned to take an assistant's job with the Philadelphia Eagles. I played in a charity golf tournament with Bob Hope, had my picture taken twice by *Sports Illustrated*, filmed some TV messages with other athletes in Arizona and spent a weekend in Dallas with the other players selected to Playboy's All-America team.

By my senior year we were no longer playing just for the fun of it but to prove a point and be a national champion. We won our first four games, beginning with a 44-24 victory over Western Carolina, the top-ranked Division 1-AA school, and then prepared for Alabama. The Crimson Tide were ranked No. 9 in the nation, while we were ranked 18th. Alabama head coach Ray Perkins was asked by reporters a couple days before the game whether I had the ability to play in the NFL. Perkins, who had coached in the NFL, said: "I don't think anybody will take a shot at him. I think he would have a tough time in the NFL simply because the guys are a lot bigger in the NFL than in college. And I don't see the NFL utilizing the same kinds of schemes, roll-outs, that he uses in college. His only weakness is his height. Some people don't think height means that much, but I'll guarantee you it does. It's just a big disadvantage. I think he would make a super, super Canadian Football League quarterback because of his movement. He's got a real strong arm, he's very smart, and he's highly competitive."

The game was televised nationally on ABC, but a funny thing happened the day before. Gerard and I were late for practice.

BARRY GALLUP:

Keith Jackson and Frank Broyles are doing the game for ABC. We're out there on Friday practising and Jack Bicknell asks me to get Doug and Gerard because Keith Jackson wants to talk to Doug. I knew something was wrong because Doug and Gerard were always the first ones out on the field. I went to get them in the locker room, and they're not there. They had missed the bus. I called the hotel and it wasn't that they were fooling around, they were playing chess. They had a couple hours at the hotel, and they lost track of time.

JACK BICKNELL:

There was no question about those two kids. They were everything you'd want in an athlete and they blew it. It was comical. From then on I said, "Let's make sure Doug's here before we go." Anybody else, I'd have left them. He was not the kind of guy who would ever do anything that wasn't team orientated and wasn't the way it should be. Anybody could make that mistake.

Frank Broyles was saying, "What are you going to do?"

I said, "Are you serious? I'm just going to make sure he sits next to me on the bus when we go to the game." I've left many kids, and I've benched kids, but they're the kids who have had a track record of not doing what they're supposed to be doing. This was just a mistake and it was nothing to be thinking about.

We made a great comeback from being down 31-14 early in the third quarter to win 38-31. I tied the game on fourth down and one at Alabama's 12-yard line on a little play-action pass to fullback Jim Browne — No. 32, of course. It was a real gutsy call by the coach. With about three minutes to go in the game, we went up 38-31 when Troy Stradford breaks a 42-yard run. Darren and Gerard made two great downfield blocks. Defensive back Tony Thurman had three interceptions but the last one saved the game with about a minute to go. They ran a flea flicker-type play with the tailback throwing a pass deep to a receiver. Tony just came out of nowhere, covering all kinds of ground and laid out, catching the ball on his fingertips to ice the game. It was probably one of the most emotional wins we ever had.

In the next game against North Carolina, I had one of my greatest games in college. I threw a BC-record six touchdown passes in just over two quarters and ran with the ball well before Coach Bicknell took me out of the game. It was one of those days where I was doing everything and I felt like I could have done anything. It was definitely my best all-around game from start to finish. Everything was on fire. I completed 28 of 38 for 354 yards. Darren had his first reception in that game.

We climbed to No. 4 in the country and had a two-week break before playing Temple. ABC and CBS did stories on me in the interval, and there was also a piece in *People* magazine. We beat Temple 24-10 and I threw three interceptions. For some reason I always struggled against Temple, which played us tough defensively. At the end of the half we were around midfield when I threw a 51-yard Hail Mary pass to Gerard and he caught it on the goal line in the middle of the crowd. That was the first time we ever tried to run that play that year. Gerard had a knack for catching the ball. It was the same Hail Mary play he caught later in the year in Miami that everybody remembered, but this game wasn't on TV and no one remembered it.

Then we played West Virginia, the school I just couldn't beat. It was always a very hostile atmosphere, and it was just one of those things where they played us tough. They were ranked No. 6 and it was a big game on ABC. They beat us 21-20 after we had them 20-6 at halftime. We were on the edge of field goal range and turned the ball over with less than a minute to go. I tried to explain to Coach Bicknell what Darren had done in high school by letting the other team score so you could try to come back for the tie or the win if they missed the extra point. But in the 15 seconds or so that I had to explain that situation, I couldn't get my point across. They ran out the clock.

We beat Rutgers 35-23 and I completed 70 percent of my 30 passes. Then we played Penn State. It was a pretty frustrating game, although Darren had a great day with a couple of huge catches for long yardage. We moved the ball up and down the field but had a bunch of turnovers. I threw two interceptions and we had three fumbles, but we still scored 30 points. However, Penn State had 37. It was the game in which I became the first player in college history to surpass 10,000 yards in total offense, but it was kind of bittersweet because we lost. I suffered a slight shoulder separation and a win could have shot us back up in the national ratings after we had fallen to No. 11.

We blew Army out 45-31 and that was the game in which I became the first collegian to pass for more than 10,000 yards — and Darren was almost the receiver on the historic play. I called an audible and threw it to Darren for about a 30-yard touchdown, but it was called back for holding. It wound up being a great catch by Kelvin Martin on a slant route on the next play that put me over the 10,000-yard mark. It would have been cool to have Darren catch his first touchdown pass and put me over the 10,000 mark.

We beat Syracuse 24-16 and we knew if we won we were going to a New Year's Day Bowl game. It was informally announced that night that we were going to the Cotton Bowl, which was kind of exciting. We could have held out for the Sugar Bowl and done a winner-loser job with Miami in which the winner went to the Sugar Bowl and the loser to the Fiesta Bowl. However, the school decided we needed the New Year's Day Bowl game as a definite and took the one in hand rather than waiting.

There wasn't a lot riding on the Miami game. The Heisman voting had been done by that time, so it was just a big-time game played in the Orange Bowl in which Bernie Kosar and I were going to let it fly. This was the game I threw *The Pass*.

Miami was the defending national champion and was coached by Jimmy Johnson. Bernie was only a sophomore but highly rated. He and I were two guys who threw the hell out of the ball, and that's the way the game developed. It was blustery and rainy, but the first few drives felt so easy. I completed my first 11 passes. We just walked up and down the field and led 14-0. Then Bernie started doing the same thing, coming back the other way. He completed 11 in a row and the score was tied 14-14. It was one of those games where you felt the team that had the ball last was going to win it. We led 28-21 at the half and the battle continued that way right until the end. We led 41-38 with less than three minutes remaining, but Bernie led them back and they scored inside of a minute on a one-yard touchdown run. I remember just wishing they would hurry up and score and leave us a little more time, but they didn't.

They started celebrating on the sideline, thinking they had won. We took it on the 20 with 28 seconds left and I hit Troy Stradford on a seam route for a 19-yard gain. A holding penalty against Miami stopped the clock. I came right back and hit Scott Gieselman, who ran out of bounds at the Miami 48. I didn't even use the darn timeouts. I saved them, thinking I might need them, and wound up not using them. I threw a pass to Peter Caspariello at about the Miami 25-yard line, but it was incomplete. There was only six seconds left on the clock.

The last play of the game we called was 55 Flood Tip. Everybody lined up out to the right. I remember the coaching staff sending out Shawn Dembrowski with the play, but I knew what they wanted. Shawn would have replaced Troy Stradford, but I made Troy stay in, even though I didn't realize he had a pulled hamstring. At first when we lined up for the play, there was no one covering Kelvin Martin, who was the outside receiver. The DBs were way off. They put a man on Gerard's nose and on Troy's nose and they were bumping them. But they left Kelvin alone and he probably would have made it to the end zone first.

The ball was snapped, but the play was blown dead for a

penalty. But then the officials waved it off. I didn't bother re-huddling. I stayed at the line of scrimmage and yelled out the snap count. I told Peter Caspariello to go down the backside. I decided I was going to drop back, try to buy some time, roll to the right, let the guys get there and throw a jump ball. I also thought once I rolled to the right that I'd have a chance to look back down the left sideline and if everybody drifted, I'd have the tight end down the backside.

When I rolled out to the right, I didn't have time to look to the backside. I just let it heave to Gerard. Turns out the tight end was wide open and I might have had a chance at that. When we snapped the ball, at the last second the guy that was on Gerard walked out and covered up on Kelvin. That made Gerard the guy that got down the field first.

It's so funny to watch the tape of Gerard just chugging down the field with his head down. He didn't even bother turning around and looking until he got down to the end zone. Because I was rolling right and the DBs kind of froze, he got behind them at about the 10-yard line. At the five-yard line he turned and kind of backpedalled as he saw the ball coming toward him. The defensive back, Tolbert Bain, who should have been covering the tight end down the backside, drifted across the corner and jumped for the ball. He collided with the free safety, Darrell Fullington, who was also jumping for the catch, and it went through cleanly to Gerard — although Troy said Fullington tipped it. Gerard said he tried to catch it in his stomach, but the ball slipped down and he trapped it against his thigh and fell into the end zone. When he landed he saw there was writing on the ground underneath him and knew he'd scored. Then he showed the referee he had the ball.

Officially it was ruled a 48-yard pass, but I actually threw it 65 yards. The amazing thing for me was I didn't even know who caught the ball. I saw the ball fall over the heads of the two defensive backs and thought it fell incomplete. A second or two later I saw the official's arms in the back of the end zone go up and rule it a touchdown. I started shaking my head and laughing. I jogged down the field but never made it to the pigpile in the end zone. I ended up jumping into the arms of Steve Trapilo, one of our offensive linemen. I was in Darren's arms at one time. A good five minutes later I made it to the locker room and asked our strong safety, Dave Pereira, who caught the ball. He told me Gerard did, and I kind of shook my head and said, "That figures." There's some great footage of the lockerroom scene with Gerard getting Gatorade poured over his head, me getting water poured over my head and me and Gerard yelling and hugging. It was wild.

JACK BICKNELL:

He knew exactly what we were going to try to do and a play like that is luck, although it had worked one other time during that same year. We had practiced it every Thursday and it's just a play that everybody has where you go down the field. But what Doug does is he buys time. He drops back and then he scrambles a little bit to allow the three receivers on the one side to get down that far, then he just put it up. I'm convinced that the Miami defender didn't think he could throw it that far. He had gotten just about three yards in the end zone and figured, "There's no way this guy is going to throw it over my head with a 65-yard pass," and he threw it over his head and our kid was there to catch it.

That game was a fantastic football game. If you look at the stats or if you look at the list of the future NFL players that played in that game on both teams, you'll find an unbelievable cast of characters. The game was just back and forth, back and forth. It seemed like the last team to have the ball was going to win it and that's what happened.

It was a fantastic play, but I remember the game and I say the pass was just one of those things. Gerard Phelan calls it The Catch. *There's no question that something like that is just a fortunate thing, but Doug deserved to be in that position. When he pulled it off, that was just unbelievable what happened to him after that — the attention and the national exposure.*

It happened to be on a Friday. It happened to be at dinner hour. It happened to be that everybody in the country that liked college football had the game on and it was the only game on in those days. I think people all over the country saw this little quarterback — in their mind he was a little guy playing with all these big guys — just do this superhuman type of stuff. It was really a great thing.

TOM COUGHLIN:

The day he threw the pass to beat Miami I came home from practice and opened the door and my wife and my four children were sitting there in the family room crying, and I thought, "Oh my God, what's happened here? Has there been some kind of tragedy that I'm not aware of?" I said to my wife, "What's the matter?" She looked at me and said, "He did it again. He did it again." Here they had been watching the game on television and he threw the pass that beat Miami. He was capable of doing things like that that no one really thought he could do.

There was some extra seats on the charter and the coaches allowed Laurie to fly back with us. That was kind of unheard of, but she had a plane ticket anyway and just flew back a day early. There were thousands of people at the airport — not just college students — and Gerard and I and our girlfriends were shoved into a state trooper's car to keep us away from the mob. It was just a wild, wild scene.

The next day in Miami I was called the Midget Moses in one of the papers. In the issue of *Sports Illustrated* they ran a story headlined, "It Wasn't a Fluke. It Was a Flutie."

ABC wanted to interview me the next day, but I told them I was too tired and asked Gerard to make the appearance. CBS interviewed me the following day and I attended a Cotton Bowl pep rally and was interviewed for four hours. Jack then shut off the media interviews.

JACK BICKNELL:

After that Miami game and The Pass and the Heisman Trophy stuff, it got stupid. I mean it got to the point where it was affecting the kid. Not affecting him with his head — he didn't get a big head — but it wasn't as much fun for him. He was under the gun all the time and then I said, "That's up to me to control that." Up until that time it had been wide open. Then it got to the point where it was just out of control. There were so many demands on this kid that he couldn't concentrate. We had just beaten Miami, we're going to the Cotton Bowl and wouldn't it be embarrassing if we limped into the Cotton Bowl after losing to Holy Cross, a team we should beat.

That was a time I just said, "Okay fellas, that's it. I'll handle all interviews and I'll set the schedule." I had done it with the sports information director Reid Oslin. He handled all the requests. I didn't want to get involved with all that stuff. Then at that point, I said, "Wait a second, from now on I'll make those decisions," and it was only for a two-week period. Then it was over and then there was no problem. I felt at that point I had to make sure things were done the right way.

We had one more regular-season game to play on the road at Holy Cross and it was kind of hard to stay focused. David Letterman wanted me on his show. I just said, "Can't we do the Letterman Show next week or whenever?" I had just gotten back from all that travel and I didn't realize how big of a deal it would have been to do the Letterman Show. It ended up I never got the opportunity to do it at a later date, which was kind of disappointing looking back on it, until I made an appearance on his show in 1998.

All three networks wanted to interview me. So did Johnny Carson for the *Tonight Show. Sports Illustrated* had me on the cover again.

The Heisman was being announced a few hours after the Holy Cross game and they had all these plans arranged for me to get to New York for the award presentation. I played terribly in the first half and it was kind of close, but in the second half we blew them out like we should have from the beginning and won 45-10. The great thing was Darren had a great day. I called an audible in the third quarter, and there was Darren breaking down the sideline, and I hit him for the touchdown. It was like a piece of cake. It was his first collegiate touchdown. We did a nice high-five on the run and it just completed the day to get Darren in the end zone. On the next possession, Darren ran an inside trap and broke a tackle or two and went 25 yards up the middle for a touchdown. It was a great run. That was more deserving of a touchdown to me. The other one, I did the work. I checked it off and Darren just went down the sideline. It was too easy, but he came right back and scored one on his own.

He actually should have won game MVP. It's a big rivalry game and they hand out the O'Melia Award as MVP, which I won. I had won it once before in my freshman year. Darren was a freshman this time and there were five people who voted on the award. Two voted Doug Flutie, two for Darren Flutie and one put D. Flutie. The decision was made to give it to me, but Darren was very deserving of winning it at the time.

There was a big mob of people who swarmed the field after the game. I did a live interview, and as I was going to the locker room, I remember looking at the crowd and hearing a voice just yell, "Doug." In the middle of the crowd I still recognized the voice of Laurie. For some stupid reason she had come down to the field. I don't know why, but I worked her through the crowd and whisked her out of there. After I showered up we headed to a van waiting to take us to the airport to go to New York. In addition to the two of us there was my family, Jack Bicknell and his wife, Barry Gallup, quarterback coach Sam Timer, Bill Flynn and his wife, BC president Rev. J. Donald Monan, Tom Lamb and Reid Oslin. It was kind of humorous because as we took off, a whole tray of hors d'oeuvres and drinks fell on my dad's lap. When we landed I was met there by a helicopter and Laurie and I were flown to New York City. We were supposed to go to the Downtown Athletic Club, but the pilot figured we had some time and radioed to the control tower at LaGuardia Airport to ask if he could take us on a fast tour of the city.

"For Doug Flutie, you can go anywhere you want," was the response from the tower.

When the tour was over, we jumped into a limousine to go to the Downtown Athletic Club. I was definitely the frontrunner for the Heisman. I just had the feeling they wouldn't have gone through all the trouble to get me there if I wasn't going to win the award. The last few minutes before the Heisman was announced, we were all sitting in the room and I kind of got nervous thinking, "What happens if I don't win it?" The Heisman was something I never dreamed of winning. It was something that was so far out of reach that you don't really dream of winning it. I was always concentrating on the football seasons and that just kind of happened. That was the most amazing feeling. I totaled 2,240 points in the voting, almost twice as much as runnerup Keith Byars, the running back from Ohio State. Brigham Young quarterback Robbie Bosco was third.

I remember thinking I won the Heisman Trophy and nobody could take that away from me. It didn't matter what they would say about my height or whether I played in the NFL or played professionally or even if I didn't play another down of football. I had won the Heisman Trophy and that was something I was going to be proud of for the rest of my life.

There was a celebration at the dormitory when I returned at midnight and a cake from my teammates. After winning the Heisman, I appeared at the halftime of a BC basketball game and received a standing ovation. Mayor Raymond L. Flynn invited me to turn on the Christmas lights at the Boston Common, which is a big park downtown. Then I had to fly to New York for Heisman activities. I did the *Today Show*, taught Mayor Ed Koch how to hold a football, spoke at the National Football Foundation Top Scholar Award and then traveled to Washington, D.C., to go to the White House. It was the 50th anniversary of the Heisman and they awarded a mini-Heisman to President Ronald Reagan. They took me into the Oval Office and I met the President and Vice-President George Bush. We talked a little bit about football on the way out from the Oval Office to this press room. It was like three guys hanging out talking football, and it was a great feeling. George Bush turns to me and says, "How about this Gerry Faust guy, they're about ready to lynch him at Notre Dame?"

It cracked me up that they were just football fans, just regular guys. That was kind of a fun thing for me. I felt like I was being treated a little bit special and it was a nice feeling.

It was kind of cool they did a *Saturday Night Live* skit on me. They did a spoof in which Eddie Murphy was Bishop Desmond Tutu and they somehow broke the Heisman Trophy while doing this interview with me. They try to weld it together but end up melting it. I was at home and a friend called to tell me this skit was going on. I caught it in the middle of the skit and saw the end of it and I didn't really think it was that funny personally. I thought it was kind of stupid, but it seemed like everybody else thought it was funny. So it was pretty cool to have that done.

There was such hype around the Boston area about the Cotton Bowl against Houston. People were just jumping on the bandwagon, loving the fact we were going to a New Year's Day Bowl. People flew down for the game and there was such a crowd at the Anatole, a beautiful hotel with a big atrium where we were staying. But I was miserable the whole week. I was really taking the game seriously. It was a fun thing in my sophomore year when we made it to the Tangerine Bowl, but now there was pressure to win. We needed to win this stupid game. I did not enjoy the experience. I was avoiding people — the bus that took us to the hotel had to drive around to the back where I took the service elevator — because they were getting on my nerves and I was sick of signing autographs. I just wanted to win this game and it made for a very frustrating and aggravating week for me. I had to change hotel rooms two or three times because all the people were finding out where my room was and constantly coming by and pounding on the door in the middle of the night and during the day to get autographs.

The people at the Cotton Bowl were fantastic and there were a lot of great events set up, but I was trying the best I could to avoid the events and the people and just concentrate on the game. I really didn't enjoy that week as much as I should have.

It was windy and rainy with near-freezing temperatures, but I came out smoking and did some really good things in the first half, throwing a Cotton Bowl-record three touchdown passes in the first half. We led 31-7 and I completed 11 of 20 passes and ran for some nice first downs. The second half I completed only two of 13 for 13 yards and threw two interceptions. I was able to grip the ball but couldn't judge the wind. I overthrew some open receivers. Houston narrowed the gap to 31-28, but then we started running the ball down their throat and pulled away to win 45-28. It was BC's first Bowl since the 1940-41 season. We set a Cotton Bowl record with 541 total yards. Fullback Steve Strachan won the game MVP, but I actually thought Troy Stradford deserved it.

My last collegiate touchdown pass was just a short one, but it was to Gerard and that was kind of fitting.

When it was all over, I felt relief, kind of like my feelings after winning the Grey Cup — of winning it all. It's more satisfaction looking back and saying, "Hey, we did it, we won, it's over with and now I can sit back and enjoy it."

Playing the Trump Card

I got up early the following morning and was driven to the airport by Jim (Hoss) Brock, the Cotton Bowl executive vice chairman. There was a storm and ice all over the roads and Hoss wasn't used to driving in those conditions. I swear I thought we were going to die, but we made it to the airport alive and flew out to Hawaii for the Hula Bowl.

The USFL conducted its territorial draft the day after the Cotton Bowl. The New Jersey Generals selected me. Shortly thereafter, they began negotiating with my agent, Bob Woolf.

There was a long process involved in selecting Bob as the agent who would represent me. During my senior year, we had at least 50 inquiries from people seeking to represent me. My father used a computer system to grade the agents. He eventually narrowed the list down to three: Bob Woolf, Ed Keating, and the partnership of John Hawkette and Ron Shapiro. My dad favored Bob because of a gut feeling he had about him and because he was in Boston and could give me faster service.

I made the decision to go with Bob Woolf without even meeting him, basing it on reputation more than anything else. I felt he was someone I could trust, someone who was considered a class act within the business. He always treated me more like a son. He was always worried about image and doing things the right way. He didn't care if it cost a little more money or I didn't make quite as much or I lost out on something. What mattered to him was the appearance and how it impacted on me.

After the Hula Bowl, I played in the Japan Bowl and then went to Nashville for the Scholar Athlete Dinner. When I came back I was exhausted from everything. I was nominated for a Rhodes Scholarship, but they didn't tell me I had to do an interview for it. Upon arriving at the airport, Bill Flynn, the athletic director at Boston College, met me and told me we had to hustle over to the Algonquin Club because they were having a reception for the Rhodes Scholarship. It was a rarity for an athlete to be nominated for the award.

The Algonquin Club is a very elegant, old-style club, and I walked into this room in my jeans and T-shirt because there was no time to change. Everybody was decked out — the guys were in jackets and ties, the girls were in evening attire — and I guess I didn't start off on the right foot for that. But it really didn't matter to me how I looked. I was relaxed. I didn't care. This is me. This is how I am. It really didn't bother me that much that I wasn't dressed up. It was just a little awkward at first.

Because of all this traveling I was doing, I just wanted to get back to school and chill out and relax. It was kind of funny and ironic that during this time period my best friend then, Bob Riley, who was a teammate of mine on the high school basketball team, invited me to the University of New Hampshire, where he had gone to school, for a visit. I took up skiing for the first time and was lucky not to suffer any injuries before signing my big contract.

My first introduction to the contract numbers Bob Woolf threw at me came in Hawaii, and the figures were around $5 million or $6 million — and that was only a starting guideline! There was much speculation about the actual numbers, but Bob refused to discuss them publicly. He let the media speculate.

I didn't realize everything that was going on with Buffalo, which had the first pick overall in the NFL draft. There was all kinds of talk in the national media and in Buffalo about whether the Bills would draft me. I had no idea three diehard Bills fans had started a group called the Draft Doug Flutie Association shortly after the Hail Mary pass. Bob Orrange, one of the DDFA's founders, told the *Buffalo News'* Vic Carucci, "This guy's like Americana, Norman Rockwell. He's like a breath of fresh air, and the Bills have got to grab on to it." The DDFA sold buttons that read "Draft Doug Flutie" at Bills games and distributed a newsletter.

The Bills had the rights to Jim Kelly, who was playing with the Houston Gamblers of the USFL. The Bills could draft me, trade the first choice or take someone else. I was projected anywhere from a first-round pick to a third-rounder to a middle-rounder. It was so up in the air because of my size. People weren't sure whether they were going to take chances on me or not.

In an article written by *Washington Post* writer Leonard Shapiro, Mike Allman, the director of player personnel for the Seattle Seahawks, said, "I'd be a little afraid to pick him No. 1, but I'd be scared as hell not to." Reed Johnson, the Denver Broncos' college scouting coordinator, said, "Any team that takes him is going to have to move him around. You have to have bootlegs, sprint-outs. Are you going to change your whole philosophy for one guy who's 5-9? When the time comes for the draft, there may be a lot of guys who excuse themselves and go to the restroom."

While talks progressed with the Generals, Bob did not hear anything directly from any of the Bills. Bills owner Ralph Wilson told the media he would match any offer made by New Jersey. The media had the deal worth $5 million for four years. Wilson told the *Buffalo News'* Vic Carucci I would be a good drawing card, but people would forget all about my college exploits if I didn't develop as expected.

"This is not to detract from Flutie," he told Carucci. "He's a very good player, but these players do get hyped up and he has had a tremendous amount of hype from the media."

A day after those comments appeared in the *Buffalo News*, I verbally agreed to a deal with the Generals, following talks the night before with Trump and Generals president Jay Seltzer. The deal was $8.3 million over six years, the first three guaranteed — the richest deal in any sports league for a rookie at the time. The Bills never made a serious offer.

Behind the scenes so much had happened that the public — and the media — never knew. Somewhere along the line Donald Trump, who owned the Generals got real pissed off and took the deal right off the table. He just pulled it and said, "The hell with this. I'm not going to do it." The problem involved a breakdown in communication during negotiations. It was pretty obvious to me the most secure thing to do was to take this deal. Now all of a sudden Trump had pulled it off the table. The guy who got Trump and Bob Woolf back to the table was Howard Cosell. He was a mutual friend of theirs and kind of calmed Donald down. A few days later they got back to the table and we got back to the same deal we originally had and I decided to go with it.

As far as dreaming of playing in the NFL, as a kid you think about it and it's more of a fantasy than anything. I always aspired to the next level. When I was in Pop Warner football, I always looked at the junior high school kids, how big they appeared to me, and how difficult it would be to play at that level; I hoped I could do it when I got to that stage. When I was in junior high, I looked at the high school kids and they were so big — 200 pounds and all that stuff — it was scary to think of playing at the next level. But I concentrated on it and when the opportunity came, I tried my hardest. Then all of a sudden, boom — I'm playing at that level.

It was the same way going from high school to college. It was just the next level to go to and the next challenge ahead. I didn't think about pro football seriously until the end of my junior year when I finished third in the Heisman balloting. I realized then that I was in the elite of college football and I was probably going to have an opportunity to play professionally. I thought even playing at the college level was going to be a reach because of my size. That's what I had been told by everybody anyway. It just amazed me that at each level I went to, I just played and did the same thing I had been doing for years, and things seemed to happen.

I was very intimidated by Donald Trump. He was very impressive. The first time I went into Trump Tower to meet him in his office in the penthouse, I was with Bob, my father, and Gerard Phelan, whom Bob also represented and whose USFL rights were owned by the Generals. We sat down in Donald's minitheater and watched this film on the Trump empire.

Bob Woolf wrote about it in his book *Friendly Persuasion*:

> The lights went down and the curtains parted and for the next 20 minutes, we were shown a slickly produced, visually attractive, highly impressive presentation detailing the triumphs and achievements of Donald Trump. It was impressive. It was his commercial. Maybe he wanted to make sure we knew the extent of his accomplishments. It was his attempt to earn our respect and create the right atmosphere before our negotiations took place. Only after we had seen the film in its entirety were we shown into Mr. Trump's office.
>
> Power and influence hung in the air like cologne. A scale model of Television City, Trump's latest project involving roughly 75 acres of Manhattan's Upper West Side along the Hudson River with plans to develop the entire area plus erect the world's tallest building, was spread across a table like the future.
>
> And the vista was fabulous. From the room-length windows you received a panorama of New York City — it was all displayed before us, a beautiful and expansive sight. The World Trade Center, lower Manhattan, Greenwich Village, Chelsea, the Empire State Building, the glass and steel towers of midtown, Central Park and beyond. Trump took the young football star over to the window for a closer view.
>
> "There's ABC, NBC, CBS," he said, motioning to the surrounding skyscrapers that housed the three networks. "The city is at your beck and call. This is your city, Doug," he confided. "It's at your feet."
>
> I thought we'd be heading downstairs for lunch at a fancy place like 21, but Trump had something else in store; he sent out for sandwiches. A bag lunch with a billionaire. It wasn't a bad touch. He had tried to temper a potentially intimidating situation by showing us he was a regular guy.
>
> But basically he was looking to gain our respect. I can't blame him for doing this. Trump is a good negotiator.

Bob told the media the opportunity to play in New York was a major factor in my decision.

"It's very, very important to be in the same backfield with Herschel Walker, to be with the Generals and to be associated with Donald Trump," he said. "From my point of view [regarding commercial opportunities], it probably meant more to me than Doug."

The Bills wished me luck — sort of.

"God bless him, I guess," Bills general manager Terry Bledsoe was quoted in the *Buffalo News*. "I think the possibility that some people are going to go another way is inherent due to the fact our draft is in April. If we had formed a conviction on Doug Flutie and acted upon that decision and failed to get it done, I would feel badly. But this is one of the things that happens when you have another league out there, especially one that goes to training camp in January. It's a potential happening. I wish we, as a league, don't lose anybody [to the USFL], but I don't think that's practical."

The Bills eventually chose Virginia Tech defensive tackle Bruce Smith with their first choice and he became a big part of their success — along with Jim Kelly, who joined them when the USFL folded the next year. The Los Angeles Rams selected me in the 11th round.

Two days after I verbally agreed to the deal, I received a hero's parade through the streets of Natick on what was billed as Doug Flutie Day. Natick had a population of some 30,000, and the parade drew an estimated crowd of 10,000, including 1,000 parade participants. They named a street in my honor called Flutie Pass.

Almost two weeks after the verbal agreement, the deal was formally done. My family and I went to New York to announce the signing. We were walking on the street and Bob Woolf pulled up in a limo. As he and his family got out, we went in and toured New York. Bob made it feel like it was a really big deal to me. He made me feel special and made me feel like I was important to him and his family.

Bob had pushed Donald Trump into publicizing the signing. He also talked about this aspect in *Friendly Persuasion*.

I needed to make Trump understand how good he would look by signing Flutie. He'd made big media splashes with the Grand Hyatt Hotel, Trump Tower, Trump Plaza and his Atlantic City casinos. But, I assured him, "If you go public with word of Flutie's signing, you will get more exposure this weekend than you have ever had in your life."

Finally persuaded, Trump made the announcement at 10 a.m. in the lobby of the Trump Tower. The two-story waterfall in the building's atrium served as the backdrop for the conference. Reporters swarmed around the podium. Photographers' cameras flashed. That night, Trump was on the nightly news on all three networks. Newspapers headlined the story. The photos showed the handsome countenances of Trump and Flutie. Dan Rather introduced a clip on the evening news by calling the Flutie deal "the biggest contract in pro football history." My client was newly wealthy and Trump was thrilled to pay for the privilege of signing Doug.

So by the end of the day, Trump was calling me a genius — me, who had just cost him $8.3 million. I had done my job.

Here I am, just turned 22. I was very naive; I was a guy saying, "Yes sir," "No sir," and I was just trying to be polite about things. I was saying, "Yeah, I'm gonna do the best I can and all that stuff." I look at some of my comments and quotes and I feel like slapping myself. I should have been a little more aggressive. Once I stepped on the football field I was fine. I took control. I did what I had to do to win. I guess it's part of maturing and becoming a leader to look back and see my demeanor and the way I handled some of that stuff. It would have been nicer to be more affirmative and more forceful in the way I did things.

DONALD TRUMP:

He gave credibility to the league. I always thought Doug had a great future with the team. I always felt he was a great player. He was always somebody who could move the ball. Maybe he didn't have the

physical stature of some of these perfect guys, but he had the ability
to move the ball a lot better than them. You had some of these guys
coming out that had all the physical attributes, that could throw the
ball 100 yards and everything else, but they didn't have his spirit."

Bob said the contract was one of the most difficult of the
more than 2,000 sports deals in which he had been involved. It
totalled 50 pages and contained all sorts of clauses and contin-
gencies, including injuries, a merger of the USFL and NFL and
the demise of the USFL.

"Because of the newness of the league and all the contingen-
cies that could happen, I had to make sure that Doug was pro-
tected," Bob told the media. He added the contract was "deserving of a Doug Flutie."

I was just very intimidated by the whole situation, and unfortunately I didn't enjoy that year as much as I should have, or
enjoy getting to know Donald Trump.

When I signed the contract, I thought all my worries and
concerns financially were over. I thought that was more money
than I could imagine. You don't realize that half of it is going to
taxes or a percentage is taken by your agent. It winds up being a
lot less than you think it's going to be, but all of a sudden I had
a lot more money. The one thing I did splurge on was a new car
— a 928 Porsche. I had never owned a car through high school,
college, any time. If I went anywhere with Laurie it was in her
car — she began working full-time after high school as a legal
secretary — and she ended up paying most of the time because
I didn't have any money. The Porsche was the one car I'd always
wanted and I bought it. I gave my parents some money and
bought a house for them in Natick. I was able to be there when
members of my family needed money or were in financial
trouble. At least there was a little safeguard there.

A few hours after the press conference, I flew to Orlando
where the team had its training camp. There was a huge media
gathering at the airport, much to the dismay of the team's assistant media relations director, Gary Croke.

GARY CROKE:

A lot of the media was calling me for information on his flight: What time is he coming in? What airline? Of course, I was trying to avoid all that because I didn't want it to be a huge mob scene at the airport. We just figured we'd allow him to come in the next day and do it the proper way and set up a press conference. We didn't want him inundated with cameramen and people of that nature at the airport, and unfortunately they found out what flight he came in on, so myself and two security people from the Generals showed up to escort him off the plane.

There was already maybe five or six TV crews already at the gate. We actually were able to get on the plane before anyone got off. We were able to get on the runway to the plane before Doug, our president Jay Seltzer, and Jim Valek, our GM, and tell them, "Look, when you get off this plane it's going to be chaos because of the TV crews and reporters. As soon as you get out of the airport, we're going to try to whisk you straight through, out to the cars, and don't talk to anybody."

Well, best-laid plans didn't happen that way. As soon as we came out it was just a mob scene. They just basically leapt on Doug and stuck cameras in his face and asked him a barrage of questions. It was like a rock star type of atmosphere. We had the security guards trying to hustle Doug through. Through all the madness we lost our head coach, Walt Michaels. Somehow he got caught up in the back of the group and was cornered by more media people. We had to send someone back to get him, rescuing him from the media, then we finally got out to the curb and threw Doug into a Cadillac. We had three Cadillacs and threw Walt and our front-office staff into the others and took off toward training camp. From the time he got off the plane until we got him into the car it was bedlam.

I was two weeks late for training camp and Walt Michaels made the rest of the team go through another week of double sessions so I would learn and catch up in a hurry. I'm sure that made me an instant hero with my teammates.

Brian Sipe, who was the returning starting quarterback, came up to me and was polite. Brian was traded after my second day there to the Jacksonville Bulls for a draft pick in 1986 and territorial considerations. He had two years left on a $2.3 million deal. I was thinking I could learn from a veteran like Brian, come along slowly and eventually get a chance to play, but obviously when you spend that much money on a guy, they want you to play right away and make an impact. It was a rude awakening to the realities of professional football.

WALT MICHAELS:

If someone can tell me how you can do more with a quarterback who comes in late, let me know how you can do it, I'd try it again. There's only so many things you can do with a quarterback coming in late. We didn't know what he could do best and he had no idea about our system and what we were trying to do with a pro-style offense. Doug did not have a background in classic, NFL, dropback-style quarterbacking, which is what we had in for Brian Sipe. You can do a lot of things, but you not only have to coach Doug, you've got to remember there's tight ends and there's wide receivers, there's Herschel Walker, a running back, there was Maurice Carthon, a fullback type of guy. There was a whole lot of other people besides Doug.

That's what people don't understand a lot of times. How long do you think it takes a quarterback to really get ready to play in the pros? You're fortunate if you can get a great one ready within a year, two years. I had Joe Namath with the Jets and by the end of his third year he started coming on. The fourth year we won the Super Bowl. [Dan] Marino got in there and just about at the end of the first year or second year, he started doing some things. [Johnny] Unitas didn't come on till a little later.

It was not anything against Doug. Many people think Doug could have done this or done that. No, no, no. It was too much of an adjustment for him to come in at the last minute. We didn't even know for sure if he was in great condition or in shape. We weren't sure how much he'd been throwing and whether we'd give him a sore arm.

That's all we needed to do was get Doug into too much throwing in one week's practice and find out that he had a sore arm. Now what do we do the rest of the year?

Herschel Walker was a good friend early on. He was making really good money, too. Herschel and I became very close friends in that year. I kind of needed Herschel there as a buffer and to help me with the transition. Clarence Collins also was a very close friend of mine and helped me through training camp.

The Generals immediately began hyping me up with radio ads that said: "Flutie's here, so what are you waiting for? Get your season tickets now!" Season ticket subscriptions rose by 6,000 to 33,000, and ABC announced plans to kick off its season by showing us against the Birmingham Stallions.

The first exhibition game was against Orlando, and I threw interceptions on my first two passes. I tried to gun an in-route, *boom*, I hit a linebacker in the chest. I try to throw a slant route, *boom*, I hit a linebacker in the chest. Both were picked off by Jeff Gabrielsen. It was only an exhibition game and I wound up doing some good scrambling and throwing some nice balls. We ended up winning 24-14. I completed 7 of 18 for 173 yards, including a 64-yarder to Clarence Collins. It was a typical rookie debut. I took my lumps. I had a shaky start, but I bounced back.

Eight days later I made my regular-season debut in Birmingham and we lost 38-28. I was definitely nervous at the start. I'm under center and we're trying to mix the run in there and do this and do that, and I just didn't throw the ball well. I missed my first nine passes and finished with 12 completions in 27 attempts for 189 yards. With 2:18 left in the third quarter I threw a six-yard hitch route to Clarence Collins. It was low and in the dirt and he reached down and made a really nice catch. I walked up to him and said, "Thanks, I really needed that one." We were down 31-7 at that point and I started going with a no-huddle and calling my own plays. I began using the shotgun and just going into a hurry-up offense. *Boom*, I was in my element. We moved the ball up and down the field, scored 28 points, and got within three. We had a chance and I threw an interception, my third of the game. We were running and gunning for the whole fourth quarter. There I found my niche. It was like all of a sudden, yeah, that's it, just do the stuff you've always done. Get in the shotgun, go no-huddle, throw the hell out of the ball.

The following week the coaches came to me and said, we've got to start going into the no-huddle. We started the game against Orlando in a no-huddle offense. I was in the shotgun, calling my own plays and we were off and running. I threw four touchdown passes, three in the first half, and it was like night and day from the previous game. We blew them out in the first half and in the second half we went back to the old offense and didn't do squat. We won the game 28-10 after leading 21-0 at the half.

WALT MICHAELS:

My offensive coordinator, Chris Palmer, had a background in Connecticut, and I said, "Chris, you get up there and get everything you possibly can that Doug's effective at doing and did at Boston College, because that's what we have to go with. We don't have time to indoctrinate Doug into a lot of things because Donald Trump is not going to be sitting around patiently waiting for us to do something. We've got to win regardless of who says what, why, or anything."

We incorporated much of his roll-out styles, sprint-outs, and, when he had a chance to, scrambling. But we told him, "Don't start your scrambling too early, Doug, or these big guys are going to catch you. Start your scrambling toward the end of the game when defensive linemen are tired, when they're not as fast, not as fresh." Once he was starting to get into shape, he was fine.

We never really got back to a full, wide-open attack like that again. I loved Herschel and he ran the ball great, which is what we ended up doing better than anything that season. He set a pro football record with 2,411 rushing yards and was the league's most valuable player.

My favorite win of the season came in the third game of the season. It was our home opener at the Meadowlands and it attracted a crowd of 58,741, the largest ever to watch the Generals play. The visiting team was the Los Angeles Express, who were led by Steve Young, the other big-money quarterback in the league.

We won 35-24 after falling behind 24-14 with 1:33 left in the third quarter. We went into a no-huddle situation and started throwing the ball and scrambling a little bit. I scored three rushing touchdowns, including the go-ahead one with 2:57 left in the game on a two-yard run. It capped off a 78-yard drive in which I hit on three of four passes for 63 yards, including an 18-yard underhand flip to Clarence Harmon. I only completed 7 of 19 passes for 100 yards, but jammed a finger on my throwing hand early in the game. I was the game's top rusher with 97 yards on nine carries. The overall performance earned me player of the week honors.

In the opening quarter we used a play we put in that week. It was an unusual formation, lining up seven players to the left and center Kent Hull in the middle of the field to snap the ball to me in the shotgun formation. There were two receivers to the right. The play didn't have a name, but Walt Michaels was thinking of calling it the Tower — as in the Trump Tower. The first time we ran it I threw a two-yard pass to Maurice Carthon and had a 15-yard personal foul tagged on. A few plays later we tried it again and I ran for 11 yards. In the second quarter, we did it again. I threw a pass to Kent for 12 yards, but the play was nullified because of an illegal procedure.

WALT MICHAELS:

Chris Palmer came up with it. We got to talking: "What can we do differently and impress Donald Trump with Doug's ability to scramble and do things?" We moved the line over. We ran what's considered a perfectly legal formation. We alerted the officials. Of course, we'd snap the ball on one side and throw it back the other side and we'd spring it on somebody hoping that they weren't ready for the formation. We didn't do it that many times because once they see it on film, you weren't going to get away with it.

*That was Donald's style. I didn't begrudge him. It's his team. He
owned it. He wanted to see certain things. He wanted input — he
had a right to do that — and as a result we were trying to give him
something that he could talk about, and it was exciting and he did
talk about it. It was different. It was kind of, "Let's see what he
thinks," and in the meantime I felt after we had done it that he liked
it. It was a combination of, "Let's see if we can get something done."
We have to play against the opposition with a young quarterback —
a scrambler like Doug can do very well — and all the crazy things
we thought could happen. There were a whole lot of reasons for it. We
knew we couldn't do it often, but we got it done and we made
everybody wonder every week what we were going to come up with.*

We were 3-3 after our first six games and people became frustrated and worried and started criticizing me. Whenever we were
in that running mode, I never got into a rhythm. I was under
center, throwing the ball in third-down situations and there was
never any rhythm to it. I always did my best when it was the
two-minute offense, last drive of the half, last drive of the game;
all that. I'd get into the shotgun and start letting it fly. That's
when I succeeded.

We beat Houston 31-25 in our seventh game and then won
our next three. We split two of our next four games, leading to a
home game against Memphis. We won 17-7 and Herschel gained
209 yards for a total of 1,967 to surpass his mark of 1,812. But my
day — and what turned out my season and USFL career — was
over with 12:12 left in the first half.

Reggie White ran me down on a bootleg. I didn't see him
coming and he wrapped me up and body-slammed me into the
turf. I knew right away my left shoulder was messed up. I just
got up, walked to the bench and sat down. At halftime, ABC
announced I had broken my collarbone and was out for the season, which only had three games left in it. Laurie was up in one
of the press boxes with Donald and Ivana Trump and she
thought, "Oh, yeah, sure. Doug's not hurt." I had never been
injured before.

DONALD TRUMP:

I wouldn't want Reggie White falling on me. Doug really got clobbered. Reggie White is a strong guy. I thought Doug would come back because that's Doug spirit, but I wasn't sure about that season. He was badly hurt.

Ron Reeves took over for me and won the next game, but we lost our final two regular-season games and finished as the wild-card team instead of the first-place team, which we should have been. I should have been out for six to eight weeks, but it was my non-throwing shoulder. I had rested my arm for a few weeks, and I was throwing the heck out of the ball. It just felt great. I went to Walt Michaels and told him I felt great and that I could play. He said, "There's no way. It's not healed. I know the doctors are telling you that you can play." His primary concern was protecting me. He thought Donald Trump had put pressure on the doctors to say that I was healthy to make me play. You don't have to convince me to play. I wanted to play, and I thought I could.

I was throwing the ball great all week. I expected to start that game and finally at the end of the week, Walt came up to me and said, "I'm not going to let you play because you're just going to break it again." Looking back on it and seeing what other guys have done with broken collarbones, Walt was probably right. I've seen guys come back just a little too soon. It was probably the smart thing to do even though I felt like I was 100 percent.

WALT MICHAELS:

I personally delivered the X-rays to New York to an orthopedic friend of mine who had done much more work than our [team] orthopedic man. I had nothing against our orthopedic man. He was a good guy, [but] I did not know for sure how much pressure may have been put on him. I felt there was. I said [to the New York orthopedist], "Would

*you look at these X-rays?" Before I got back to sit in the office and do
everything, he called and said: "I'm not going to tell you not to play
him, I'm going to tell you don't even let him practice. If he were to
fall, slip and with bodies falling around and he put that arm back, he
may refracture it. He could cut and sever an artery, sever a nerve,
puncture a lung. There's too many things. That thing is not totally
healed."*

*I had Richard Todd with a broken collarbone when he was with
the Jets. It took Richard six weeks before he could even practice, so we
didn't play him until the seventh week and mostly in the eighth
week. And Richard was a much bigger guy. I was definitely afraid. I
didn't want anything like that possibly on my mind — no matter
what anyone said — that Doug Flutie went into a game and I let
him in there and I could have kept him out as the head coach. I didn't
care who said anything because I had checked it with another doctor
who had more experience with sports injuries and, in particular,
collarbones.*

*I'm sure Doug realizes it now and I said, "Doug, you'll thank
me for this years from now. You may never play again if that thing
were to shatter and break downward, however it may happen." I'd
still do it again whether it would be Doug Flutie or Joe Blow. Whatever the reasoning was behind Donald Trump saying he was fine,
well, Donald Trump was not an orthopedic doctor who should have
recommended anything on that. And the strangest way it happened
was that the team orthopedic said, "Walt, I don't think see there's
any way he could be ready." And he came to me two days later and
said, "Walt, I've reevaluated the X-rays and I think you should play
him." That's when I went and checked again. Donald Trump didn't
particularly like that I did that and I'm not sure he really realized
even today that I did that, but I would do it again.*

I dressed but didn't play in the playoff game, and we lost.
The great thing was Walt Michaels thinking about my future
and not about that particular game itself. I never lost a home
game in the pros and, in fact, never lost a game at all in New
Jersey, going back to college.

I finished my rookie season with 134 completions in 281 attempts — a 47.7 percent average — and 2,109 yards, throwing 13 touchdowns and 14 interceptions. I also rushed 65 times for 465 yards.

WALT MICHAELS:

I'd like to have known what Doug would have done in those playoff games if he didn't get hurt. We were beginning to get comfortable with him. He created other problems for coaches and he created other problems for defenses. He makes you sit up a little later to plan things that he could do that a dropback quarterback can't. You've got to change some things you're doing. It's not him necessarily that you've got to coach. You've got to start coaching those other guys to start doing something different. You say, he's replacing Brian Sipe, the quarterback, but there's 10 other guys on the field. Those big tackles who have to protect that guy, now look what they have to do when they don't know where he is behind them.

In early August, New Jersey and Houston merged. Donald Trump said collectively it would probably be the best team in football. Houston head coach Jack Pardee and his staff took over from Walt Michaels and his staff. The offense would be radically different. We'd be going from principally a running team to one that featured a run-and-shoot, which was more wide open.

Laurie and I were married that summer at St. Patrick's Roman Catholic Church in Natick, and it was reported on the wire service. A crowd of some 300 gathered and Coach Bick rearranged practice so the team members could attend the reception.

The following May the trial began in the USFL's $1.32 billion antitrust lawsuit against the NFL. The USFL accused the NFL of monopolizing football and conspiring to destroy it. The lawsuit had been lodged 19 months before and the NFL unanimously agreed the previous December not to consider any merger and or settlement with the USFL. The USFL had no TV contract. ABC, which had telecast the league in the first three years, didn't like the fall schedule idea. Neither NBC nor CBS, which televised the NFL, wanted the USFL. The USFL claimed the NFL prevented the networks from bidding and that its contracts with all three networks constituted an illegal monopoly. The USFL wanted an injunction to stop that and $440 million in damages, which would have been tripled in an antitrust lawsuit.

During the trial, we had a couple of minicamps in New Jersey. We had four quarterbacks: Jim Kelly and myself, Todd Dillon, and Danny Barrett. Both Todd and Danny later played in the CFL. Danny, in fact, was traded to British Columbia by Calgary a month after I signed with the Stampeders. When I left Calgary to join Toronto, Danny signed with the Stampeders after leaving Ottawa. Danny and I always had some interesting games.

There was all this talk about the battle between Jim Kelly and myself for the starter's job. Jim was an excellent quarterback. Todd Dillon was his backup, and Jim considered him a very capable backup. *Sports Illustrated* did a cover story on Jim as the next great quarterback in pro football and indicated he dwarfed me physically and verbally. I said in the article that Jim treated me well, that I didn't think there was a problem between us and that we could coexist.

A few days later the *New York Daily News'* Paul Needell had a story headlined "Kelly Warns Flutie," in which he stated I would have to beat out Todd Dillon for the backup job. Jim said in the article I can "win Heismans and everything and still wind up third string." He was just reinforcing that Dillon was a good quarterback. However, it came across that he thought Todd was better than me and I would be the third-stringer. I think more than anything he was trying to boost up his buddy, Todd Dillon, at the time. Todd and I are good friends and we get along great. Jim and I get along great. I run into him every now and then. There's never been any problems with me and Jim Kelly or Todd Dillon.

John Jenkins was the offensive coordinator, and coincidentally, we hooked up again 11 years later when he became offensive coordinator of the Toronto Argonauts.

JOHN JENKINS:

Doug was in the learning process, whereas Jim and Todd had been in this system with me. For Jim to make that kind of remark, he was underestimating Flutie's competitiveness tremendously. Jack Pardee was the head coach and was very reliant on me to call the shots offensively and this thing — Jim Kelly, Doug Flutie — would have come down to who's making the plays, who is the guy going into training camp that deserves the job. That would have been it. You can't give Doug Flutie a better scenario than that in my opinion...I had seen Kelly improve and develop and become accustomed to what he was doing in this offense, whereas Doug was merely going through the learning process, and that's one thing nobody can help.

Bob Woolf was pretty upset about the way he thought Donald Trump was treating me at the time. Donald Trump had sunk a lot of money into me and had a lot of high expectations. I went out and worked my butt off and we were sitting in first place nearing the playoffs before I got hurt. All of a sudden he's ready to ditch me and let Jim Kelly be the quarterback after merging with the Houston Gamblers. Bob felt Donald was slighting me after all I had done for him. You can't help injuries. They're going to happen occasionally, and Bob just didn't think I was treated fairly when the two teams merged. Like I said, I was a naive kid and I didn't know what was going on. I was just doing what I was supposed to do.

On July 30, the jury found the NFL guilty of monopolizing pro football, but awarded the USFL damages of only $1, which was tripled to $3 in accordance with such lawsuits. The USFL was also awarded $7 million in legal fees.

DONALD TRUMP:

When I went into the league in the second season, I never thought it was going to make it in the spring. I always saw it as a litigation that would be successful. And I was right, but I was wrong because we only got a dollar.

The league announced plans to challenge the decision and there was talk that training camps would open as scheduled in two weeks. The quarterbacks and receivers were training in Houston at the time. I was hanging out with Scott McGhee and Todd Dillon. Todd, Scott and myself had come back from a workout and were watching TV the day they announced the decision of the lawsuit. The phone rang and Scott answered it and said something like, "Scott McGhee, Job Search." In other words, he knew he was out of a job and looking for one.

The owners had a scheduled meeting five days after the jury's decision to decide whether to go ahead and play or fold. Some players like Jim Kelly wanted a definitive answer. Jim had a chance to play for Buffalo, which owned his rights. The owners met a few days later in Washington to decide what to do. The day before the meeting, Donald told the media he might let Herschel, Jim and myself out of our contracts. He said that even though he had a legal right to our services, he didn't have a moral right to stand in the way of our careers.

Jim Kelly joined Buffalo, Herschel Walker joined Dallas, which had his rights, and I went back home to finish off my communications degree and wait for an offer from the NFL.

"Da Bears"

The Rams had Steve Bartkowski and Dieter Brock, a former standout in the CFL who had just undergone knee surgery, and Steve Dils. Howard Cosell wrote in his syndicated column that the Rams needed me desperately and if they didn't there were other teams who did. Howard added the real reason I was sitting at home instead of playing for some team was because I had become the sacrificial lamb "in all the ugliness between the USFL and NFL. Certain people in the NFL may want him to sit out a season or more and force Trump to pay him, to punish Trump, if you will, for the lawsuit."

Howard had testified in the trial that Roone Arledge, who was an executive with ABC, had confided to him that NFL commissioner Pete Rozelle put pressure on him to drop USFL coverage. Roone Arledge said under oath he said no such thing.

Howard ended his column by writing it was sad for me not to be allowed to play in the NFL. He said it was against the public interest because "the fans will be deprived of watching an exciting, young quarterback in action this season and sad, too, is what this tells us all, once again, about the NFL."

I had a potential opportunity to play basketball for Boston College. Gary Williams was the head coach and he needed a new point guard because Michael Adams had just graduated. It wound up I got permission from Donald to do it and then at the last moment he realized I was serious and vetoed it. I would have loved that because that was a team that made it to the final

Sweet 16 and I could have been a part of that. Dana Barros, who made it to the NBA with Boston, came in as a freshman. He probably would have taken over fairly quickly, but it would have been fun.

It was a frustrating time for me. *USA Today* did a story on me as the world's richest unemployed quarterback. Bob Woolf told the reporter David Leon Moore: "Call it a vacation for which Doug is paid $1.3 million." Laurie said, "It's tough to complain, but it's frustrating for Doug to sit here and watch while his friends play."

Because of the injury to Brock, the Rams made a move to acquire Jim Everett. He was a rookie out of Purdue but declined to sign with Houston. The Rams told me after the USFL freed its players they didn't want me because they didn't want to upset their quarterback situation. After hearing of the trade for Everett, Bob said in the *USA Today* article: "It looks like the Rams told us a lot of BS." The Rams made me a token offer of 50 grand and basically told me to "sit tight, we're going to deal you somewhere." I felt the Rams were afraid of making a mistake and probably didn't even look at one reel of film of me.

Bob was not sure whether the NFL's disinterest was an evaluation of my talent or because of my contract status with Donald Trump. I figured it all had to do with my height. That was the only knock on me. I wasn't a roll-out or option quarterback at Boston College. I was a dropback, pocket passer. I stepped up and threw through seams like everybody else did.

I could afford to sit around and wait. I wanted to play in the NFL just to silence the critics who said I couldn't, but in terms of my financial security it was too important to pass up on the money. In between completing my degree, I kept in shape running daily, lifting weights and working out with the Boston College team. On the anniversary of the game against Miami, *USA Today*'s David Leon Moore did a front-page story on me. The headline read: "Flutie Legend Was Secured A Year Ago." Reid Oslin, the sports information director at BC, was quoted as saying, "It does look a little funny, this guy driving up in a $50,000 car and running off to class with his 98-cent notebook."

While the Rams didn't want me, some teams did; particularly Chicago, whose general manager, Jerry Vainisi, and head coach, Mike Ditka, both liked me.

JERRY VAINISI:

My daughter went to Boston College the same time Doug Flutie did, and I kind of followed him and I just really liked him as an athlete. I thought overall he was an exceptional athlete. While he was short, that didn't really bother me because he had big, large hands, so he could grip the football and throw it and he had terrific arm strength and everything and I just felt he was a winner. I liked his character and all the intangibles about him, and I talked to Mike and we knew that [Jim] McMahon was gimpy from earlier in the season.

In '84 at the end of the season, we felt we were the best team in the NFL, except we lost to San Francisco in the NFC championship game because Steve Fuller had an off day and the offense was ineffective. At that time, in 1986, we still didn't feel that Mike Tomczak was far enough along to get us over the hump if, in fact, McMahon couldn't make it through the season.

We were looking around to see what quarterbacks were available, and knowing that Flutie was out there and there was the rap on him for the size and everything — and Mike liked him for all the same reasons I did — I just said, "You want me to explore Flutie and see what the Rams want for him just as an insurance policy? If it's not too high a price to pay, maybe we'll make a move." He was excited about it and I made some calls to the Rams.

On September 30, I tried out with Green Bay, which had Tom Coughlin as its quarterback coach, but then the Packers signed Chuck Fusina, who played with Philadelphia in the USFL. On October 14 at 3:54 p.m., six minutes before the trade deadline, the Bears acquired my rights from the Rams for a sixth-round draft choice and a flop of a third-rounder for a fourth-rounder.

McMahon blasted Ditka and the Bears management for acquiring me and said it wasn't sitting well with a bunch of players. McMahon was upset because Mike Tomczak and Steve Fuller were good friends of his. He felt they were quality quarterbacks and the Bears didn't need to go outside of the organization to find someone else. Jim made it difficult for me from that standpoint, making some snide remarks in the media. These were guys he had won the Super Bowl with the year before. It was his team and the players respected his opinion. It just made it a real tough situation for me.

JERRY VAINISI:

That's what really, I think, undermined the whole thing. McMahon polarized the offensive unit against Flutie. He came out and challenged management and said that we were disloyal, that if he couldn't play then we should stay with the guys who had gone through [training] camp and had gotten us there. And if he couldn't play, then Fuller should play and if Fuller couldn't play then Tomczak should play. But once we're through camp we shouldn't be going outside the body of the team and bringing in new people.

That was McMahon's opinion — and you'll get all kinds of disagreement on this point, too — but the way I saw it and the way I felt it unfolded was he was clearly the leader of the offensive unit, especially the offensive line that he would go out with every week for dinner and stuff. If he had embraced Flutie as a move by the club for us to get better just in case of injuries — as an inexpensive insurance policy — the whole attitude of the offensive unit would have been different and the end result could have been different, I think. But it wasn't.

Mike and I were part owners of Ditka's Restaurant, and Mike had his weekly television show and brought Doug with him to be one of his guests. There were TV cameras all over the place. There was a perception on the part of the veteran players that Doug was getting all the attention that they were otherwise due; that he hadn't proven himself yet and yet he's getting all this attention, and he's got the coach and GM taking him out to dinner, and all this garbage. The whole thing started off on the wrong foot.

MIKE DITKA:

I don't think it was only McMahon. I think it was other people in the organization, too, some other players. Players get jealous; they're very petty at times. I think that's what happened, especially when they saw I really embraced Doug. I embraced him because he's an outstanding person, as well as being a good football player. I base a lot of my judgments on people and he was that. I like that in a person and I think that bothered some of the players. It almost looked like there was a little vendetta against him.

We had to sign before November 21 because the rules were you couldn't sign within 30 days of the season's end. I signed a three-year deal which paid $125,000 in 1987 and $150,000 in 1988. The salary for 1986 was prorated for the remaining games. It didn't matter how much Chicago paid me. I just wanted to get my foot in the door. We came to a settlement with Trump on 80 percent of the money he owed me and he paid it over the next couple of years.

I took the number 2, Gerard's sweater number in college.

There were many members of the media at my first day of practice. Mike Ditka told the media after it was over, "I said to the players I'd like to introduce Doug Flutie. A couple of them threw tomatoes at me."

Ditka's wife invited me over to their house for a family Thanksgiving dinner. I was living in Chicago by myself while Laurie stayed at home. It turned into a nice day. We watched the football games and I didn't think anything of it. Obviously some of the players on the team were jealous about that situation and that created a little more tension.

MIKE DITKA:

I thought it was a unique opportunity to have him out for Thanksgiving dinner. I've had a couple other players out to the house over the years and it was for the same reason. I liked him, plus I thought

*that was the time they should be with somebody. He didn't have time
to go home. He didn't have time to be with his family, so I just
wanted to make him feel at home. That was my main concern.*

The whole system was backward for me. Odds and evens
were opposite for me. Everybody does evens right, odds left.
They did it the opposite way and that made things a little more
difficult for me.

I was activated November 4 after having had only a handful
of snaps in practice. We had a game against Tampa Bay in five
days and Mike Ditka was quoted in *USA Today* as saying I was
doing very well and that if the situation arose in the game he
would use me. I saw some action at the end. I ran once and lost
a yard and threw an incomplete pass. It should have been a touchdown pass to tight end Emery Moorhead, but I threw it over his
head. Tomczak started and the team won 23-3.

McMahon aggravated a shoulder two weeks later and was
lost for the season. About 10 days after that, Ditka talked about
me in an article by *Chicago Tribune*'s Don Pierson: "There's a lot
of qualities you have to look for besides how tall he is, how fast
he runs, and how high he jumps. We've had a lot of those guys
who look good in the shower. I'm not looking for them. I'm looking for football players. This guy is a football player. . . I doubt
there are many who are as good an athlete as he is overall. And,
I'll tell you what: Don't be surprised about his arm strength. . . .
Whether he'll wind up as our starting quarterback remains to be
seen. He has got the qualities you look for in a person. He is
such a good person it's unbelievable, but I just want to find out
right now where we're at so we'll be okay when that first weekend in January rolls around."

I played against Tampa Bay in the next game, and this time I
had a bigger role. Tomczak started, but I split time with him because Ditka wanted to get me into the game. I played in the second
quarter and completed two of seven for 79 yards and one touchdown, a 27-yarder to Walter Payton. I also ran two times for seven
yards, including a four-yard touchdown. We won 48-14.

JERRY VAINISI:

What he was trying to do was get Flutie ready and forcefeed as much NFL experience as possible for the remaining games so we could be successful in the playoffs, but the players saw that as favoritism. With McMahon's criticism and the lack of support by the offensive players, it became a state of who's running the asylum. Was it the inmates or the wardens? From that standpoint there may have been a little bit of forcing the issue, too, that we believed if we were going to have any chance to win that we had to get Doug ready.

A week later we played on Monday night against Detroit, which had rookie Chuck Long as its quarterback. I had no idea it would turn out to be a battle of two rookie quarterbacks. Tomczak started but bruised the tibia in his right leg in the first quarter and I was thrust into action. I had a wristband with a handful of plays. I didn't even know the signals from the sidelines but knew the plays to run. I had some completions on my first series and that led to a 41-yard field goal by Kevin Butler. The interception came off a tipped ball and a fumble, which I recovered, but we weren't hurt too badly, down 6-3 at the half. The Lions took advantage of a fumble to score a TD in the third quarter. We scored another field goal, and then late in the game, I engineered a 74-yard drive in eight plays that ended with a four-yard run by Matt Suhey with 5:49 to go. I played a very mediocre game and did a couple of good things. We won 16-13 on a 22-yard field goal on the last play of the game by Kevin. I completed 13 of 24 passes for 130 yards and one interception and ran six times for 11 yards.

"Thank God for the offensive line, for Walter Payton," I said afterward. "If they hadn't done it, we wouldn't have won the game. I didn't expect to struggle this much when I got my chance. I know I can do a lot better, obviously. I guess this was my initiation, and I took my lumps."

Looking back on the game, I remember a situation in which we were inside the 10-yard line. A play was signalled in and we had the wrong personnel on the field. I called for time and Mike Ditka just lost it because he figured I wasted the timeout. He liked me and didn't want to get too mad at me, but he was ranting at me for about 20 or 30 seconds. This is the image everyone has of me from that Monday night game. Ditka wound up getting so frustrated because he didn't want to get mad at me that he turned to Emery Moorhead and started yelling at him. Meanwhile, I'm standing there with Jim McMahon, and he and I really don't speak because we don't have too much to say to one another.

MIKE DITKA:

That's what did bother me, the timeout. Doug was talking about all different terminology and all I was trying to do was get the play and the formation to him. I knew if I could get it into him it would work and it did work. I propelled Emery Moorhead into the game to make sure he got the right formation. I've never been one for signals and we were trying to use signals at that time. I just made sure the player took it in and told him exactly what we wanted.

I had my first start six days later in Dallas and we won 24-10. I was good on 8 of 14 passes for 152 yards. I had two TDs, a 58-yarder to running back Neil Anderson and a 33-yarder to Willie Gault. The 58-yarder traveled 50 yards in the air, and the 33-yarder came on a broken play in which I slid outside a block by Jim Covert and found Willie alone in the end zone. I was really in a groove. I only played the first half and Tomczak and Fuller played the second half. There was no doubt I should be the starter going into the playoffs. I earned my shot. Here I am, a rookie, going after the Super Bowl.

The headline in the *Chicago Tribune* story written the next day by Don Pierson read: "Bears Bury Cowboys, Flutie Tosses 2 TD Passes."

"Doug Flutie gave Mike Ditka an early Christmas present Sunday," Pierson wrote. "There will be peace on Chicago's earth for at least two weeks. Flutie made enough big plays in Sunday's 24-10 victory over the Dallas Cowboys to eliminate a quarterback controversy until the Bears begin to defend their world championship against either the Washington Redskins or San Francisco 49ers."

"I think the little guy is pretty special," Ditka said. "I've thought that for a long time and the more he plays the more I know he's pretty special. He makes things happen. He's a winner. He's got great leadership quality. I'll make that decision [about the starting quarterback for the playoffs]. I'll be very sincere. I'm leaning, very, very heavily that way. I doubt that I would lean any other way. Performance speaks for itself. He makes things happen. Period."

Mike Singletary said, "Today I think Flutie gained whatever respect that might have been lacking. You don't just come into a team and get respect and acceptance. That's just the way it is. It's one thing to be a marvelous person and to throw a pretty spiral, but you've got to do it on the field. And Doug has and he did. We will be okay."

In a *Washington Post* article that appeared on New Year's Day, Ditka said I had "eyes like a deer." He jokingly admitted to having trouble yelling at me because "it's just like hollering at Bambi. I get letters from school teachers all over the country not to do it."

I showed up at practice and over my locker it read "Bambi." McMahon wasn't going to let that die, so I had to deal with that a little bit. McMahon appeared on the *Tonight Show* and said my inexperience would show in the playoffs and the Bears would have to go with Fuller.

We were 7-1/2-point favorites to win at home against Washington, but we lost 27-13 in front of a crowd of 65,141. I didn't have a good game, completing only 11 of 31 for 134 yards. The Redskins opened the scoring at 12:45 of the first quarter on a 28-yard pass from Jay Schroeder to Art Monk. I threw a TD in the second quarter, a 50-yarder to Willie Gault. Kevin Butler kicked two field goals, and we led 13-7 at the half.

It fell apart in the second half. I had two interceptions in the game, including one in the third quarter by cornerback Darrell

Green, who was beaten on Willie Gault's TD. The ball was intended for tight end Tim Wrightman but sailed over his head. Three plays later the Redskins scored to lead 14-13. After moving the ball well on our next series, we turned it over when Walter Payton, the best running back in the history of the NFL, fumbled on the Redskins' 17-yard line after defensive tackle Darryl Grant hit him. Washington responded with an 83-yard touchdown drive.

There was a lot written about the team and me. Washington safety Curtis Jordan said, "I felt late in the first quarter Flutie was flustered. He was having trouble throwing over our front people. I just don't think he was ready for this type of game. He hadn't played against a good football team . . . His height hurts him. I don't think he can see over the line. That's why he had so many of those overthrows."

"I don't think what happened today had anything to do with [me] doing too much too soon," I said. "I wasn't nervous before the game. I felt more comfortable than I felt in Dallas. It had nothing to do with me being so new. Would I have felt any different if I'd have been here a year instead of a few months? Probably not. Things just weren't clicking today. I'll learn from it, but it wasn't a situation to go in and learn. It was a situation to go in and win."

I told the media I would take some of the responsibility for the loss. "The team as a whole didn't play exceptionally well, but I'll accept part of the blame. It's a bittersweet ending for me. I was happy for the chance to be here. Where was I three months ago? I'm sorry it wound up this way. People expect big things of me. I expect it of myself."

MIKE DITKA:

I just believed that he was going to take us to the Super Bowl and win it. I came to that conclusion when I brought him there. There's an old Biblical saying, "And a child shall lead us," and I really did believe that. If we had played even close to our potential against Washington we would have beat them and went to the Super Bowl, but we had a very poor game in a couple areas, especially our offensive line that day. Why? I don't know. It wasn't Doug.

Doug really held up in the playoffs. He really played well enough to win the game. We had a couple dropped passes and very little protection for the quarterback. That was the thing that hurt. We didn't change our system at all. We stayed as it was instead of adjusting the system to fit Doug a little better by using half-rolls and getting him out of the pocket more. If we would have done that I think we would have really enhanced his value tremendously, but at that time it was already into the season, although we could have devised a package weekly and tried to work on it.

I believed in what we were doing and I believed he could execute that as well as any other quarterback we had. That didn't bother me at all. I just felt, why change if I believed in it and I thought he could do it. I never worried about that.

Patriot Games

In the off-season the Bears had me on a weightlifting program. I felt real stiff and I didn't feel like I was throwing the ball as well as I did the year before. I didn't like the way it felt and that really aggravated me in hindsight. Here I am trying to work hard and lift and get a little stronger and impress people, and it wasn't the best thing for me. I think this is where I first developed the problems that led to my elbow tendonitis problems in Calgary.

I came to camp after they had drafted Jim Harbaugh and I was low man on the totem pole. Basically I was in a position to be traded. It was a very frustrating time for me. It just wasn't a comfortable situation. I went to Mike Ditka and he told me that as long as he was the head coach I wasn't going anywhere. He really believed in my talents and my abilities and was going to stick with me. Tomczak was the starter, McMahon had shoulder surgery and wasn't ready to play yet, and I was the backup.

Then came the players' strike. I went to a player rep meeting in Chicago and I realized that some of these guys just didn't know what they were doing and what they were talking about. Everyone stayed up and gave their point of view until five or six in the morning. The strike was basically over by then. These guys were ready to go back in. I was amazed at the lack of direction as far as the reps were concerned and the people involved in the union. I just shook my head.

Billy Sullivan, the owner of the New England Patriots, and his son, Patrick, who was the general manager, wanted me to play for their team and were prepared to make a trade. It was a chance to go home, so I jumped at the opportunity. The only negative was they wanted me to play that week against Houston in a strike game. I initially told them I didn't want to do it, but they said it was a condition of the trade.

I was kind of rolling the dice and figured the strike would end so I wouldn't have to play in that game. So, I did it and New England traded an eighth-round pick in 1988 to acquire my services.

MIKE DITKA:

Believe me, I didn't initiate it. It was brought to me by somebody in the Bears organization — but it's not worth mentioning who — that "This was a chance we can go with our people, the Sullivans really need him," and this and that. So I'm thinking maybe this is best for Doug, he's going back home, and I rationalized myself into saying it was a good deal for him. I never knew if it was a good deal for him. I don't know. I regretted doing it at the time, but I did it because I thought — as silly as it sounds — it would be the most humane thing for him. There was like a vendetta against him from some of those players, and it was very unfair to him. And I figured if this is what it's all about I don't want to beat my head up against a wall, and there's no use letting him beat his head up against a wall, so why not let him go to New England and enjoy himself.

RAYMOND BERRY (PATRIOTS HEAD COACH):

My concern was winning games, management's concern was staying in business, and Doug Flutie was fulfilling both roles. He could win for us, plus he was the most well-known local player in professional football at the time. Doug Flutie was the big name out of Boston, so it was a natural that he would really bring a lot of interest to the fans there and get people buying tickets.

The strike had ended three days before the game, but the owners locked out the players and didn't allow them in until the following Monday. I played in the strike game in Houston and did extremely well, completing 15 of 25 passes for 199 yards and one touchdown and running six times for 43 yards. I impressed the heck out of the coaching staff by learning a new system in a couple of days.

The veterans came back the day after the game, but at least I was home in New England. For the rest of that year I basically sat on the bench and didn't get an opportunity to play. We were one game away from going into the playoffs if we could beat Miami in the last week and some other teams lost. The wrong teams won and we didn't have a shot at making the playoffs, and played Miami in a useless game.

The next season I was in the best shape of my life going into training camp. I felt great. Tony Eason, who was No. 1 on the depth chart, spent most of the season on injured reserve after suffering a shoulder problem and an elbow injury. Steve Grogan was No. 2, Tom Ramsey was No. 3 and I was No. 4. Steve started the first four games and had his best outing in the season opener in which we beat the New York Jets 28-3. We lost our next three. Steve played very well, but couldn't play every week. The problem was he'd get banged up. In the off-season he had to have neck surgery to repair a herniated disk that was affecting his throwing arm. If he didn't have the surgery, his career would have been over.

Tom Ramsey started the fifth game against Indianapolis in New England and he didn't play badly. People dropped some balls on him and he didn't get a lot of support from the guys on the team. It was a close game and he played very well, took his reads and delivered the ball, but nothing was really happening.

Nearing the end of the third quarter with the score tied at 7, I started warming up. As soon as I took my jacket off the place went nuts. When it came time to go in the game, I trotted on the field and it was just a great feeling. We ran the ball on first and second down. I kind of scrambled on third down and dumped the ball off for a few yards, but we had to punt. On our second drive I came out slinging it and threw the ball extremely well. They tried to blitz me, figuring I was a young quarterback. I moved the team 70 yards and hit Stanley Morgan for a touchdown.

They tied the game on a touchdown and took the lead on a field goal, but we got the ball back with two minutes to go. We then put together an 80-yard drive in nine plays. I completed all six passes in that drive for 41 yards. The key play came on a third and one from the 13-yard line. I came over to the sideline and we still had a timeout. They had to be thinking we were going to run the ball, get a first down and take a shot or two to get into the end zone or kick the field goal to tie it.

As soon as I got to the sideline, I said to Steve, "I may be crazy but what about running the bootleg?" Raymond Berry had a grin on his face because Steve had just suggested the same thing to him. Steve kind of nodded and said to go for it and do it. I ran the naked bootleg and just walked in the end zone with 23 seconds remaining. We won the ball game 21-17. That was like my initiation as far as the Patriots were concerned. I completed 12 of 16 passes for 132 yards and was named the AFC's Offensive Player of the Week.

The following week we went to Green Bay and got the crap kicked out of us, losing 45-3. I played hard but didn't play well. I was pretty high-strung. The thing I remember the most about that game was throwing an interception and making a good tackle on the play. I was all worried I wouldn't be the starter the following week at home against Cincinnati, but Raymond Berry stuck with me.

RAYMOND BERRY:

We changed our whole approach to what we were doing from that point on. We were going to run this big running back, John Stephens, play good defense, and we were not going to ask Doug Flutie to do a lot of complicated things in the passing game. Once you establish that run, they've got to defend it. And then you fake it and you'd pull the defense in and you open up receivers, and Flutie knows what do with it. We just had a very successful season from that point on with him playing quarterback, but we were not putting the whole load on his shoulders.

We beat the Bengals 27-21 — they were undefeated at the time — then lost 23-20 in Buffalo, leading up to a home game against Chicago. It was a big deal because it was the first time the Bears played the Patriots since crushing them 46-10 in the Super Bowl two years before. There was a lot of talk about revenge for the Super Bowl loss, and for me personally it was a big deal because it was the Bears, my former team. I got along with a lot of the players, except guys like McMahon who were cold to me. Right away, McMahon started mouthing off, calling me "America's midget," making a big deal about the game and trying to downplay me.

A lot of the guys from Chicago I was close to — Neil Anderson and Willie Gault and Mike Singletary — came up to me before the game and asked how I was doing and said they were happy things were going well for me. There was a lot of talk before that game about how I didn't get along with my teammates in Chicago or how they didn't like me and all that. I didn't know how I would be received by them during the game or pregame especially. Right away those fears were removed and it was a really nice feeling. A lot of people in the media recognized it and saw there were no hard feelings. It was just McMahon who was doing all the talking and making it seem that way. It wasn't a true reflection of the entire team.

We stayed in a hotel room the night before a game, even if at home — we did the same thing in Chicago — and I talked to Raymond Berry about wanting to go deep on the first play. We decided we'd do it with Irving Fryar against Vespy Jackson. Irving Fryar couldn't sleep the whole night. He said he was so fired up about it he wanted to just blow by him. On the first offensive play for us, I dropped back and Irving just blew by Jackson. He caught the ball and went 80 yards for a touchdown in front of their sideline. It was our longest TD pass of the season. That touchdown was one of four I threw in the game. I didn't have that many completions but made big gains. I should have had a fifth TD, but I underthrew it a little bit and it was knocked away.

McMahon was injured early on and Tomczak came in. He and Ditka were arguing and fighting throughout the game. Harbaugh replaced Tomczak for a couple of plays and threw a couple of crappy balls. Tomczak went back in. There was just all this turmoil on their sideline and on our side we're blowing them out. I was surrounded by a bunch of guys who were just happy to have me around and were genuinely happy for me to do well against Chicago. We crushed them 30-7, giving them only their second loss in nine games. They had five straight wins going into it. We improved to 4-5.

It was just a great feeling being on the sideline. Ditka always had some classy things to say about me from Day One and was the same way after that game.

MIKE DITKA:

I can honestly say when they kicked our ass up in New England, I wanted to say, "I told you so." I didn't feel bad about getting my butt beat by him. Two days later I had a heart attack. That's how bad it bothered me, it gave me a heart attack. No, I'm just kidding.

We won our next three games, beating Miami twice and the New York Jets once. It was around this time the national media started to focus on me again. First came an article in *USA Today* by Greg Boeck. It was titled "Doug Flutie: Happy At Home With His Family And Patriots."

"Life back in New England is sweet for Doug Flutie, quarterback of the Patriots, hero of the Patriots," he wrote in the article. "After a year in New Jersey and another in Chicago, he's been back a year now among friends, family and fans." The article detailed the places I hung out at, such as Casey's Diner and the Natick Sports Club, and how relaxing it was to be with my family and friends.

Sports Illustrated followed USA Today with an article headlined "Standing Ever So Tall: Doug Flutie, the Patriots Home-
grown Hero, is Beating the Big Guys and the Doubters." Paul
Zimmerman, who wrote the article, started it off: "There has to
be a place in pro football for Doug Flutie. If there isn't, then something is wrong with the sport." It detailed the team's turnaround
with me and the success of other previous "little guys" playing
quarterback in the NFL, such as Eddie LeBaron and Frankie
Albert.

RAYMOND BERRY:

*It was an extremely difficult situation for a head coach to be under,
and yet I didn't pay any attention to it. In retrospect it created a real
problem for me playing a local hero like Doug Flutie, with all the
people wanting him to play and be a success, and I'm the head coach
and I'm in charge of handling his career the way I think is best for a
football team and it doesn't coincide with what the fans think. That
was basically the dynamics of it. On the other hand, my approach to
coaching was I was never trying to run a popularity contest. My
number one job as a coach is to do what is best for the football team.
And whatever it is, you've got to do it. It doesn't make a difference if
the public doesn't like it, the owner doesn't like it or anybody else
doesn't like it. You've got to live with yourself and you've got to
respect yourself, and that was my whole rule of thumb in making
any decision, whether it involved Doug Flutie or whatever. The
dynamics of it being in Boston, it was a loaded situation. It was a
time bomb.*

Just when all the hype was happening, we lost to Indianapolis on a missed field goal that would have tied the game at the
end. We then beat Seattle 13-7. It was a very mediocre game
played on a sloppy day. I had no idea it would be my final start
of the season.

The night after the Seattle game, I was at home decorating
the Christmas tree with my wife in the family room. The phone
rings and it was Raymond Berry calling. He told me the team

wasn't being explosive enough and he had a gut feeling to make a change for the starting quarterback; it was either going to be Steve or Tony. It kind of shocked me a little bit, and I really didn't respond to him too much. As I sat around that night and the next day, it really started to bother me. So on my day off, I went in and started to talk to him a little bit. He reiterated what he said, and obviously I was frustrated.

The teams we beat were playoff-caliber — Seattle, Cincinnati, Chicago — and they were close games. Raymond Berry was very frustrated that we weren't being explosive enough, and my only comeback to that was, "How do you expect to be explosive when we are throwing only 10 times against Seattle, 11 times against Miami?" When the situation called for it — whether it was a three-point game or whatever — and we needed to eat up some clock, we'd run some bootlegs or I'd complete a ball or two. That's how we'd win the game — by running the clock out or scoring the points at the right time.

The next day at practice I didn't take any of the snaps. Steve and Tony were taking them. Tony came up to me and asked what was going on. He wondered if I knew anything about it and who would be starting. Steve was out there winging the ball and doing his thing. Steve had a good, long rest through the games that I had started, so I'm sure he was in a position to make the playoff run if we needed him. Berry opted to start Tony, but I kept my mouth shut when the media asked me about the move.

RAYMOND BERRY:

We were in contention. We still had a chance to make the playoffs, and for the first time in two years Tony Eason was totally healthy. It way my decision, pure and simple, that a healthy Tony Eason would give us a better chance to go all the way than going with Doug Flutie. Tony Eason's ability to operate a complete pro passing game at that stage of his career was way ahead of Doug at that point just because of years of experience. But this is not a decision that I would then or would now say I'm going to debate with you about. As a head coach at the time I'm using my best judgment and using one rule of thumb: What is best for our football team? This is the decision

I had to make. Tony Eason was well and healthy and with his skills and experience would give us a better chance of going all the way that year than we would have with Doug Flutie. And it's not like saying Doug Flutie can't get the job done. It's like Tony Eason, in this particular case in my opinion, is the guy we need to go with because he gives us the best chance of winning.

We played Tampa Bay and won 10-7 in overtime on a 27-yard field goal by Jason Staurovsky. The temperature at game time was 18 degrees Fahrenheit and the windchill factor made it feel like minus 25. Tony completed 16 of 27 for 155 yards, most of it coming in the second half when he hit on 13 of 19 for 129 yards.

We played Denver in our final game. If we beat them we were in the playoffs and if we lost we were out. It was plain and simple. Tony was the starter and completed 12 of 16 for 94 yards. He suffered an injury in the second half and I thought I'd have a chance go back in. However, Raymond Berry called on Steve Grogan. He threw the ball extremely well and made some big plays, but we didn't stick the darn thing in the end zone. We lost 21-10. Late in the game, Steve came over to the sideline and talked about throwing a Hail Mary-type pass. The game was basically over and we had to score twice.

The knock on me all year was that I didn't have the arm strength; that I wasn't as strong as the other guys as far as throwing the football. Steve turned to Raymond Berry and suggested putting me in because I was the only one who could reach the end zone. Raymond Berry raised his eyebrows, turned to me and asked if I wanted to do it. I said yes, went out, rolled out a little bit, stepped up and threw it about 68 yards in the air. It was tipped around in the end zone and then intercepted. What I was most proud of was that I went in, threw the hell out of that ball and gave our guy a shot at catching it. It got tipped and they intercepted it. It was no big deal. I went down, made the tackle and caused a fumble, but they recovered it. It was an indication of my competitiveness.

It was a very frustrating thing for me not to be able to take that team to the playoffs. In New England they still question Raymond Berry's decision to bench me and put Tony Eason in. A radio talk show host called Eddie Andleman loved to talk about that and still stirs that up every so often. I don't know. I would have liked to have had the opportunity to throw the ball more when I was in there. Overall I completed 92 of 179 passes for 1,150 yards. I had 8 touchdowns and 10 interceptions. I ran the ball 38 times for 179 yards and one TD.

We won primarily on our running attack. John Stephens rushed for 1,168 yards on 297 carries and was named the league's Rookie of the Year and was selected to the Pro Bowl. Our offensive line was fantastic, blowing people off the ball. We were running the ball so well, we tried to stick with that. When I did throw the ball it was always third-and-long situations, and I didn't have a good completion percentage. We didn't throw the ball a lot and it was tough to get into a rhythm. Throughout the year the best we moved the ball was in our no-huddle situation. Whenever it got down to the end of the half or the end of the game, we'd move the ball because I was able to throw on first and second down, which is a better situation than third and long.

I was named the team's Unsung Hero by the fans, the radio station carrying the games and the Quarterback Club. That description kind of fit the role I played that year. Not a lot was expected of me, but I wound up starting a bunch of games and helping the team win.

The great thing about playing for the Patriots was being at home, living out of my house and having my family and friends around. Everybody came to the games. It was just a comfortable atmosphere for me.

Lary Kuharich, the head coach of the Calgary Stampeders of the Canadian Football League, and Bill McKay, who was the team's chairman of the board, approached me around Easter in 1989 about playing for their team. They had my rights on their negotiation list, and we went to a Celtics game with our wives and Randy Vataha, who was working with Bob Woolf. Bob was away in the Caribbean. I kind of shook it off because I was in a pretty comfortable situation, so I didn't really take them seriously, and re-signed with New England earning $375,000 a year.

LARY KUHARICH:

I had met Doug years before when I was with Temple and was trying to recruit him out of high school. We tried to tell him about the good things about the CFL, and although it didn't pay any dividends for me in Calgary, it did for me with the B.C. Lions.

The quarterbacks at training camp were Tony Eason (who had signed a two-year contract), Steve Grogan, Marc Wilson (who was signed as a free agent in the off-season), and myself. Tony was No. 1 and I was No. 2. Tony started the first three games, beating the New York Jets in the opener and then losing to Miami and Seattle. I was given the chance to start the fourth game against Buffalo. I played my ass off, but we got beat 31-10. I completed 15 of 41 passes for 176 yards and had one touchdown and one interception. I ran the ball seven times for 43 yards. Then we played at home against Houston and I started again and won 23-13. I played very well, completing 9 of 18 passes for 145 yards and running six times for 24 yards. It was nothing flashy, but we weren't throwing the ball a lot.

We went down to Atlanta — and we were the better team — and for the first time I really felt like the coaches had confidence in me. In the first half I threw the ball extremely well and completed some big passes up the field. I had sprained an ankle against Buffalo and wasn't as mobile as I should have been in the next two games. I felt really stiff and didn't move around very much, but I finally had my confidence back as far as standing in there and throwing the football.

Early in the second half I threw an interception on a post route. Our offensive coordinator had these certain plays where he liked to throw it deep no matter what. I tried to pump the safety off and just let it wing to the post route, and basically wound up throwing it in the safety's lap. And that's just not my style. I don't like just a throwing-it type of route and that's the type of route that it was. It was still my fault for putting it there and not throwing it away or over the guy's head. We got the ball back and I threw another interception on a tipped ball that went over the receiver's head. We started moving the ball again and were still leading when the coordinator decided to run another one of these pump-it-and-throw-it-deep balls. I told him on the sideline I didn't feel comfortable doing that and I just might dump it to the tight end. He told me to "just throw it," with a kind of aggravated look on his face. Sure enough, I pump it and throw it and get a third interception.

We only threw it once more in the game, a little hitch pass. In the first half I finally felt like they had confidence in me and were letting me throw the ball; now I throw some interceptions, the confidence is gone and we're not going to throw it anymore. On our last series I came up short on a quarterback draw and we had to punt it. They got it deep in their end zone with no timeouts, converted a fourth and long when the defensive back fell down and got into a position to kick a 22-yard game-winning field goal with nine seconds on the clock. We lost 16-15. I completed 12 of 30 passes for 172 yards and had one touchdown and three interceptions, but two were passes I didn't want to throw. For the rest of the season I was benched and basically didn't see the field again. Either Steve Grogan or Marc Wilson started the remaining games.

The only time I played again, which was very frustrating for me, was against Indianapolis in the 13th game of the season. Raymond Berry had messed around with a shotgun offense, where we just spread it out, no backs, all the stuff that is so innovative that Pittsburgh did in 1996, that we did later when I was in the CFL. In practice Berry put me in the shotgun. I did some sprint-out passes, some quarterback runs and some different stuff to spread people out. Marc Wilson had gotten sacked, and we were deep in our end. Raymond Berry put me in and told me to run that offense because we were going against the wind. I ran a quarterback trap right up the middle for nine yards and got us back into a third-and-five situation. I ran a sprint-out pass and dumped the ball off to Hart Lee Dykes, and he dropped the ball. We ended up punting and we never went into that offense again. We never even attempted it. That was the last time I played with the Patriots.

O' Canada

Raymond Berry was fired after the 1989 season and Rod Rust, the defensive coordinator, took over in late February. I was vacationing in Florida early in March, visiting Bob Woolf, and I got a phone call from Rod. He told me the team was having a minicamp that weekend and I wasn't invited. I was still under contract, but they were going to let me be a free agent. It was kind of shocking to me.

ROD RUST:

The decision I had to make — and I made it in concert with other people — was whether Doug was going to be our starting quarterback or not. There was no way in New England Doug Flutie was going to be a backup. That's an impossibility. He has to be a starting quarterback and there's all kinds of evidence that that's the most logical approach in New England. I couldn't make that assurance he'd be the starting quarterback. I didn't know that he would be. I called him because I wanted him to know what the situation was. I owed him that courtesy. There's no question about it.

You have to understand another thing. I was — and remain — a very big fan of his. I think he's a great competitor. I couldn't make the assurance in my own mind he'd be the starting quarterback and I knew because I had been there all those years, there is no way he can be a backup for the Patriots. He has to be the starter. It just befits his stature in New England. It's that simple. That is a compliment to

Doug, not an insult to him. It's a high compliment. The fans won't let him sit on the bench there, nor will the press, so you have to decide: "Do I want to go with him or I'm not quite sure yet, I want to see who else I have." You can't do that there. That won't work there. He's too much a fabric of New England football — and with very good reason.

I had looked around the NFL and didn't have a lot of options there. I started talking a bit with the British Columbia Lions, who had acquired my rights after Calgary took me off their negotiation list. Lary Kuharich, who became the head coach of the Lions after the 1989 season, immediately put my name on the team's negotiation list, just ahead of the Toronto Argos, who also put in a claim.

The Lions had the league-leading quarterback in passing yardage the year before in Matt Dunigan, who was earning a base salary of $210,000 a year. He was involved in a contract squabble pertaining to bonus money and was traded to Toronto on March 20 in a six-for-one deal. Once there, Dunigan was signed to a new deal. The Argos were courting Major Harris at the time. He played U.S. college ball at West Virginia and had finished fourth the year before in the voting for the Heisman. The day after acquiring Dunigan, the Argos traded Harris' rights to the Lions, but Murray Pezim, the Lions' owner, told the media they could fit both of us in the salary cap if my asking price was lowered. The Lions flew me up in June and let me take a look at the facilities and the team and all that. I was met at the airport by the Lions' publicity director, Roger Kelly.

ROGER KELLY:

I had just started working for the Lions, and [general manager] Joe Kapp and Murray Pezim were supposed to meet him at the airport and pick him up. I think I asked Joe twice that day if I needed to come out there and he said, "No, don't worry about it." Being the conscientious individual that I am, I decided I'd better get out there.

There's a whole horde of media guys of course waiting around, and no Joe and no Murray. In the end, I was the welcoming committee for the Lions. We go running through the airport and I'm thinking, "What am I going to do?" I've got my little Cavalier, or whatever I had then, way out in the middle of the frigging parking lot, and I've got media guys chasing us. Literally, we're running.

I get out there and we just dive into a rental limo. A private camera crew jumps in with us and I'm saying, "What am I going to do?" I've got Doug Flutie here, Joe and Murray aren't here and we go around the block a couple times and I say, "All right, you guys get up to the hotel and then I'll just get in my car and follow you guys up there." Doug got his room and I go to get him, and we come down, and then Murray and Joe show up finally down in the bar. They sit down with him, and then I take off and they get him to practice the next day.

I wasn't an expert on the CFL by any means, but I did have some knowledge about its history. I knew of the Toronto Argonauts, the Winnipeg Blue Bombers, the Edmonton Eskimos and the Roughriders. I didn't know if it was Ottawa, which was called the Rough Riders, or Saskatchewan, which was also called the Roughriders (Ottawa folded in 1996). I knew there were no fair catches in the league, that it had three-down football, that the field was bigger and that it had huge end zones. I didn't know too many of the players. I knew that Joe Theismann had played for Toronto in the early '70s. I had heard Vince Ferragamo had gone up there to play for Montreal. I knew that Warren Moon had come from the CFL, but growing up I didn't pay too much attention to the names or know any of the players. I hadn't heard a lot about the CFL until my senior year when we were playing Alabama and its head coach, Ray Perkins, said I would make a good CFL quarterback.

I went to watch practice, and it was kind of at a rinky-dink little college — Trinity College — that they were using for a facility, about 45 minutes outside of Vancouver. I kind of shook my head at some of the facilities, but when you looked at the guys on the field they were great athletes. Mark Gastineau, who was a key member of the New York Jets' Sack Exchange, joined the team as a free agent that year. Mark had his share of problems before and after that, but as a person he was fine. I never had any problems with him. Major Harris was there. I talked to some of the guys, and they were shaking their heads watching Major, who was such a fantastic athlete. He could throw the ball a mile and run, but he had trouble learning the system; he didn't really read coverage. The guys were kind of surprised at him, including the coaching staff. Some of the guys were saying, "Doug, we can't even understand him in the huddle. He can't call a play in the huddle. You've got to come here and help us out."

I was going to go back to Boston because the contract talks between my agents and the Lions' management weren't working out. That's when Murray Pezim intervened. He called me over to his house, which was situated just off the downtown core. The house had an outdoor swimming pool and an indoor swimming pool, which were identical. Both had Jacuzzi tubs that overflowed into the main pool. The indoor pool had a current machine that you could swim against. Murray treated me like a king for a couple of days and even cooked for me. Murray loved to cook.

Murray was a real character. He described himself publicly as the "world's greatest promoter." He said all kinds of crazy things and didn't care what people thought. It got down to him asking me what would it take to get me to play in B.C. We worked a deal for about $350,000 U.S. annually for two years. It was the highest salary in the league and the first in American currency. The contract called for $150,000 to be registered with the league as part of a standard player's contract, and $165,000 to be paid as part of a personal services deal. The remaining monies were for bonuses.

Murray announced the signing in his office in the early evening and proudly proclaimed: "The B.C. Lions are going to kick the crap out of the Argos, and Doug Flutie will be there. Tell Dunigan that Gastineau is looking for him."

LARY KUHARICH:

It was very close to camp when things started getting encouraging that we could sign Doug. We went into the negotiation process — Joe Kapp was the GM and he was talking to Randy Vataha — and it took us a week into training camp before we signed him. I was so excited about having him. I thought he'd be tremendous for the CFL and have tremendous success there — and it's been proven out beyond anybody's forecast.

Murray drew some criticism from some parts of the league for his spending, but he told the media, "I'm not concerned about the [salary cap]. If we're not creative [as a league], we're going to die. We're trying to create interest and bring fans back. Do you moonlight at all? Why shouldn't [Flutie] be allowed to hold another job?"

Normie Kwong, the general manager of the Calgary Stampeders, called the deal "disturbing." He told a Toronto reporter: "It's unfortunate [Flutie's signing] destroys the whole spirit of the salary cap, but he will become an attraction for the rest of the league."

Hugh Campbell, the Edmonton Eskimos' GM, was quoted as saying: "I've always been liberal in letting teams do what they can to put the best team on the field. I'm not against the salary cap, but they have to market that team in Vancouver. If they have done anything extraordinary, I'm all for them."

The Lions played an exhibition game against Edmonton three days after I signed. I watched it from the press box with the offensive coordinator — he was only there for a short while and then basically quarterback Joe Paopao and I wound up running the offense — and Joe Kapp. The following week I dressed for an exhibition game in Winnipeg against the Blue Bombers. When I went into the stadium, I kind of shook my head. I thought, "I guess it's okay, it's kind of adequate." To me it looked like a small college stadium, but I just kind of accepted it. The game attracted a crowd of 34,000, which was a record there for a pre-season game. Major Harris started and I entered the game in the second half. My first thought was, "Damn this field is big. There's so much room to run around." I scrambled a few times, I threw the ball well and it just felt like it was fun. There was a lot of room out there to do things and guys would get open. It really felt pretty easy, even though I didn't have a good grasp of coverage and what people were doing in the league defensively. They ran pretty simple coverages so it wasn't that complicated.

It was a fun game for me to play. I remember starting to scramble, getting outside the pocket, turning the corner really quick, turning it up and I'd still have 10 yards to the sidelines. I wasn't even using the extra space on the field. It was just a fun atmosphere to play football. We won 32-20 and I completed 8 of 15 passes for 102 yards, ran the ball six times for 61 yards and had two TDs.

In only two weeks after my signing, the Lions sold 2,000 season ticket packages. There was a lot of hype and not just in Vancouver. There were reporters and camera crews from various parts of North America. One article written by a *New York Times* reporter indicated how I had gone from one BC team to another.

The thing I remember most about that training camp was Major Harris. That whole year he was a comedian, just a fun guy to be around. He made everybody laugh. He was always comparing you to somebody. He kept calling me a Peter Brady lookalike and called Jim Mills, one of our offensive linemen, Big Bird.

We opened at home against Calgary on Friday, July 13. Rickey Foggie, who starred at the University of Minnesota, started at quarterback. I relieved Rickey in the second quarter, trailing 27-15, and we tied the game 35-35 with one second on the clock on a Hail Mary pass to Ray Alexander. The game ended tied at 38. It was a heck of a way to start my CFL career. It was also kind of funny because Ian Sinclair, our center, came up to me on the sideline and told me I finally did a Hail Mary pass for him. He had played for Miami in the Hail Mary game, which he told me about the first day of training camp.

IAN SINCLAIR:

When Doug signed, the media was all over him and that Miami game kept coming up and the questions always to me were: "Will you ever forgive him? Do you still hate him?" I never had bad feelings toward the guy. He did beat us and I was kind of pissed off at him for that, but my answer back to them always was, "I won't forgive him until he does it for us." I was saying it 90 percent jokingly. What do you really say? What answer can you give? I don't dislike the guy or never would because he beat me in a football game. The first game he plays for us he throws a Hail Mary to Ray to win the game, so it kind of became a bigger joke and something we kind of laughed about and kind of carried on for the rest of the year almost.

We played in Edmonton next and lost 41-23. We returned home and beat Winnipeg 24-23 on a 42-yard field goal in the final minute of the game. Rickey Foggie replaced me in the fourth quarter after I suffered a rib injury when tackled by James (Wild) West.

I missed the next game against Saskatchewan, which we lost 36-25. Rickey started and Joe Paopao relieved him in the second quarter in his first game action in almost three years.

I started the next game on the road against Winnipeg and we lost 28-14 with Joe in relief. It turned out to be a memorable experience for more than just the outcome of the game. It began before we even left. Joe and I wore wristbands with cards attached to them containing the plays. I gave my wristband to Joe to put in his attaché case and he put it in the car and left it there when we went to the airport. We were getting ready to go on to the field for the pregame warmup when I asked Joe for the wristband. He suddenly realized that he had forgotten them. He and I made up or own makeshift wristbands with plays and that got us through the game without any problem.

The next day Kuharich came by our lockers and asked for our wristbands, which we were supposed to turn in after the games for new insert cards. I looked at Joe to follow his lead and

Joe said, "I threw mine out." I looked at Lary and sort of agreed that I had thrown mine out, too. Lary lost it. All of a sudden he went off the deep end and told us we should know better. He informed us we were going to be fined before he stormed out of the room. I said to Joe, "Don't you have them in your briefcase?" He said, "Oh, yeah," and we went back in for the team meeting. Kuharich was up front and I walked in and laid down these wristbands with the cards on them. Now Kuharich couldn't understand what was going on. He was pissed. He stopped the meeting and called both Joe and I out to go upstairs to his office. Lary said he didn't know what was going on and that he couldn't trust us. He even called us traitors. He turned to me and talked about how his wife had invited my wife over to his house and all this other stuff. I just shook my head. I couldn't believe it. I tried to explain to him what was going on before leaving the room. Joe was ready to quit. He had had enough.

The next day Lary sent us a formal letter that was kind of a retraction for the fine, but it didn't come across that clearly. The whole issue was straightened out, but it was a typical example of how people get frustrated and upset at trivial things when you're losing football games. It was a very frustrating time for me.

We beat Saskatchewan in our next game, then lost to Hamilton and Ottawa. Four days later we played in Toronto and when I was asked about my play by a reporter, I said, "I'm still coming into form. The game is still so new, every day I feel something different. I'm just scratching the surface. Believe me it will come."

We were blown out 68-43 by the Argos. I started, Joe came in the second quarter and then I returned later in the game. We combined for a league record in points scored in a game, surpassing the 103 set by Calgary and Hamilton in 1982. We scored 50 points in the fourth quarter, breaking the old mark of 43 set by Hamilton and Saskatchewan five years previously. I had 21 completions, 3 TDs, and 288 yards. My statistics were better than Dunigan's, but I was unhappy with my performance and told

reporters afterward: "I'm relying too much on my athletic ability. The bottom line is that I've got to get the job done and I'm
not. I'm not aggressive enough when I'm on the field. I can't
continue to screw around."

Five days later we played the Argos at home and lost 49-19.
I started but injured a ligament in my throwing hand and Joe
relieved me. I came back in the third quarter when Joe was injured. Looking back on it, this was a low point in my career.

After the game, Murray promised to make changes. The next
day, Lary was fired. Three days later Joe Kapp was fired and Jim
Young, one of the greatest players in Lions history, was named
interim coach and GM. Jim started out the season as director of
community relations. Jim coached the team against Edmonton
and we lost 32-13. Murray hired Bob (Obie) O'Billovich, who
had been the head coach of the Argos from 1982-89 and won the
Grey Cup in '83 over B.C., as head coach and director of football
operations. Jim Young was given the title of Vice-President of
Marketing and Business Operations.

Kuharich ran a pretty stagnant offense. He allowed me to
call my own plays, but he ran an offense that was very NFL-
style. There wasn't a lot of movement and people weren't getting their running starts (what we call waggles). O'Billovich came
in and put me in a system that was a little more suited for the
CFL. He did some things with turnback protection and put in
some option routes where people were reading the routes. All of
a sudden, I had a lot of success.

BOB O'BILLOVICH:

*We did a good job of putting him in a system that was best suited for
his ability. When I first got there we were going to start out with Joe
until Doug felt comfortable in what we were doing and got a better feel
for things. He was definitely the guy to build our future on and as
those remaining games went on, he would become the guy. He responded
in a very positive way and started feeling good about himself and everything and started performing the way everyone including himself
thought he could.*

In our first game with Obie, we won 34-4 in Hamilton to snap our five-game losing streak. Joe started, I followed him, then Major came in. We lost 37-34 to Saskatchewan in our next game with Joe starting. We then played Ottawa at home and lost 42-26.

We rebounded to beat Calgary 33-25 and concluded the Alberta trip with a 30-8 win over Edmonton. It was my best game as a professional with 384 passing yards and 3 TDs. I was asked by a *USA Today* reporter during this time about my CFL experience and my response was: "I miss home a lot more than the NFL."

We returned home and played Calgary, losing 54-29. I was injured in the second quarter and replaced by Joe. We closed out the season against Saskatchewan at home and won 35-28. I didn't play because of an injury. Joe started and was hurt in the first quarter. He was replaced by Major Harris.

We finished with a record of 6-11-1 but won three of our last four. It was kind of a rough year. We had a really poor football team overall with a lot of problem cases — guys that were involved in drugs or weren't showing up to practice everyday, things like that. I was just happy to get the year over with. I finished with 207 completions in 392 attempts and 2,960 yards, with an additional 662 yards rushing, which was eighth best in the league.

Vancouver was a first-class city — the stadium was unbelievable — but I wasn't happy. I was thinking to myself that I just wanted to finish the two years and get the heck out of this league. I wanted to get back to the NFL or do something else. That was a very frustrating year.

Next season it seemed like the entire operation — the front office, everything — was run just a little smoother, a little bit better, and Obie was a fun guy to play for. We had training camp in Kelowna, which is a beautiful city about four hours north of Vancouver. I was excited about the season, but like I said, it was a very frustrating season throughout the first half of the last year. I wasn't sure by this time about the CFL and what I was going to do in it.

Well, what a difference a season makes. I threw for 6,619 yards

— the most ever by anyone in league history by almost 1,000 yards — and had 466 completions in 730 attempts, which was a personal high for me. I threw 38 TDs and 24 interceptions. I also ran the ball 120 times for 610 yards. I won just about every honor that year, including my first league MVP.

We opened with a loss in Calgary, then beat Winnipeg in overtime on a 32-yard field goal by Lui Passaglia on the last play of the game. That was the first of six overtime games we played that year. We beat Edmonton 37-36 at home and everything was going well. We were looking forward to the games. Each week I was feeling better about myself and enjoying myself. I couldn't recall a point in my pro career when I felt so much at ease.

We had the Argos next up on our schedule and there was all kinds of hype. The Argos were undefeated and averaged 35 points a game. They had Notre Dame star Raghib (Rocket) Ismail, who had been signed for four years and more than $18 million by Bruce McNall, who owned the team with Wayne Gretzky and John Candy. The Argos had a celebrity status to them, but we had Murray. He did his own hyping. Prior to the game Murray drove up in the Rolls Royce of Vancouver financier Jim Pattison and brought out a trophy he had made to give to Rocket as a memento of the evening. Murray handed the Argo players hats that had the inscription: "Don't Mez with the Pez." The game attracted a crowd of 53,527, which is a huge number in the CFL.

We won 52-41 in overtime. Murray was so excited he took his shirt off in the game and threw it into the crowd.

We lost 34-30 to Calgary in overtime in our next game and a week later played the Stampeders for the third time in six games and lost 37-28 in OT, our third overtime in a row, which was a league record.

We had a real shootout in our next game, winning 50-47 in Regina by scoring two TDs in the final minute. It was probably the most amazing comeback I've ever been involved in. Jay Christensen caught a TD pass from me, and I ran the other one in from a yard out to win it. I completed 37 of 50 for 478 yards and had 5 passing TDs. Kent Austin was good on 30 of 53 for 404 yards and 5 TDs.

BOB O'BILLOVICH:

Doug took us right down the field. He developed a patent on being as good as anybody that's ever played in [the CFL] in the two-minute offense. I was so impressed with the way he brought us back, his competitiveness and the leadership he showed. I remember telling him after the game on a personal basis that I was really proud of him, that he showed the kind of athlete and competitor and professional that he is by the way he brought the team back in that fourth quarter.

We played the Argos next in Toronto and they beat us 34-25 in front of a crowd of 39,508. My brother Darren joined our team after being cut by the Phoenix Cardinals in training camp. He had played a few games for the Cardinals the year before, then was put on injured reserve with a broken bone in his left foot that required surgery. He had played two years with the San Diego Chargers before that. I saw Darren in Seattle when the Cardinals had a pre-season game there. We talked during that period how the season was going, but when he was released we were talking more regularly. I let the Lions' management know when Darren became available right away and they didn't hesitate in bringing him up. The team had him on its negotiation list because Bob O'Billovich's brother Jack, who was the team's western scout, had seen Darren play and liked him.

About a week later Darren signed with the Lions. *The Vancouver Province* ran a story headlined, "Lions Tune Up a New Flutie." Ironically, about two or three weeks later, the Cardinals called back wanting to re-sign Darren, but it was too late by then.

We beat Ottawa in back-to-back games. In the second game, Lui Passaglia became the CFL leader in consecutive converts for a career with seven conversions. Tony Kimbrough replaced me in the fourth quarter when the game was well in hand and even scored a TD on a 17-yard run.

Our next game was against Winnipeg and marked Darren's first game after two weeks on the practice roster. In hindsight it was a good idea to let him just work out with the team for a couple of weeks and then people saw his athletic ability. It was a better way of doing it because it eased him into it. I was gung-ho to get him in there right away. Obie told Darren before the game he was playing because of his own abilities, not because he was my brother. Darren was the all-time leading receiver at Boston College with 134 receptions for 2,000 yards, and he had NFL experience. He could play and was about to prove it.

We won 36-23. I had a good game, rushing for two TDs and throwing for two more. Darren caught three passes for 63 yards.

When he got in the game, I was the one that got apprehensive. It was just like that in college. I wanted to get him the ball and whenever he was open, I babied the ball at the start. On the very first play against Winnipeg, we called a hitch screen to get the ball to Darren to get him involved. I threw the thing over his head out of bounds. Even in the Miami game — the one with the Hail Mary — Darren got in for his handful of plays. I had him open on a little out route, and I bounced it to him. It's because I knew it was Darren. He always just lines up and plays. I'm the one who didn't play as well when we played together. Darren had some unbelievable games, but I was the one who got nervous about playing together.

I wanted him to do well so badly I was nervous for him in that game. My wife had a video camera one day, filming some of the practice, and I said, "Keep that film with the two of us on the same team because you never know when it's going to end." Darren sort of had that same feeling like, "What if I go out and drop five balls?" There was pressure on him to have some impact right away, plus the pressure of being my brother.

I always worry more for him than me. I watched him in his high-school championship games and stuff and I was a nervous wreck on the sideline. I always want him to do well. In my own mind I can control what I do, but I can't control what Darren does. I have to have faith in his ability.

We lost to Saskatchewan 49-47 in our next game, in which Kent Austin threw a club record six TDs. He was good on 35 of 54 for 451 yards. I was good on 28 of 39 for 406 and had three TDs. I scored from a yard out with 1:31 left to make it 49-47. We made the two-point convert, but it was called back on a penalty. Darren led all receivers in the game with 13 catches for 175 yards.

We defeated Hamilton in the following game 37-27 and were lucky to score a TD in the fourth quarter when Jay Christensen recovered my fumble in the end zone. After the game, Ticats head coach John Gregory told the media: "Flutie should be disallowed. It's unfair when a guy has four eyes. Our guys did absolutely everything they could."

We played in Calgary next and beat the Stampeders 49-34. I passed for over 400 yards for the fifth time that season and threw three TDs, breaking Joe Paopao's 1981 club record of 28 in a season. Darren caught 12 passes for 226 yards, including 51 on an easy TD.

We lost 45-38 at home to Edmonton in our next game, in which both teams combined to set a league record with 1,248 yards in total offense. I completed 36 of 55 passes for 582 yards to move past Warren Moon as the all-time leader in passing yards in a single season with 5,676. When Moon, who was with Houston, was asked about me breaking the record, he said: "Flutie's talents are tailor-made for the CFL. It doesn't surprise me. I'm glad it's somebody who works hard both on and off the field."

We kept the overtime thing going in the next game when we beat the Eskimos 39-38 on the road. Lui Passgalia sent the game into overtime with a field goal and won the game with a 23-yard single as he angled the kick out of the end zone with time expired. Obie told him to do it. Edmonton's punter, Glenn Harper, was in the end zone hoping to kick it out if he could and avoid giving up the single.

We beat Saskatchewan handily in our second-last game and closed out the season with a loss to Hamilton, which had the worst record in the league. The loss prevented us from clinching first place in the West. We had all kinds of injuries at the receiver's position. Jay Christensen suffered a separated shoulder in the game and Matt Clark fractured a thumb. We had already lost Mike Trevathan with a broken jaw. Ray Alexander caught 10 passes to total 104 on the season to break Mervin Fernandez' record of 95 set in 1985. Darren finished with 52 catches for 850 yards.

Murray Pezim was quoted a couple days later in *The Vancouver Province* as saying the loss cost him $1 million because he lost a chance to hold the semi-final game at B.C. Place, which he expected to be sold out. Murray even tried to buy the rights to play the game in B.C. It turned out to be my last game as a Lion at home.

We travelled to Calgary and that's where Larry Ryckman first approached me about coming to play for the Stamps. We were seated together for some strange reason at the Western Conference All-Stars reception. It's usually held in the city of the conference champion that year. The conversation was nothing serious and I just let it roll off my back. It was no big deal to me. Unless you're sitting down talking contract and numbers, I don't consider that tampering. But Obie did. He heard about it from Jon Volpe and issued a complaint to the league. Nothing ever came of it. Larry had purchased the financially troubled Stampeders late in the season and was looking for a marquee player. He originally had his sights on Desmond Howard, the Heisman Trophy winner from Notre Dame.

The game was billed in *The Vancouver Province* as "Rich Man, Poor Man," referring to my salary and Danny Barrett's. We lost 43-41 after leading 31-15 at the half. We walked the ball up and down the field the entire first half of that game. I threw the ball well, ran with the ball a lot, all that stuff. They were always a very stingy defense. The bottom line was they came back in the second half and scored four touchdowns, including three in the third quarter, using a six-pack of receivers for the first time against us that season. We made three turnovers in the third quarter.

DARREN FLUTIE:

The week leading up to the game, I didn't prepare myself the way I usually do. I'm someone who gets into a ritual type of thing. I have certain things I do in the middle of the week and then as the game gets closer, I do different things. I didn't follow that pattern. I was still young back then. It just ended up I didn't play well, that was the bottom line. I had had a good game against Calgary earlier in the year. The next game we played them was in the playoffs. I attracted a little more attention. I wasn't going to sneak up on anyone and they played me very well and I didn't play well. I've used that as motivation for every playoff game since then. Doug carried us through that whole game. We scored 41 points, and he basically did all that on his own. I felt really bad for him.

I scored a TD on a three-yard run to bring us within two. Darren and I were sitting on the sidelines with more than three minutes left, and we had the ball on the 47-yard line with a strong wind at our backs. We could have gone for the field goal — Lui Passaglia was four for four in the game, with his longest being a 40-yarder — but Obie elected to punt it and pin them down deep and hopefully get it back.

We never did. They just ran the ball and ran the clock out. It's very difficult to run the clock out in the CFL, but they did it.

That was the last playoff game Darren and I played together on the same team in the CFL — although we've had some interesting matchups against one another since then.

Stamp of Approval

My initial plans were to let my contract run out and take a peek at the NFL, but now I was playing well in the CFL and was worth more in that league. Murray Pezim said in a newspaper interview early in the year he thought it would take $1.5 million over three years to sign me. He said he was pretty confident he could do it and was willing to do whatever it took to make that happen. He said his only concern was that some NFL team would offer me an "obscene amount."

I kept telling Obie: "I really don't want to leave. I want to stay. I want to play in the Dome. I want to play with Darren. Just get a little closer in money and I'll stick around." He didn't budge.

While all this was going on, Bob Woolf was dealing with the so-called Rocket Rule. It was approved in late January by the board of governors and exempted one player from each team's $3 million salary cap, but the exemption was taken away if that player moved to another team. The rule was named for Rocket Ismail, even though he was exempt from the cap already because he had been under contract before the rule was conceived. Bob talked publicly about contacting the CFL Players' Association to find out what the rules and regulations were because in his opinion this rule was very restrictive.

"I know the Rocket made a great impact on the CFL last year but I don't think he was chosen rookie of the year," Bob told Frank Zicarelli of the *Toronto Sun*. "Doug is a superb player. Why isn't he given a special status? It's a shame. Doug accomplished a lot last year and it seems to me that he's being punished."

The league modified the rule six weeks later to allow marquee players to move to another team.

"I'm pleased to hear the league has changed the rule, not just for Doug, but for other players as well," Bob told Zicarelli. "Right now, I'm talking with two [NFL] teams. The chances of returning to the Lions are not good, and I would hope some other CFL team would come forward. I'm maintaining an open mind."

Larry Ryckman publicly said once he was sure I wouldn't sign with B.C., that he planned to pursue me. I had offers from Houston and New England of the NFL and the Stampeders, which financially was the best. Larry was telling the media he felt confident Calgary would sign me. He made me an attractive offer unlike a regular CFL contract, offering personal-service incentives. The three-year deal plus an option year had an annual escalating salary which would rise to more than $1 million in 1994. Never before had any player in the league earned that kind of money. There was also the option of owning a piece of the franchise once the contract expired. I believed it was the best situation for me, my family and my long-range plans after football.

BOB O'BILLOVICH:

When I was in the States for the Senior Bowl and the Coaches Convention, the only thing I told Murray from what I'd found is that I didn't think there was any genuine interest in Doug Flutie as a quarterback down there, that it was all a smoke screen by his agents talking and that it was strictly going to come down to a dollars-cents thing. It's possible that maybe he could have gotten signed by somebody down there as a backup. I didn't think that's what Doug wanted to do because if he did he would be making less money than we offered him to start. I never did feel like the NFL was ever a threat.

I felt I did enough homework on that that I knew what was out there, and that the only way we could get derailed on what we were trying to do was if somebody in the CFL— and the only guy I had any suspicions about was Ryckman — would do something like he did. I felt confident that we would keep him in B.C. because I thought B.C. offered him a heck of a deal and one that they could honor as far as having the stadium that could afford to pay Doug the kind of money that he was hoping to get. As it turned out, he wanted even more, so when Calgary paid him that it surprised me because I didn't think Calgary had the resources to pay that kind of contract to him. At least in B.C. you could justify it.

Calgary signed me on March 23 at the Calgary Convention Centre at a media conference that was televised live on The Sports Network — Canada's equivalent of ESPN— and fed via satellite throughout North America. Larry called me "the Wayne Gretzky of football" in describing me to the media. He said I had the same "magical mixture of personality and ability" as Gretzky. He said my signing was probably the biggest sporting event in Calgary since the Calgary Flames of the National Hockey League came to town in 1980 from Atlanta. "The deal will go down in history," he said.

I was asked by the media about being a savior and my response was that I had never stepped into a normal situation anywhere before. All I could do was go out and play football the best way I could and not get bogged down with all the other stuff.

I wanted to wear No. 22, but it belonged to a retired Stampeders great named Tom Forzani. Junior Thurman, a cornerback who was entering his fourth year with the team and was nicknamed the Thurmanator, wore No. 2. I was given No. 92 — symbolic of the year — at the press conference. I chose No. 20.

Murray needed a quarterback now and told the media he called up Larry after the signing and asked for Danny Barrett in a trade. When Larry wouldn't do it, Murray called him Chicken Ryckman. Obie and B.C.'s president Frank Gigliotti met with Larry and Wally Buono and worked out a trade about a month later, sending Danny Barrett to B.C. for guard Rocco Romano the rights to center Jamie Crysdale and $300,000 in a stock. The stock dropped significantly after the trade and Larry wanted the deal revised, but Murray refused.

As part of the deal the Lions also agreed to let the Stamps

play against the Argos in an exhibition game in Portland, Oregon on June 24. The game was originally to be between the
Lions and the Argos, but now would be a Grey Cup rematch —
albeit with a new starting quarterback for Calgary.

ROCCO ROMANO:

*The whole situation was frustrating because I found out about the
trade firsthand from the media in B.C. instead of the organization.
The organization in B.C. was the last to confirm it. When I was
traded from Ottawa to B.C. in 1990, I had a no-trade, no-cut clause
put in my contract because I was tired of being bounced around the
league. When I was traded to Calgary, I thought the trade was still
intact, so that's what I was most upset about. But, it ended up that
part of the agreement was null and void because Lary Kuharich
wasn't there anymore. That clause was signed between me and Lary
Kuharich. Once I got to Calgary, we kind of cleared all that matter
out of the way. One of the first guys I saw in the locker room when I
got to Calgary for training camp was Doug, and he gave me a big
hug and said he was happy I was there and I said I was happy he was
there and I was happy to be on the same team again.*

I went into training camp and was sold on the fact I was
going to have to work my ass off. This was a team that went to
the Grey Cup the year before with Danny Barrett, who was very
well liked by his teammates and by the town, and now I was
replacing him. It was a little bit of a sticky situation at first, but I
went in and worked my tail off. Right away the guys acknowledged that I was working hard and decided to deal with it and
we went along. Allen Pitts and Derrick Crawford and Carl Bland
were all receivers who were very close with Danny Barrett and
now I had to earn their respect.

We played that exhibition game in Oregon and I got a real
charge out of that. I thoroughly enjoyed playing that game. I
played well, we won and it was a big thrill to go back to the U.S.
and know that people down there didn't forget about me.

WALLY BUONO:

When you look at Carl Bland, Derrick Crawford, Allen Pitts, Dave Sapunjis and Pee Wee Smith, you're putting an awful lot of speed and skill on the field. Every one of them could burn you with the home run. Then you put Doug back there, and you make the combination fairly lethal. It was obvious in preseason. Right then and there you knew the makings were there, that it was just a matter of how far and how much they were going to do.

We kicked off the season with a win at Taylor Field in Regina against Saskatchewan. It was a game in which I reached the 10,000-yard passing plateau faster than any player in league history. Eight days later we beat Hamilton. In two games we had a net yardage of 1,182, which represented the greatest back-to-back amount in Stamps history.

DAVE SAPUNJIS:

Over the first two games, we got a flavor of what Doug was truly about and all of a sudden there was an excitement generated around the team because we knew the opportunity was there not only to be a great team but to win the Grey Cup that year.

Our third game marked my first return back to B.C. since the trade. Two weeks before, Murray had billed the game as Chicken Thursday — as in Chicken Ryckman — and planned to hand out chickens to all the fans in attendance. He told the media, "You won't believe what will happen on the night of the chicken. There will be chickens coming out of everywhere, all in honor of that chicken Ryckman. This is life in the wild west. The division is going to be a free-for-all. Calgary will be there, but so will we."

The fans weren't given chickens as promised. We won the game 37-19 and it marked my first victory over Danny Barrett, who was injured in the game.

We returned home and beat the Argos 28-26 on a 35-yard field goal by Mark McLoughlin with six seconds left on the clock. We lost our next two: 30-21 in Saskatchewan (in which I set a team record with 63 pass attempts, surpassing Danny Barrett who had the old mark of 57 the year before) and 32-11 in Ottawa.

We came home to play B.C. and it snowed. It was the first snowfall in August in 46 years in Calgary. We beat them 44-23. Next came my first game for the Stamps against Edmonton in Commonwealth Stadium. There is an incredible rivalry not only between the two teams but the two cities, which are about three hours apart with Edmonton in the north and Calgary in the south. Edmonton is called the City of Champions because of the five consecutive championships the Eskimos recorded from 1978-82 and the four championships the Oilers of the National Hockey League won in five years.

Lanny McDonald, the onetime captain of the Flames, talked about the rivalry in his autobiography, *Lanny*: "This rivalry is between cities, mayors, concert halls, Commonwealth Games, Olympic Games, the oil companies, theatres. It's a rivalry that dates further back than the life of the Flames or the Oilers. As a kid I remember hearing about the Calgary-Edmonton rivalry between the football teams. Even then I was anticipating what was to happen later in life: I cheered for the Stampeders, not the Eskimos."

We won 45-38 in overtime and I set a Stampeders record for a quarterback with 141 yards rushing. Edmonton had the lead at the half and in the final minute, but Andy McVey tied it with a four-yard run with 19 seconds on the clock. Pee Wee Smith scored the game winner on a seven-yard pass from me in overtime. It was the Stampeders' first regular-season win in Edmonton in 12 years.

Then came the traditional Labor Day game against the Eskimos. Everybody told me your season was measured by your Labor Day game against Edmonton. The game attracted a record crowd of 38,205 at McMahon Stadium. Edmonton led 20-18 at the half and won 34-21. I had 32 completions in 44 attempts for 417 yards and 2 TDS, but I also threw 6 interceptions. A couple of them weren't my fault — they were tipped balls, and one at the end of the game was thrown up for grabs — and just some stupid stuff happened. Edmonton took sole possession of first place at 5-2, while we slipped to 4-3 after our third loss in the last four games.

Everybody tells you which games are going to be important, but the bottom line is the next game is the most important. Once it's gone just move on to the next one. Winning and losing the championship is the only thing that matters. You talk about Labor Day games. You talk about the home opener. Whatever it is, the next game is always, for one reason or another, the most important game in the world.

We rebounded after our Labor Day loss to beat the Argos 31-0 in Toronto, then we returned home and beat Winnipeg 57-29 in the highest single-scoring output ever by Calgary. We lost 17-16 in Winnipeg in a game that was rainy and windy. In the first half nothing could go wrong, and in the second half, nothing could go right. Dave Sapunjis had a good game, catching 7 passes for 116 yards, including 93 yards on 5 catches in the first quarter.

We won our next four games, during which I set team records for single-season passing yardage, pass attempts and pass completions. Furthermore, I became only the second quarterback in league history to pass for more than 5,000 yards in a season. Warren Moon had done it in 1982 and 1983 with Edmonton. Our streak came to an end when we lost against the Ticats in Hamilton.

We closed out the regular season at home, beating Saskatchewan and finishing first overall in the league with a 13-5 record.

I finished with 5,945 passing yards — from 396 completions in 688 — attempts and posted 32 TDs and 30 interceptions. I also had 669 rushing yards in 96 carries, which was a personal best at that time. It was a very intense year for me and there was a lot of pressure to win it all because of the contract. Larry Ryckman and I got along great. There wasn't a problem getting paid. Wally Buono was fun to play for as a head coach. The offensive coordinator was John Hufnagel, who was an all-American quarterback at Penn State and was on Denver's roster for three years before joining the CFL as a player. John was the closest coach I ever had to Tom Coughlin as far as being disciplined and organized and having everything in order. He really paid attention to detail. He and I hit it off very well. I was a hard worker and he demanded a lot out of his quarterbacks. It was fun. We just had a great time that year.

JOHN HUFNAGEL:

Each quarterback puts his personality to it and then with his ability and with the things he did, it allowed us to grow. Sometimes the growing happened in the office as far as the game plan and other times it happened just with his great football instincts. He made them work and then we made them into a play. Doug was good at doing a lot of things. He was very, very good at doing things that were meat and potatoes to him. Obviously Allen Pitts and Dave Sapunjis comprised a lot of that meat and potatoes stuff.

Throughout the year I had a real good friend in Dave Sapunjis. We became really close. I could talk to him about anything. Dave was born in Toronto and played college football at the University of Western Ontario, which has one of the best football programs in Canada. Dave set new standards as a slotback in the league. He was named the outstanding Canadian in the 1991 Grey Cup game and he really took off from there. He caught 77 passes in 1992, after only 7 the year before, and 21 the year before that. He totaled 1,317 yards, which was about 13 times his amount from 1991.

DAVE SAPUNJIS:

The year before was my step into feeling confident on the field and knowing I could be a star in the league. When Flutie came and because he was so smart on the football field and so gifted, it made it so much easier for me. There were times on the field where receivers are going to catch a ball they shouldn't because there are two or three guys that might be around them and you need a perfect pass. Flutie would give you the perfect pass and he accounted for a lot of extra catches I probably wouldn't have had from other quarterbacks. It was my year to step into the limelight and at the same time, it was the Stampeders' year to step into the limelight and Doug just made it a lot easier for everyone.

We played Edmonton in the playoffs and everybody talked about the Labor Day game — how it was the benchmark — but none of that meant a hill of beans. Whichever team won was going to the Grey Cup, which that year was in Toronto.

It was one of the coldest games I'd ever played in. The wind was blowing all over the place, so I ended up running a lot that day. On one play I sprinted out, even though it was supposed to be a pass. I took off and ran for 15 or 20 yards, and then I pitched the ball to Derrick Crawford who ran for another 20 yards. It was a day where we played extremely well and should have had a lot more points on the board. We had a third-down situation where we came up short late in the first half. We dominated the first half but were only up by a little bit. I was kind of frustrated at that.

After the third quarter, I thought we were in great shape, but then they put a touchdown drive together going into the wind. That put us behind and frustrated the heck out of me because, up until then, nobody had done anything into the wind as far as scoring points. Now all of a sudden we had to score, but we did have the wind at our backs. It was kind of a safe situation where we should score some points. We got the ball with about three and a half minutes to go, and I threw an interception on the run, trying to force it in. Larry Wruck picked it off.

I looked at the clock and there was a little more than two minutes to go. One of our defensive linemen, Srecko Zizakovic, came up to me and said, "Don't worry about it, Doug, we're going to get the ball back for you defensively." I had full confidence that our defense was going to get the ball back. Edmonton got a couple of first downs and then we finally stopped them. We came back on the field with a minute and 18 seconds to go and the fans were on their feet. It was the first time that I had ever felt like the crowd for one of the home teams in the CFL was trying to urge the players on and really initiate what would happen. Yeah, the crowd would cheer when things happened well and when things didn't, the crowd booed. But it was usually a reaction type of thing. Here was an instance where I honestly felt the crowd trying to urge the team on. That is the way it's supposed to be.

On the first play of the drive, I threw just a little middle screen to Sponge. He made a nice little run and got it out toward midfield. That play got the momentum back for us. It made everyone believe that, yeah, we were going to score. I hit Carl Bland on a little eight-yard pattern and the ball bounced off his shoulder into the air and very well could have been intercepted. It went laterally into the chest of an Eskimo player, and he dropped it. That was the pivotal play of the drive. It should have been an eight-yard completion, but it could have been an interception that ended the drive. We were now in a second-and-long situation, and I called a play to the wide side of the field that I would normally run to the short side of the field. I was thinking that Carl Bland would be open on an in-route, but he actually got a little rub on Allen Pitts' defender. Al spun it up the sideline and was wide open. I threw the wheel route, which is like an out and up, to the wide side of the field. Al made a really nice catch and took it down to the 15-yard line. That was the play that got us into a situation where it was no longer a fire drill. It was no longer a hurry-up situation. We just had to get it into the end zone. With the wind the way it was and the way the ball was blowing all over the place, I was trying to be as conservative as possible. I kept the ball in my hands from there on out.

DAVE SAPUNJIS:

I've played with Doug enough that you could see when he was in his own element. You hear a lot now about players and athletes referring to being in the zone. He was in that zone and he wanted to control that drive and no matter what the play was or what his call was, if he saw an opening, he'd tuck the ball under his arm and run down the field. There was a couple plays in that drive where we'd be running our patterns expecting to get open and catch the ball and we'd turn around and here comes Flutie 10 yards behind you running with the ball. But, that's part of what Doug was all about — being creative — and there's not a better quarterback I've ever seen that is as creative as Flutie with the success he's had.

I called a little trap play with the full intention of faking a handoff and running a naked bootleg. I did and ran for about eight yards. All I was thinking was, "Let's get the first down." There were still around 30 seconds to go, which was still plenty of time. Since the clock stops after each play, I was thinking, "Just make the first down." In fact, I was kind of hoping I might even come up just a little short of the first down on the second and two. As a result, we could go for it on third down and get even closer to the goal line for the first down if you can understand that thinking. I called a quarterback sneak. We spread them out and I found a little seam off tackle. Instead of just getting a couple of yards, I wound up getting five yards, moving us down to the three-yard line. That got us the first down, which made it a situation where all I had to do was run a couple more quarterback sneaks to get in the end zone.

Part of the success of that quarterback sneak was I just don't run the play straight ahead. I look for a soft spot in the defense. I gave our right tackle, Kenny Moore, a signal to get his attention, and he understood exactly what I was talking about. He fanned out and took the outside defender, which created a nice, big, wide hole. I started wide, cut it up and was able to get five yards out of it. On the next play the same situation occurred, and Kenny made a great block and drove the guy into the end zone. I just followed him in.

The play began with about 20 seconds or so on the clock and when I got back in the huddle I was trying to fix my shoe. While getting tackled on the previous play, somebody pulled one of them off. I had a double knot in it and didn't have time to untie it. Our center, Doug Davies, reached down and tried to get my shoe on. I finally just said the heck with it, got to the line of scrimmage and stuck my foot down in toward the toe as far as I could with the heel being out. When the ball was snapped, I took off to the right. On my first stride, the shoe went flying off. I just took two lateral steps — one north and one south — wrapped up the ball with both arms arms, dove through and went into the end zone.

WALLY BUONO:

When Doug had control of the game, he was going to take care of it himself. When you look at great players in the history of sports, when big games are on the line, they usually step up. I don't think Doug in any way was going to be denied now that he was so close. Doug wanted to win a championship and he was so close to losing it prior to that drive that when he got down there, you knew he was going to put it in the end zone.

It was a great feeling of satisfaction, like lying exhausted on the field of battle. I knew my job was done. We had tied the game. All we needed was the extra point and I was just thankful we were in the situation we were. At that point I knew we were going to the Grey Cup. When I got to the sidelines, I didn't want to put a jacket on. I didn't want to do anything until I saw our kicker, Mark McLoughlin, kick the extra point. Then I was satisfied. We still had to kick the ball off and there were a few seconds left on the clock. Gizmo Williams ran around in circles trying to make something happen until we finally pulled him down. There was no time left on the clock.

It was so darn cold that in the postgame interview on the field we went live and my lips were half-frozen, so I couldn't even speak. After the interview, I ran toward the locker room and had so much adrenalin pumping through me. Like I said I was exhausted as I landed in the end zone, but I was so fired up that we had won and were going to the Grey Cup that running off the field I must have sprinted and jumped about 10 feet in the air. I had a little home video camera in the locker room in case we won. It was a fun atmosphere to be around.

I couldn't really sleep too well that evening. I sat up most of the night and actually put together a little highlight film of the game — including both the offense and defense. I put it to music and brought it in the next morning. But a really weird thing happened that night. I was lying in bed and one of my feet felt like it cramped up. But it wasn't a cramp, it was something else. My foot was in a half-pointed position and the middle joint just locked up and would not move. I couldn't put any pressure on it because it was in an odd position and hurt like hell. I started jumping on one foot and tried to work it out and get it loose again. Unfortunately, it wouldn't. I decided to lie down and sleep, hoping it would relax.

I woke up at about five in the morning and it was the same way. Now I was getting really nervous. I was about to call our trainer, Pat Clayton, but I decided I may as well wait a couple hours until he was up. I spent the next hour or so just kind of manipulating the foot, trying to work it out and doing what I could to see if something would spring it loose. I had no idea what the heck it was. All I was thinking was how am I going to explain this and what if they can't fix it? The Grey Cup was that week. I got out of bed and took a hot bath, which probably wasn't the best thing because there was probably swelling already in it. I should have been icing it. Eventually it relaxed a little bit, and I kept working it with my fingers. All of a sudden I hit a spot just below my ankle. I felt a little tendon or something in there that I was rubbing and, *boom*, my foot released. I was perfectly fine and it never happened again. I went and told the trainers about it, and they couldn't understand it either. I still to this day don't understand what it was.

There was a great atmosphere around the locker room that day because we were all going to the Grey Cup. We all went down to this Western clothing store and bought the long rider jackets and the hats and the boots and the whole works. I guess it was kind of a Calgary tradition that we all wore Western attire

on the road so that when we showed up in Toronto for the Grey
Cup we would look like we were from the West. It was kind of
cool.

We were facing Winnipeg in the Cup. We felt we were better
and had outplayed them in the regular season. They had Matt
Dunigan at quarterback — he left Toronto as a free agent after
the previous year because the Argos couldn't afford to keep him
— and there was the whole bit about the two of us. All of a sudden it started coming up in the media that I couldn't win the big
game. The media had to write about something, so all of a sudden they started writing about that stuff. Matt had been to the
Grey Cup the year before and won it playing with a shoulder
that had to be frozen. I hadn't been to the Grey Cup before and I
guess that's what kind of sparked it. Then again, this was only
my third year in the league. I know Matt was a great quarterback, but I started wondering what the heck these people were
talking about.

Winnipeg was stubborn and would run their system. They
wouldn't go with a nickel package. They'd leave their regular
people on the field and try to cover receivers with linebackers,
or running backs with linebackers. What we did a lot was put
Derrick Crawford in the backfield to make a linebacker cover
him. Derrick just had a field day. The first play of the game he
ran a corner route for a long gain. He caught a bunch of balls
and had a great game. Derrick probably would have won game
MVP, but he never ended up in the end zone. Dave Sapunjis
made a great catch on a touchdown and won Canadian player
of the game. We threw the ball up and down the field. We could
have set all kinds of records. I threw for 480 yards and came out
in the middle of the fourth quarter. The whole second half we
played very conservatively, just trying to hold on to the lead.
Our defense had a phenomenal game shutting down Matt and
the Winnipeg offense. It was a very enjoyable game to play because we were moving the ball so well. We even had a 70-yard
touchdown called back.

WALLY BUONO:

The uncanny thing about that whole game was that Doug dealt with Winnipeg's pressure unbelievably. They had two guys free to him almost every play because of what we were doing and what they were doing, and it never phased Doug. It never bothered him. It never let him get away from his game plan. He was in one of those rhythms when no matter what you did, it wasn't going to be wrong.

DAVE SAPUNJIS:

In the second half the game was almost boring because you just knew that we were dominating and there was not a chance for Winnipeg to beat us. All of this stuff could be attributed to having a strong team and now having Flutie with us. By Grey Cup time that was a whole season with Doug and we knew exactly what he was about and we knew he was a player that was better than we thought he was and that gave us that extra element to go out and dominate games.

It was just one of those days where everything went perfectly. It was a big game and we won the Grey Cup. I can remember after it was over standing on the field with Sponge and looking at the fans behind our bench and acknowledging them. It was just a fun atmosphere. Right at the end of the game when I came out and Steve Taylor came in, I put my Grey Cup champions hat on, and I was just so relieved.

I don't know how to celebrate after winning a championship. I don't enjoy it enough I guess. I enjoy it by being satisfied and by being able to relax. I enjoy my off-season and knowing that we've won it all. I think I look at it too realistically and realize that next year we've got to do the same thing, that people are going to have even higher expectations. It's just a very satisfying feeling for me — a very comforting feeling — winning it all.

The most aggravating part of the whole post-game thing was

being taken to a room to talk to media people. As a result, I missed the whole celebration in the locker room. This was a mistake I'll never make again and I didn't make when we won it with Toronto in 1996. After that game, I just went straight to the locker room and enjoyed the win; I enjoyed it with the guys on the team.

Cold, Hard Truth

During the off-season, I was in Calgary for a charity hockey or basketball game between our team and the Eskimos. While standing around the front office I overheard one of the people saying how Larry Ryckman had told him he had wasted a million dollars or something along those lines on me. He figured to recoup a portion of the contract from endorsements, so he wouldn't have to spend all that money paying me, and it didn't happen.

In Canada, there is not a lot of money for CFL players to be made in commercials or endorsements. I was always under the impression — and maybe it's from my NFL days, maybe there's a different mentality in the CFL — that if I do a commercial or endorsement, I make the money. This is where the first real conflict between Larry and I came into play.

Larry was under the impression that he deserved that money — that he was giving me the opportunity to play — and if I went and did some commercials or whatever I'd bring in money and give it to him. It would be a kind of way to recoup some of the money from the contract. I didn't see it that way. That was probably the first time I got aggravated at Larry. It was probably just Larry trying to motivate somebody in the front office to get more done or to stir things up a little bit.

Larry had purchased the rights to the Cup from the Argos, hoping to win it all at home. We came back planning to repeat what we had done the year before and finished the regular season with a club record 15-3 mark, which included winning our first 10. We also totalled a league record 646 points in a season and I set a club record with 416 completions. Dave Sapunjis became the first Canadian to catch 100 passes.

We played Winnipeg in the season opener in a rematch of the Grey Cup. We won 54-34 after leading 20-7 after the first 15 minutes and 34-17 at halftime, in which I scored a 50-yard TD on a sneak with eight seconds to go. Overall I threw for three TDs and scored two on runs. We followed up with wins over Sacramento — which became the first American-based team in the history of the league — B.C., Toronto, Winnipeg and Ottawa. In defeating Ottawa, I set a club record with 556 passing yards. We then beat Ottawa again, Hamilton, B.C., and Edmonton on Labor Day.

Four days later we played in Edmonton and lost a chance at the league record of 11 wins at the start of the season by losing 29-16. I completed only 16 of 34 for 124 yards and threw three interceptions. I remember sitting there in the locker room; it was probably one of the hardest losses I'd ever endured. I honestly thought that year we'd go undefeated, considering the way we were playing and the team that we had. The loss just stuck with me the rest of the year. It just really irritated me.

We won our next four, beating B.C., Hamilton, Saskatchewan and Toronto. We finished off the regular season with two losses in our final three games, including a 39-21 drubbing against Edmonton in the last game. Edmonton got on a real good roll toward the end of that year. Damon Allen was playing very well. The Eskimos were running the ball very well and Allen was running the naked bootleg off it and throwing the occasional deep ball.

We played the B.C. Lions in the first round of the playoffs. It was a hard-fought game in which we struggled to win 17-9. Then we moved on to the final against Edmonton. This was the game everybody seems to remember when talking about my career in the CFL because it was played in the wind and snow and cold. We lost 29-15.

The temperature at kickoff was minus 23 to minus 30 degrees, and by the end of the game it was minus 44 with a windchill that made it minus 80. In the first half the heaters were working on the sidelines. The snow was falling pretty good. The field was sloppy and slick and that created problems because people were slipping and sliding all over the place. When you play Edmonton, you have to run routes that have double moves on them: You start in and then come back out; you start out and come back in.

We moved the ball very well in the first half, but we missed a field goal and botched the hold on another attempt. The play that sticks with me more than any other came on a second down at the eight-yard line. I stepped up in the pocket and it parted like the Red Sea. I started to take off and then I saw Derrick Crawford wide open. It just took me too long to get rid of the ball and when I threw it to him, it was intercepted at the back of the end zone. The interception took away seven points, which coupled with the blown field goals meant a loss of 13 points. Still, we led 13-8 at that point.

We came out for the second half and I think they turned off the heaters at halftime. It was so darn cold the propane had thickened up and had stopped flowing. We came out of the locker room and were sent back because they wanted to clean off the field. That extended the halftime, which allowed the heaters to sit there inoperative for that much longer. They never cranked the heaters back up for the second half. Consequently, the heaters basically were blowing out cold air. The Eskimos scored to go ahead and we marched the ball right down the field only to lose the ball. On a straight dive play our running back Tony Stewart held the ball and somebody was on top of him ripping at it and finally pulled it out. I was ignoring it because the play was dead in my mind, but they ruled it a fumble. It became a crucial turnover because Edmonton marched the ball down the field again and scored to lead by two touchdowns. Basically, they put us away.

The last few drives we started to go no-huddle and now I didn't have the 20 seconds between plays to stick my hands back in my pouch to keep warm. I was going every play and grabbing the ball and throwing and moving. I had run the ball a few times and had gotten tackled in the snow. My hands were out in the open and I couldn't even feel the ball hitting my hands. I was in the shotgun and I was just catching the ball and running around and scrambling because I couldn't throw. I only threw if I was going to get tackled and even then I just threw it into the ground for an incompletion. The amazing thing was we moved the ball this way. It actually pissed me off because I thought I should have started running all over the place earlier instead of trying to throw the ball with the receivers slipping around the way they were. We probably would have been better off if I just took off and ran all the time.

On a third down and goal from about the six late in the game, I came over to the sideline and asked Huf what he thought. He told me the play, but I told him the best option was letting me run a quarterback draw or something like that because I couldn't even feel the darn ball. As I was standing there I looked at our backup, Steve Taylor. He had this big old parka and these big mittens on and I asked him if his hands were warm. He said yes, so I asked him if he wanted to take a shot at it. My thinking was to let Steve go out and stick it in the end zone. In the meantime, I would run over and try to get my hands warm for the two-point conversion. Then we would go for an onside kick. Unfortunately, Steve threw a pass that went incomplete. The game was basically over.

Afterward, the media made a big deal out of that situation — that my hands froze and that it cost us the game and all that crap. In my opinion, we had one play and it was a third down. I thought Steve could run just as well as I could and he was in a position to throw the ball if needed. The bottom line was the receivers weren't going to be able to get open or run. The best opportunity should have been to just run with the ball.

DAVE SAPUNJIS:

When Doug took himself out of the game to try to warm his hands, the game was over. We couldn't move the ball all game. They were up by two touchdowns and we had to score at least twice and at that point the game was pretty much over and Doug wasn't warm and he couldn't keep his hands warm. They were frozen and when your hands get frozen you don't even know if you're holding the ball on the football field, so he had to whip over and try to get warm and then come back in. He took a lot of flak for that and really wasn't that deserving because at that point the game was over. That weather took a lot of life out of us and it took a lot of life out of Edmonton. It was just not a great football game by either team. It was the most miserable day I've ever played football in and it just kind of zapped your strength and zapped your motivation to a certain degree and threw Flutie off a little bit. You talk about being in the zone the year before when we won the Grey Cup, well Doug was in a zone on the football field. In this game you could see he was having trouble trying to find that zone to get going and he never did, but no one ever did.

WALLY BUONO:

The game wasn't lost on that drive where Doug couldn't finish it. That was kind of the tragedy of the whole thing that he took all the heat, whereas the team didn't get the game out of whack in the first half because we had plenty of opportunities to do that. The guy that gets all the glory usually gets all the blame. Doug took a tremendous amount of flak. He was branded as a guy that couldn't play in the cold, which was ridiculous. I don't think he could function. If you knew Doug at all, he's never going to let you pull him. He's not going to pull himself out. That's not characteristic of him at all. His hands were frozen. I bet you they were more than frozen. I bet you they were just numb beyond where he couldn't even feel the football. A player sometimes takes his lumps and he goes on and I think Doug's proven over and over again that that was just an unfortunate situation that happened to a great athlete.

JOHN HUFNAGEL:

The thing that people didn't realize was how extremely cold it was. How we got the ball down to that position was because Doug was doing a lot of running himself. He was getting his hands wet and

cold because of picking himself off the ground and everything, and
his hands were just frozen. It came to a point where he couldn't grip
the football. It was unfortunate. He came over to try to warm up his
hands and our heater wasn't working and he had no feeling in his
hands. I had to make the decision and did what I felt was the right
thing to do and put a guy in there that had some feeling with the
football. If I realized the amount of criticism that Doug would have
to take over the next few years, I would never had made that decision
because I thought it was very unfair.

   That became a trademark of my CFL career. Never mind the
6,000 yards and the Grey Cup championship the year before,
now all of a sudden I couldn't play in the cold weather. The previous year we beat Edmonton in a cold-weather game where
the wind conditions were much worse than the snow conditions
in '93, but '94 was the coldest game I think I've ever played in.
I've won games in the snow dating back to high school and I
even played in college against Alabama in a snowstorm. All my
life I've played in bad weather. I remember playing for B.C. in
Saskatchewan and kicking the crap out of Saskatchewan in a
snowstorm that was 10 times as bad as the one we played in
Calgary.
   That ended that season and it irritated me the way people
remembered things about the game. I think I completed 22 passes
for well over 200 yards and Damon Allen completed 8 of 19
passes for 216 yards (it's just that a couple of them happened to
be to Jim Sandusky because he ran these hitch-and-goes in the
snow and the DBs would fall down).
   We came into the '94 season with the same kind of expectations. We started the year up in Saskatchewan and lost 22-21.
We were up by a mess of points after scoring on three of our first
four possessions, got conservative in the last 10 minutes of the
game and didn't make some first downs. They had one touchdown drive. They blocked a kick for a touchdown, scooped up a
fumble for a touchdown and scored a touchdown on the last
play of the game.

It was only the first game of the year and no big deal, but John Hufnagel and I both learned not to be conservative. No matter what the score, no matter what the situation, you've got to stay aggressive and try to score as many points as you possibly can. We took that attitude and blew some people out during the course of the year. We took some criticism at times for running up the score or leaving me in a little too long or things of that nature. It's the same philosophy Don Matthews had with the Argos: No lead is a safe lead in the CFL. I think it was a lesson well learned that opening day in Saskatchewan.

We beat Baltimore 42-16 in the second game, then played Winnipeg. The Blue Bombers came into the match having defeated Edmonton 50-35, (a game in which Matt Dunigan threw for a CFL record 713 yards). I was all fired up for that game and we routed them 58-19. I threw for five TDs and ran for two more. We beat B.C., Ottawa, Sacramento, Saskatchewan and Toronto, which unbeknownst to me at the time was where the seed was sewn for my future as an Argonaut.

BOB NICHOLSON (ARGOS PRESIDENT):

My first interest in Doug Flutie was August 25, 1994, when Calgary came into town and we had a great crowd. Doug Flutie proceeded to put 17 points on the board by the end of the first quarter and we had three. He just scrambled and threw; I mean, he was just incredible. I just watched through the whole game and I had to swallow my pride and go and shake Larry Ryckman's hand at the end of the game, which we lost 52-3. I just shook my head at that time and said, "This is one guy we've just got to get here in Toronto."

We finished with three consecutive wins to lead the league with a 15-3 mark. We went into the playoffs and we were smoking. We played Saskatchewan in the first round and just lit it up from beginning to end to win easily. It was fun. It was a playoff game, guys were loose and relaxed and we were just flying around. The next week we played B.C. and offensively did the same thing, moving the football up and down the field. We held the lead for almost the whole game. However, they moved the ball as well as we did.

It came down to the fact that we needed to stay aggressive. We had the ball on our own one-yard line. We were up by five and I ran a quarterback draw to get us out of our own end. I busted it upfield for some 60 yards. We were stopped on the next series and lined up for a field goal. Mark McLoughlin missed it and we got a single. They got a couple of first downs before fumbling. Again, I think the lesson to be learned is don't be conservative. Both Huf and I realized that and tried to stay aggressive, but we did run the ball a little more than usual while moving for a few first downs. Everything was great: We were eating up the clock, there was under a minute to go and we were finally stopped.

The play that stands out in my mind was the pass I had to make to Vince Danielsen on a corner route — it was just off Vince's fingertips. It was a little bit overthrown and he made a great effort to get to it. However, I'm so used to seeing Vince stick one paw up there, the ball hitting his fingertips and him pulling it in anyway. Vince has real strength in his hands. He made a catch against Sacramento in '95 at the back of the end zone that was just amazing. But this time the ball was just a bit overthrown and he couldn't get to it and pull it in. We had to kick a field goal.

I don't think we had a field goal blocked all year. Mark had struggled that day and had missed a couple, but he hit this ball solid as a rock. And I knew it as soon as he kicked it that it was good. I looked up and all I heard was another whack right after that, which was Ray Alexander's arm blocking the ball. They did a little pyramiding and Ray Alexander went flying up in the air. It squirmed off to the side and I batted it out of bounds to avoid them scooping up the ball and running. Now, all of a sudden, all control of the game is out of my hands. That for me is the most frustrating feeling in the world. I'd rather be on the field trailing then off the field with the lead. I like when the control is in my hands or in the offense's hands.

With the kind of day Darren was having, they were going to make some plays. Danny McManus found Matt Clark for a big gain. I guess the biggest play of the drive came with about 15 seconds left. They were on our 25-yard line and needed a big play. They could have run three plays for about eight yards a play, but it just felt like they needed a big one to get close. Darren made a diving grab and even though he took a big shot from our safety, Greg Knox, he held on to the ball at the five-yard line. It came down to the last play of the game and I just remember standing next to Huf. He had his arm around me and the two of us knew it was totally out of our control. They ran what I think was supposed to be a pick play and our defense read it. Both guys jumped the receiver that Danny Mac probably was going to throw to and it left Darren open. Darren turned and broke off his route in which he was supposed to go to the corner, but because he found himself open, he just stopped there and put his hands up. Danny Mac found him and stuck it in there and Darren caught the ball for the touchdown.

I just saw a mess of people, the ball being caught and the arms going up for the touchdown. I started shaking my head and walking across the field to find Darren. I figured it was Darren who made the reception just because of the position of the field and where the ball was caught. I asked him if he had caught the ball and he responded, "Yeah." I jokingly said, "You asshole." Then I kind of slapped him on the head and said, "Good job," and left the field. All the media wanted to know what we said to each other. Darren said, "He called me an asshole." It was all in jest but I guess some people took it the wrong way.

DARREN FLUTIE:

I remember just briefly bumping into him and him asking me if I was the one who caught it. At first I was a little surprised he asked that because of course I was the one who caught it. I thought it was obvious. At the time I was a little excited. I said, "Yeah," and then he patted me on the head or something and called me an asshole and walked off the field. That was it. I mean like he would really call me that. I would just take it for granted that no one would think he would call me that and mean it.

I love my brother and I think the world of him and if I'm going to lose a game that way, I want it to be Darren catching that ball not somebody else. There's never been any resentment one way or the other as far as winning and losing and who did what in the game. Usually after the game we can sit down and gripe about this play or that play. We don't talk about who won or who lost. We talk about specific plays more often, what exactly happened and what we were thinking. We never claim bragging rights or stick it in each other's faces.

The Grey Cup game took place about 10 years after the college game against Miami when I threw the Hail Mary pass. After Darren made the catch in the Grey Cup, some reporters referred to it as "The Catch."

Season in Hell

In the off-season I negotiated an extension of my contract, which was going into its option year. I decided my entire future was going to be with the CFL, that I was not going to try the NFL after the '95 season but rather stay put and keep what I thought was a secure situation and build a new home in Natick. Basically, I wanted to do the right thing for myself and my family.

I signed a five-year deal — four years plus an option — starting at $1 million Canadian a year and rising up to almost $1.5 million. It was all guaranteed with Ryckman.

Steve Taylor had gone to Ottawa, and Jeff Garcia, who was the No. 3 guy, moved up to No. 2. Huf really liked the way Jeff worked and some of the things he could do. You could see Jeff was going to be the No. 2 guy the next year. So it was Jeff and me in a year that I thought we had the same high quality on our team. We came out and won our first seven games, but I experienced some problems with my throwing elbow.

In the first couple games my elbow and arm felt great, but in the third or fourth game of the year against Baltimore I had to keep warming up on the sideline to get loose. It got progressively worse in that game and I didn't feel like I physically threw the ball really well because my elbow was bothering me. After that game we were getting ready to play in San Antonio, and during the week it was really bothering me. I rested it for a couple days, and then I threw the ball and my arm felt pretty darn good. I threw kind of hard just to test it that day. During the pregame warmup, it had gotten a little bit sore from throwing the day before. At the end of the warmup, I was standing at center field and spun around and threw a tight spiral. *Bang*, it hit the cross bar from 55 yards out. It felt great. Jeff, Huf and I had always tried to hit the crossbar from 15, 20 or 30 yards out.

The second or third pass of the game, I threw a ball and something just went in my elbow. I knew something was definitely wrong. I came off the field and told Huf I didn't think I could throw but then I picked up a ball on the sideline and could sort of throw the ball still. I figured what the heck, maybe it's not as bad as I thought. I'll just keep throwing. I went out and played the rest of the first half, but every time I threw the ball it was like somebody taking a knife and jabbing it into my elbow. I finally got so frustrated with it that in the middle of the second quarter I came off the field after having thrown an interception. The ball went nowhere near where I was trying to throw it. I turned to Huf and said, "You've got to put Jeff in." Jeff started warming up and was ready to go. We got the ball back and then I said, "Give me one more shot."

I started throwing these little dump balls to the running backs and we marched the ball down the field. We scored just before the half to get ourselves back in the game. I figured, oh, what the heck, I can go through the game this way. I might have thrown one or two balls up the field, but the rest of the game I completed 19 out of 22 because I was just dumping the ball off to people. However, we were moving the ball. We came from behind to win the game when Vince Danielsen made a great catch in the end zone. It was just unbelievable. We got through the game and I decided the whole next week I wouldn't throw.

I went and got an MRI and they said they couldn't find anything. They said it was probably tendonitis and to just rest it. I waited until the pregame against Birmingham before I started throwing and it wasn't as bad as it was in the game against San Antonio, although it was sore. But, it was nothing I hadn't felt before, so I figured it was okay. I went out in the first half and by the end of the first quarter it was miserable. I couldn't throw the ball. It was the middle of the second quarter and my whole forearm had swollen up like a balloon. I came over to the sideline and told Huf I had to go out. It was probably the series before that I woke up to the severity of the problem when Sponge saw my arm and said, "Get the heck out of here. What are you doing? You're crazy, you can't keep going." I was only about six yards away from 30,000 career passing yards, so Huf told me to throw a hitch screen, get the 30,000 and get off the field. We basically did that. I threw the hitch screen to Pee Wee and went out. Jeff went into the game after that.

Jeff struggled his first couple of series and then settled down. He threw a touchdown pass that should have won the game for us, but Matt Dunigan, who was playing for Birmingham, brought his team back to win. From there on Jeff was the starter. It was a great offense that Jeff stepped into and we didn't miss a beat. Jeff played extremely well. Although we had just as much success with Jeff on the field, things did change a little bit. Jeff has a tendency to throw the ball up field a little more than I do. Subsequently, he will hold on to the ball a little more. He takes a couple more sacks maybe, but in return he makes a lot of big plays going up the field. It was just a little different twist of basically the same offense. In the meantime, I was in a situation which I had never been in before.

I got my elbow checked again and they said the tendon was definitely torn — it was pulled right off the bone — and I was going to need surgery. Right away Patty Clayton said to me, "Let's not mess around with this thing, let's go to the best." At that time and for the last 10 years, the best had always been Dr. Frank Jobe in L.A. He became famous in the sports world after he did reconstructive surgery on pitcher Tommy John.

I went down to L.A. to get it checked out and sure enough he agreed surgery was needed. I was a little skeptical because I'd sat around for a week and it was feeling pretty good. I was thinking if I wait three or four weeks maybe it would heal up and I would be fine. I was told later — and this is probably what I did the first week — that by resting it you start to get scar tissue, which is not a strong thing. It's also a bad thing because it can shorten the tendon and it won't heal properly. I think that's what I had been doing — letting it rest and, just as it started healing, ripping it again.

Dr. Jobe told me one of two things would happen in surgery: if it was just the tendon, which he thought it was, he'd go in and repair it by drilling two holes in the elbow, taking a suture, putting it through the end of the tendon, pulling it through the holes, kind of tying it off in a knot and letting it heal. The suture would be strong enough to let me do everyday activities but obviously not for throwing a football. That would take a good six months to heal. If both the ligament and tendon were torn, he would have to take a ligament or something from my other wrist and put it in my right elbow. That kind of scared the heck out of me. He was talking about a year and a half of rehab for something like that. He wouldn't be able to find out until he was in there and looking at it.

My first thought was what if I can't come back from this? What if I can't play again? As soon as I got out of the operation and started thinking about the rest of the season, the next year and my future, all I wanted to do was get back on the field.

When I woke up after surgery the first thing I did was look at my left wrist. There was only the cast on my right arm. That indicated to me that Dr. Jobe didn't have to do the second part of the operation; it was just the tendon. That was the first encouraging sign. The second thing was it felt pretty good. I could move it without a lot of pain. Obviously I didn't have full range of motion, but my first objective was to try to start getting that back. I was hanging out in L.A. because they wanted to check the surgery at the end of the week. By that time I had already taken the cast off to take a peek at the stitches and everything else, but it felt reasonably strong. I could open and close car doors with my right arm and I started slowly working on stretching it and trying to get some range of motion back. Dr. Jobe was saying it was going to be six months before I was ready.

While I was in L.A., I was sitting at a bar and got them to switch to the TV channel showing our game that week. It was the weirdest feeling in the world to be in California watching the Calgary Stampeders playing football without me on the field.

Before I left L.A., I played some pickup basketball down at this little outdoor court at Laguna Beach. I still had this soft cast on my arm but I got the urge because there were some guys playing. I shot around a little bit and played left-handed just for fun.

There were only eight weeks left in the regular season at this point. By the time I got back to the locker room about eight or nine days after the operation, some guys wondered if I had even had the surgery because I didn't have a sling or cast or anything on my arm. The stitches were gone and there was just a faint, long scar. You couldn't really see it because it was underneath on the inside part of my arm. The guys were kind of shocked that it didn't even look like I had an operation.

JOHN HUFNAGEL:

Doug's first day back from the operation he said, 'I'll be back for the playoffs,' and he worked extremely hard at rehabbing it. The closer the playoffs came he kept reinforcing that thought. It was an absolutely amazing recovery.

When you're injured, you feel like you're on the outside looking in all the time. All of a sudden you're out of the circle, out of the loop, and even when you're around the locker room or around the coaches' offices, you feel a little bit out of place. I was still trying to talk to Huf and and do some game planning if possible — just anything to keep me involved — but it was no longer my game. We played Toronto one week and I ended up doing the ESPN 2 broadcast for that, sitting in the booth. That was another strange event.

I wanted to give it my best shot anyway at coming back before the end of the year. Within a couple weeks of the operation, I had gotten the full range of motion back. I started doing some squeezing exercises with the football to just try and hold it. Just for fun, about two weeks into it, I picked up a ball and kind of flipped it over to Sponge. Of course right away Sponge yelled at me for throwing and said, "If you're ever going to try to come back you're not going to do it that way, just wait. Make sure you're ready before you go, don't damage it."

I started doing some soft tosses. I was working with Patty Clayton in the training room doing some paddle-type exercises in the water. By rehabbing it and trying to strengthen it to get back in a position to play, I was able to occupy myself so I wouldn't think about the other possibility of not playing again. I was so focused on trying to come back and play that I wasn't thinking whether the elbow was going to be 100 percent or whether or not I could make it back and all that stuff. At about the three-week mark, I was lobbing the ball back and forth anywhere from 10 to 20 yards, just to get a feel for it. I did it in a very slow, deliberate motion, and there was no pain at all, which I hadn't felt in the last five years. Then again, I wasn't pushing it so I didn't know how strong it was.

My instructions from Dr. Jobe were to stop if there was any pain at all in what I was doing. That's basically the approach I took. At this point I had enough strength in my arm to do things, so I started running wide receiver for the scout team (the formations used by the opposing team you're playing in your next game). Like I said, you want to be involved and participate in some way when you have an injury. I started practising with the team, just running routes, messing around and having fun basically. Wally even gave me scout player of the week one time for catching a lot of balls. It just made me feel like I was part of the team again.

At the end of six weeks, I went back to Dr. Jobe to see whether or not I could take a shot at coming back. Basically I gave him the day of the Grey Cup, which was an extra three weeks from when I actually wanted to come back and he said he thought it would be strong enough by then. To me that meant it was okay to go out and throw now.

I started trying to throw the ball with a little bit of zip. I still was afraid to throw the ball up the field. I remember throwing a couple of slant routes in practice. I threw it right on time in a hole and completed the passes. It just made me feel good, even

I played high school football in Natick, Massachusetts, about 17 miles west of Boston. I've worn No. 22 whenever I could because it was the number of my favorite childhood pitcher, Jim Palmer.

Four games into my first season at Boston College, I played the final quarter and impressed the coaches enough to become the starter from that point on.

I remember thinking I won the Heisman trophy and nobody could take that away from me. It didn't matter what they would say about my height or whether I played in the NFL or played professionally or even if I didn't play another down of football. I had won the Heisman trophy and that was something I was going to be proud of for the rest of my life.

Donald Trump stands in the background while I answer questions at the press conference to announce my signing with his team. He paid me $8.3 million, a record contract at the time for rookies in any league.

I chose the late Bob Woolf as my agent. He became like a father figure to me and always made me feel special.

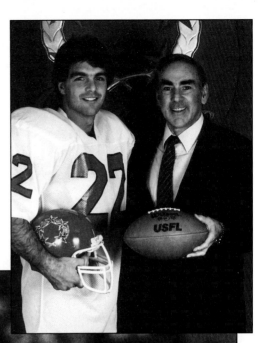

I played for the Chicago Bears in 1986, but was traded to New England the next season, and it was a comfortable atmosphere being at home and playing in front of family and friends.

Murray Pezim, who described himself as the world's greatest promoter, hams it up with me after he signed me to play for his B.C. Lions team of the Canadian Football League in 1990.

Calgary Stampeders' owner Larry Ryckman and I were all smiles when I signed with his team after two seasons in B.C. Four years later, Larry ran into financial problems and didn't pay me the personal services money from my contract.

The Toronto Argos acquired my rights in 1996 and there were high expectations for me to turn around the team right away.

Here I am celebrating our Grey Cup win with my daughter, Alexa.

We won the Grey Cup in what was billed as the Showdown in Snowtown. Joining me on the victory podium are wideout Paul Masotti (88) and Mike (Pinball) Clemons (31), a running back who enjoyed a career year as a receiver. The ribbon on the trophy was later digitally added to the photograph and the Argos sent it to their season ticket holders.

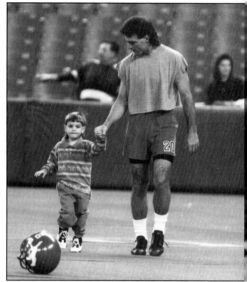

This is a picture of Laurie and our daughter, Alexa, when she was a baby. Laurie and I met in our sophomore years in high school and she's supported me all the way, through the good times and bad.

My son Dougie and I enjoy some time together at the SkyDome in Toronto the day before a game in 1995. He's the happiest kid I've ever seen.

I had been prepared to finish my career in the CFL, but was pleased to sign a contract with the Buffalo Bills in early 1998. It was great to have another shot at the NFL.

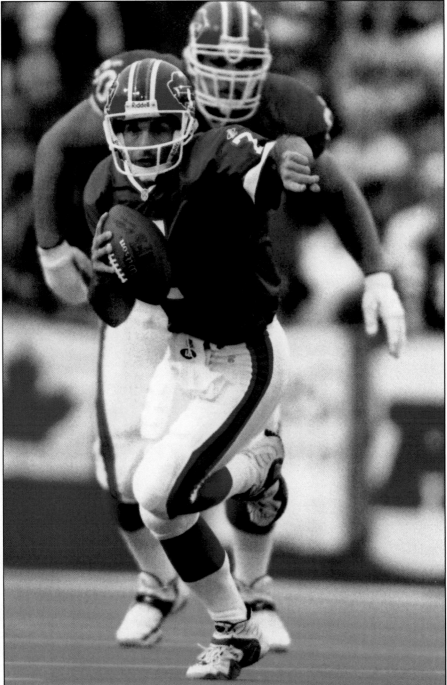

Jack Boland/Toronto Sun

We had a great game against Jackonsville on October 18, 1998 winning 17-16, with a TD in the dying seconds of the game. The guys just made some great plays. This game was a bit of a turning point for me — people began to realize I could play in the NFL after all.

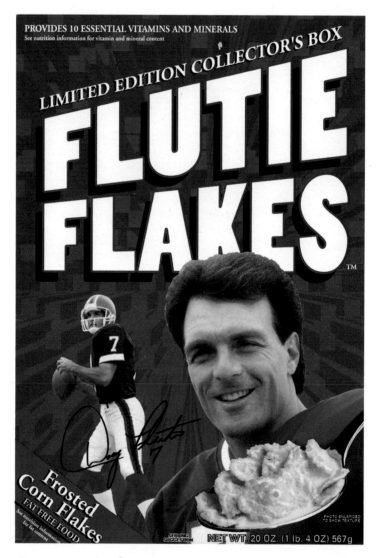

I was amazed at the response to Flutie Flakes. Over 100,000 boxes were sold, and they even became collector's items. I was especially pleased, as a portion of the sales goes to the Doug Flutie, Jr. Foundation for Autism.

though I wasn't really throwing the ball hard. I decided at about that point I wanted to take a real shot at making it back for the playoffs. In order to do that I had to at least get some playing time in the last regular-season game, which was in Toronto. I kept biding my time and trying to throw a little further, a little harder, but being as careful as possible.

Jeff had a sprained ankle and I started the first couple of series against Toronto. The game was really Shawn Moore's to play, but I wanted to get on the field to at least try it. I completed 11 of 16 for 129 yards, and my legs felt great. I had really quick feet that day, with a lot of bounce in my step and ran five times for 42 yards. I was just excited to be on the field again. Overall, it was a success. I threw a couple of nice balls, but I didn't have to gun anything in there (or at least was careful that I didn't have to). However, the problem was we didn't have a bye-week. If we had that one extra week to rest, it would have been great.

We had Hamilton the following week in the playoffs bye-week, and that week in practice, I made a point to throw some deep balls to let the guys know I could do it. The day before the game, with the media around, I threw a Hail Mary pass of about 55 or 60 yards at the end of practice just for fun. I could throw the ball up to 65 yards, but my elbow wasn't really 100 percent just yet. It looked impressive enough that it opened some of their eyes.

WALLY BUONO:

The reason we went with Doug was that in our minds he was the starter. We didn't feel the starter lost his position because of injuries. Doug has shown us in practice he could do what we felt he had to, to allow us to win.

I don't think it had anything to do with not playing in a while, but I threw four interceptions in the first half. My best attribute has always been that I've been a very patient quarterback. I dump the ball off, take what they give me — I know it sounds like a cliché — and am very patient and very careful with the football. For some reason in that game I wasn't. They forced me to try to throw the ball upfield, which was fine with me, but I didn't get the ball in there. I think the bottom line was that I was taking a big, elongated throwing motion rather than a quick, snap throw. I believe that was to protect my elbow. I wasn't doing that intentionally. I notice that now looking back on it. It just took too long to get the ball from me to the receiver because of the nature of my release, which was slow and deliberate.

People actually booed us coming off the field, and I don't know if it was directed specifically at me or the team. Here was a situation where I had done all I could over the last three or four years, and because of one half of football, people were down on me and that mentality really bothered me.

At halftime I said to Huf, "Do what you've got to do. If you've got to put Jeff in, put him in." Huf and I had a real unique relationship. If I had gone to him and told him I definitely wanted to play the second half no matter what the circumstances were, he would have left me in. There's no doubt in my mind. I left the door open and took a little of the pressure off him so he could make a decision. If I hadn't have said anything and he had to make the decision, it would have been a real tough thing for him to do. Sure enough he put Jeff in during the second half.

JOHN HUFNAGEL:

He understood it wasn't happening for him and he didn't want to bring down the team. I also knew after the game that he overcame the mental part of it because his throws that were intercepted were deeper balls. I think that's what he was hesitant about throwing. He got that out of his system and got ready to play the next game.

Hamilton's defense was good. Jeff completed only a handful of balls in the second half, but the key was that we ran the ball well enough and Marvin Coleman intercepted a couple of passes and ran them in for touchdowns. That iced the game for us and we won the game and moved on.

We were getting ready to play Edmonton in the western final. Everybody was bringing up the snow game and the fact that we'd lost the last two years. It just amazed me how even local media guys, who deep down want you to win, had to take that stance of "whatever sells." I didn't understand it.

I didn't know what the coaches were thinking, whether they wanted to start Jeff or myself. They basically came and said, "Whoever has the best week in practice is going to start." I was upset with myself for throwing the four interceptions. I took the attitude that I was going to rear back and throw the ball as hard as I could, snap off the throws and use a quick release. If I reinjured my elbow, so be it. If the tendon popped off again, I had the entire off-season to rehab it and get ready for next year. I called Dr. Jobe and asked him what was the worst thing that could happen if I hurt it. He said I could snap the tendon off, in which case I would have to have the surgery again. I had a great week of practice and earned the start against Edmonton.

WALLY BUONO:

In the [Hamilton] game, Doug's biggest mistake was he tried to do more than he thought he should do. I think if he had stayed within himself and within the game plan, he probably never would have got himself in so much trouble. Jeff came in in the second half and we pecked away and pecked away and, in reality, I would say what won the game was the defense, not so much the quarterbacking change. I think the quarterbacking change helped prevent any more big turn-overs, but if you look at that game and analyze it, the reason we won was because of defense.

John and I talked about it and, again, Doug was the starter. It was his job and his team and Jeff was there as a support. John and I had made up our minds because that was the right thing to do. As coaches you've got to be able to portray confidence in your players. Knowing the kind of personality and competitor Doug was, we knew he would have this burning desire to make amends for what happened in the first half against Hamilton and he proved us right.

DAVE SAPUNJIS:

*As long as his elbow was 50, 60 percent, he was a better quarterback
than anyone who had played the game here in the CFL. He was
probably about 85 to 90 percent healthy and it was plenty good
enough for Doug to be on the football field. I was not surprised that
they put him out there as a starter because he's the guy who had won
a Grey Cup for us and he was the MVP of the league any time he
played a full year. There was controversy in the papers a little bit, but
that was just sort of media hype. In my mind, and in most of the
players' minds on our team, it wasn't a question of who you started.*

I was more focused, more intense than I had ever been. I
threw the ball extremely well and probably completed more than
70 percent of my passes. The first drive I think I was five for five
as we took the ball down the field and ran the ball in from the
one. The first play of the second quarter I threw a bomb to Terry
Vaughn for 60 yards, and he was tackled inside the five. I think
that was a very important play in that I reared back and just
threw the ball deep and hit him in stride. It was a perfect spiral
— a nice ball — and it kind of showed everybody that my arm
was fine.

My favorite part of the whole game was that I ran the ball so
well. I took off, made some plays on my own and avoided the
rush. There was a second-and-long play where I avoided a couple
of different pass rushers — I must have done two spin moves in
the backfield to get away from them — and dove for a first down.
It was just a real intense game. I played extremely well. We blew
Edmonton out and had about 30 points at halftime. I played a
couple of drives in the third quarter and then I went to Wally
and said, "As soon as you can pull me out of this game, get me
out so I can rest my arm for next week." That's basically what
we did. We won the game 34-3 and silenced the criticisms about
playing Edmonton in the western finals and about my arm. Now
it was on to the Grey Cup in Saskatchewan against Baltimore.

DON MATTHEWS:

A lot of people in the media were talking about Flutie at the head coaches press conference. I got a little upset and almost a little emotional in sticking up for Doug Flutie. I said it surprises me that, as much as he has done in this league and for this league, how could anyone question any part of his ability. I said if Doug Flutie never takes another snap he has done more for this league and in this league than any other player in the history of the league.

Wally Buono was taking the question and I sort of got involved in it because I couldn't believe people were questioning the things Doug Flutie could do or anything else about his playing. I'd admired him from the opposite side of the field, just like I'm sure every other coach had. I just didn't feel he had to ever answer any questions of criticism about his play because he had been spectacular.

All the people of Saskatchewan were fired up about having the game in Regina. Taylor Field is a relatively small stadium, but they added bleachers and made the capacity 50,000. Nonetheless, the facility itself is not a first-class facility. It's the worst artificial turf in the league by far no comparison. I don't know what they were thinking about when they put that turf down. I said something about it and I guess I don't have a lot of friends in Saskatchewan because of that. That artificial turf is a joke. Instead of painting lines on the field, they cut out different sections of white rug. I guess somebody wanted to save money over the long term by not having to paint the field. Lines are crooked, seams are bulging all over the place and the field has got no grip to it. It's just amazing.

My philosophy is — and I think some people get irritated at me — that if you're having the most important game of the year, you should play it in decent conditions. You would never play a Super Bowl game in cold-weather, outdoor stadiums in Green Bay or Buffalo. It doesn't make a lot of sense. For some reason the CFL wants to try to play the game in the small towns to make it more of an event because it gets lost in the bigger cities. But I think the game itself should be more important than the festivity surrounding the game. I think you should be holding those games in your best facilities, putting them on display for the rest of the nation and for the rest of the continent to watch. It's got nothing to do with playing in the cold or the wind.

Baltimore defended us better than most teams in the league, and we knew we had our work cut out for us. We played them nose to nose the first half. Wind conditions before the game were just ridiculous. They were talking about postponing the game because it was too dangerous for the temporary stands. I'm not sure what the winds were, but that's a perfect example of why the game should be at one of your best facilities. You don't need a major tragedy to happen because you have these temporary stands under conditions that cause it to be dangerous.

Baltimore ran the ball extremely well. They had the league's leading rusher in Mike Pringle, who had been voted the MVP earlier in the week. Baltimore blocked a punt for a touchdown, and they ran a punt back for a touchdown, which was the difference in the game. The final score was 37-20 for Baltimore, the first and only time an American team has won the Grey Cup. It is likely the last, too, given that the three-year American experiment ended after that season and is not expected to come back.

Some of us said that when the American teams played the Canadian teams the biggest advantage they had was on special teams. It's a situation where the Canadian teams usually put in backup guys who are probably in their second or third year out of Canadian schools. In contrast, the American teams' backup guys were probably just as talented as their first-line guys because they were all Americans and had more experience. The American teams didn't have to employ Canadians because of the employment laws in the U.S. The Canadian teams had to have a minimum of seven Canadian starters on the field at all times and 20 of the 37 players on the roster had to be Canadians. The biggest discrepancy was always in special teams and that's where it killed us in that game. We were pretty darn even across the board as far as total offense and every other category.

Tracy Ham, who didn't play in the regular-season game be-

tween our two teams, played extremely well that day. In the second half we came out and marched the ball into the end zone to
bring it down to a one-touchdown lead. Tracy led his team back
and on a second-and-long play within the pocket, we seemed to
have him hemmed in. However, he scrambled away and ran in
for a touchdown. That had to have been the play of the game,
which basically won it for them.

The wind conditions were a major, major factor in the first
half, but they died down enough in the second half so that they
were practically no factor at all. We got beat by what I thought
was a better football team that day. They were a more talented,
stronger team and that was the bottom line.

DAVE SAPUNJIS:

*People wanted to see Garcia in there, but I didn't and the coaching
staff didn't because they knew if there was one guy who could swing
the game it was Flutie. In hindsight because we lost maybe it would
have been a good idea to put Jeff in there, but that's only because we
lost. Right up until the last time we had the ball, we thought we had
a chance to win that game because we had Doug Flutie as quarterback.*

WALLY BUONO:

*In my mind and in John's mind, too, quarterbacking wasn't the prob-
lem. The one thing I know I didn't want to do was pull Doug so that
the blame would be put on him. In essence, if we had pulled him anywhere in the middle of the fourth quarter, then people would have perceived he was inadequate, that he was not doing his job, and that was
not the case at all.*

Looking back on that year, I was getting the payments on
time for my standard CFL contract of $150,000, but I had major
payments from Larry personally to make up the rest of my con-

tract. The year before he owed me a lot of money by the end of the season. Larry kept pushing it back and finally waited for next year's season-ticket money to come in to pay me.

During training camp, all this stuff was going on in the media with Larry and the Alberta Securities Commission, which was alleging Larry misrepresented the stock of a company he once owned. I went to Wally one day and told him I wanted to get traded, that I didn't think Larry would be able to pay me my money that year and that I was tired of Larry saying things behind my back. Face to face Larry and I always got along. He was an owner, I was his star player and we publicly acted like everything was just fine and dandy. And it was fine most of the time, because I was keeping my mouth shut. The only problem was I was scared sometimes that I wasn't going to get paid.

Even though I had gotten paid the year before — I had kept my mouth shut hoping that I eventually would get paid and everything would work out fine — I was just hoping that things would happen for the best the following year. When I sat down to talk to Wally and Huf about it, Huf kind of cooled me down a little bit.

WALLY BUONO:

As a team we had sold all our season tickets based on Doug being the quarterback. We were in a very awkward situation. When we were asked by Doug about trading him, we said no. Larry's responsibility was to pay Doug. The club had paid him his CFL portion and Larry had to come up with the personal services part, which he actually never did.

After about the third or fourth week of the '95 season, it developed into the same pattern with the missed payments. It became a situation where all of a sudden I was hearing a lot of other rumblings about Larry. There were a lot of things that made that '95 season a little scary as far as me getting paid. At about the fifth or sixth week, my agent started to threaten that he would have me sit out if I wasn't going to be paid. I didn't want that to happen and I didn't want it to come to that because you don't want to let your teammates down. While all this was going on, Larry was trying to sell my contract to Toronto.

BOB NICHOLSON:

I was thinking that Doug's contract was up at the end of the year and there might be a chance for us to perhaps pursue him, and then shortly after that Larry signed him to a multiyear deal. I figured that our pursuit of Doug had ended at that point in time. Larry Ryckman, I guess, in the beginning or the height of his financial problems, came to us and wanted to basically create a trade, but that there would be a significant cash payment of $10 million moving back out west, payable in four annual installments of $2.5 million. For the kind of money that Larry Ryckman was expecting to get, we couldn't justify it. It was sometime early in the '95 season, before Doug got hurt, that Larry Ryckman floated the idea by us about acquiring Doug, that he's "the one guy who will make a difference in Toronto. He'll put so many people in the seats. He'll pay for himself." Larry had a great line about how this was all going to work. Because of the number he threw at us we just kind of scoffed at it and said, "Thanks, Larry, appreciate the call."

Basically everything was fine, I was just getting frustrated at the financial situation. On the field I loved the guys I played with. I loved the coaching staff. Huf and I were extremely close. The whole team — Stu Laird and all the guys on the defensive side of the ball — seemed to get along great. It wasn't a situation where I wasn't getting along with anyone on the team. It was a situation where I was nervous that I wasn't going to get paid. And when it came to fruition in the middle of the season I just figured, what the heck, keep playing, keep your mouth shut, and at the end of the year eventually he'll work it out again; we'll restructure the payment schedule and I'll eventually get my money. Then I got hurt and was still not getting paid. The amazing thing was that I busted my ass to get back from this injury to be ready for the playoffs and was not getting paid. That was the hard part for me. I think it did a number on me mentally. It was really driving me crazy, but by keeping my focus on football and on the field stuff, everything seemed to work out. We came back, we went to the Grey Cup and we had a great year.

DAVE SAPUNJIS:

I was aware of [the money situation], but most people weren't. Doug and I had a great relationship going and he let me know what was going on. He was very frustrated about it. I think he considered all the different alternatives of what he could do — not playing a game, calling it quits, taking it public — but he was very professional in the way he kept it quiet. He had his own approach of trying to get the money out of Ryckman, but it was a frustrating thing for him and it took some of the fun out of the game for him.

You have to take care of Doug in certain ways, where you pay him his check when his check is to be paid. If he wants to go and have fun doing something, well, you let him do that. You let Doug be himself. When he's your star quarterback you don't want to shake him up at all, but that did shake him up and that frustrated him. It took some of the excitement of football out of him.

Rowing with the Boatmen

A couple weeks after the Grey Cup, I was in Toronto to sign some autographs at the opening of a sports store. I was asked by a Toronto reporter about the rumors that I would be playing for the Argos and John Hufnagel would be joining me to become head coach of the team. I said I expected both Huf and I to be back in Calgary. When I was asked about Larry Ryckman owing me money, I said Larry had been behind in payments before but had always found a way to get it done. A Calgary TV station had reported near the end of the regular season that Larry owed me money from the '96 season, but he vehemently denied it and asked for a retraction. At that point I hadn't publicly said anything about the payment problems.

The next day the CFL board of governors had a meeting in Toronto and though I didn't know it at the time, Larry talked about the Stampeders' franchise and me.

BOB NICHOLSON :

He stood up and he told everybody how much money his club would have made if it didn't have the Doug Flutie salary on his books and that it was a very viable business operation. He kind of got up and pitched his own case in front of the governors as to what a viable asset the Calgary Stampeders were and that he had it up for sale because of the various other problems he had in his life, but that Doug Flutie couldn't be part of the equation. He was clearly an-

nouncing to all there that Doug was available. What he said to everybody I don't know. He certainly came to us and said the CFL was important to him, he wanted to see it thrive and the only way it would do so was if Toronto was a strong franchise. He thought it was important Doug come to Toronto because of the closeness to Boston and everything like that. He was prepared to see us conclude a deal that brought Doug to Toronto.

In January, following the conclusion of the Alberta Securities Commission hearings into his alleged manipulation of shares in an Alberta Stock Exchange-controlled company — Westgroup Corporations Inc. — he once headed, Ryckman publicly talked to the media about me and the team and his ownership. He told the *Toronto Sun*:

"If Doug wants to go to Toronto that's fine, I'd rather him stay," he said. "The team can afford him now. The press articles that have been running lately have been saying Ryckman might sell Flutie because of the Alberta Securities Commission. I'm saying that's not a factor yet. It doesn't mean it won't be in the future. The Alberta Securities Commission thing has not stopped me from being able to afford Doug. It's all timing. Right now, we're OK, but this commission thing is certainly a big issue to me from a public perception perspective."

The Argo rumors really heated up in February in Edmonton, where the coach of the year awards were held in conjunction with the monthly board of governors' meeting. There were strong suggestions the Argos were about to sign Don Matthews as their head coach — he had an option to leave the Baltimore franchise, which had an uncertain future — and that I could also be heading to Toronto. Don officially signed with the Argos a few days later. Shortly after that, Bob Nicholson publicly admitted the team would try to sign me after Ryckman had given the Argos permission, but I had a no-trade contract and had to approve any deal. "I think it's time for Doug to move on for economic reasons," Ryckman said publicly.

Bob Nicholson told the media he was in the process of framing an offer but said an annual salary in the $1 million range was inappropriate in the current state of the financially streamlined CFL. "I know he would sell some seats but is that a few or a few thousand?" he asked. "If I knew that, it would make my decision so much easier."

About that time, Calgary Flames captain Theoren Fleury commented about me in an article written by George Johnson of the *Calgary Sun:* "The Stampeders won't die because Doug Flutie is gone. Jeff Garcia proved last year he has a lot of the same assets as Flutie. If they get Garcia signed, they'll be knocking on the door again. I've only met Flutie a couple times. He's a great player, no doubt, made for the CFL...but here's an American, coming to play, making good money and he wasn't very visible in the community. For whatever reason he didn't want to make himself available. He didn't give much back. It wasn't like you saw him out at a lot of things and the minute the season was over — boom — he was on a plane to Boston."

I never saw that article when it first came out because I was in Boston, but I think it was unfair. I do a hundred times more work in Boston in the off-season for community work or benefits than any one player in Calgary does during the off-season. It's nonstop. I would do two or three things a week in Boston, but the people in Calgary wouldn't know about it. Just because it wasn't in Calgary doesn't mean I'm not giving back to the community. Boston is my home, where I plan to live permanently and where my kids go to school. I wasn't going to stay in Calgary and be apart from my kids for six months just to please somebody up there. I play football and I'm paid to do it, but I do the things that I feel are very important to me, such as my involvement with the Autism Society, but I can't worry about that.

When there is something important that is needed, I do my part, whether it's in Buffalo now or was in Calgary then. I bet I'm willing to do a lot more charity work than people who were pointing the fingers at me. I'm sure Theoren Fleury did a lot of work in the Calgary area, but that was his home and where he was all the time. It was very convenient for him.

About the time the Fleury article came out, I went public

with my thoughts about the contract situation. Larry Tucker of the *Calgary Sun* had come to my house to do a piece about my lifestyle in the off-season, and in talking to me he let me know Ryckman finally admitted he hadn't paid me yet. Now everybody in the Calgary area knew it and Larry Tucker asked me a couple of questions about it. I gave him most of the details. I had a feeling Larry was going to write this big article about it, so I decided to be fair and called Murray Rauw of the *Calgary Herald*. Murray had been trying to contact me at the same time about the same types of things and I told him basically what I told Larry Tucker. I said that including interest, Ryckman owed me $680,000 U.S. and that I would go back to the NFL and play for $200,000 before I'd renegotiate. I said Ryckman sent me one check before the playoffs, then put a stop payment on it. The fact was everybody knew about the contract problems already, although I had never said anything about it. I had never made an issue about it, but now I was finally admitting that, yes, he owed me money and I didn't like it.

League chairman John Tory indicated the league would not become financially involved in my dispute with Ryckman because the monies owed were part of a personal services contract and not with the standard players' contract filed with the league.

Larry was quoted in a Toronto paper saying he was disappointed about some of the things I said in the articles that appeared in Calgary. He said the agreement was to pay me to the end of January, but it was going to have to wait until the Securities Commission thing was worked out, which he expected would be concluded at the end of the month.

"I've treated Doug very well, and he's played longer for me than any other team," he said in the article. "I brought him in, tripled his salary, put a good team and good coaches around him. I think that professionals like a [Wayne] Gretzky would not make those kinds of comments. I was kind of hurt. It's not the whole story. I really like Doug. He's been a friend of mine. I was very surprised Doug would speak out after the exceptional treatment that I have given him. Doug is in no risk of not getting paid. Never has. Never will be."

The Securities Commission ordered Larry to pay $492,640.14

for the costs of the investigation, although the fine was later reduced to $250,000. He was given 90 days to pay. He was also forbidden from being a director or official of any Alberta company for 18 years, although he could still own it.

While the Argos and my agent, Jack Mula, continued to talk contract, the Alberta Treasury Branch took legal action on March 5 to secure its loan of $8.5 million from the Ryckman Financial Corporation, which controlled the Stampeders and my personal services contract. A Calgary judge declared the Ryckman Financial Corporation bankrupt on March 6 and placed the company in receivership. A public receiver was appointed to liquidate the Ryckman Financial Corporation's assets. I had an attorney at the court who told the media I planned to be a claimant in the proceedings regardless of where I played football in the future.

I feel someday if and when Larry gets back on his feet that I still have a claim to the money he owes me. I wasted a lot of money with lawyers who were finding out what his situation was, sitting in on hearings and rewriting a payment schedule that would never be followed. Larry flew down to Boston even after he had declared the bankruptcy to talk about getting a payment schedule squared away. He also promised he was going to pay the money. That was just a very frustrating thing.

Jack Mula told the Toronto media I was keen on coming to play for the Argos, but the money owed to me and the uncertainty of the future ownership in Calgary stood in the way. Jack was waiting for the legal papers to declare me a free agent while still allowing me to collect money from Ryckman. I had just come back from a vacation in Florida at this time and was to meet with Jack, although I had been apprised of the developments on a daily basis. I had to petition the league, indicating I was a free agent, and I eventually got a letter back from CFL commissioner Larry Smith saying I was free to go to Toronto. My feelings were, "No, I'm a free agent. Period." The league sent back another letter saying I was free to sign with another CFL team. We sent that one back and eventually got the letter I needed, stating that I was an unrestricted free agent. We talked to a few NFL teams at the time, but nothing significant was happening.

At one time we had interest from Edmonton, B.C. and, of

course, Toronto. Edmonton made a decent offer and was going to try to do some other things to make it financially attractive. At least the Eskimos were being honest about their position and what they could afford and I liked that. The talks didn't last but a day or two because Toronto was definitely offering more money. It was a much better situation for me, but I really respected Edmonton's assistant GM Tommy Higgins and GM Hugh Campbell for being up front right away and saying, "This is the type of thing we can afford to pay you and this would be the situation here in Edmonton." I told B.C. it would probably take a salary in the million-dollar-a-year Canadian range to sign me.

I really wanted to take a crack at going back to B.C. Darren had just played out his option, but I really wanted to play on the same team with him again. Moreover, I liked playing in Vancouver when I first joined the team. They said the team was being sold, there was going to be a new ownership and that I should hang tight because they were going to be in that ballpark. The Lions ownership changed hands, but there was never any interest from the new group and turmoil reigned all season. The Stampeders had a new owner, Sig Gutsche, who owned the Hard Rock Cafe and whom I knew quite well, but he wasn't interested in paying me the kind of money Toronto was offering. I understood that and still consider Sig a good friend.

Bob Nicholson is a first-class guy, something that became evident in the way he handled negotiations and dealt with Jack Mula. Everything went great, but I was trying to buy some time to talk to NFL teams and find out if there was any interest. The Argos needed a commitment out of me right away because they needed to start working on ticket sales and other stuff for the upcoming season.

DON MATTHEWS:

I called Doug one time and told him what he could expect if he comes to the Argos. I said, "We're going to play wide open. I think what you can relate it to is you will be the point guard on a fast-break offense." I also told him, "You'll probably have more fun than you've ever had because you'll call your own plays, so this will expand your game to a more fun level than you've had in the past." All of his plays were called for him very competently in Calgary. They had very good success, but there's an element of satisfaction when a quarterback calls his own plays, and I thought this would be intriguing for Doug, which it was.

I only had a small window of opportunity to talk to NFL teams. We put in some calls and got a couple of responses, primarily from the Rams and the Raiders initially, but no one was in a position to make me an offer at that time without evaluating other people and the talent around the NFL.

It was blatantly obvious to me that I was going to Toronto. On March 14, after Bob Nicholson and Jack Mula had talked by telephone on and off for some 12 hours, an agreement was reached in principle for me to join the Argos. Ironically, the signing happened at the same time the Toronto Maple Leafs made a big trade to acquire their one-time captain Wendel Clark from the New York Islanders. Both upcoming deals had been written about for weeks in the Toronto media.

BOB NICHOLSON:

People made a big issue about the fact we got bumped out of the headlines because of the Wendel trade. I'm not sure every paper in the city would have put us on the front page either way. We still got good coverage out of it. It was sort of a historic day for Toronto. It wasn't ideal, but I certainly didn't consider it devastating that the Leafs had a big announcement the same day we did.

After the signing, an article appeared in a Toronto paper quoting Calgary center Jamie Crysdale and guard Rocco Romano, who collectively said I wasn't going to be missed in Calgary, that I didn't talk to my teammates about anything other than football and I only took the offensive line out for dinner once and billed the team for it. Rocco and I are close and always have been. Jamie is the type of person who may have said something without realizing it or maybe have had his words twisted around. I later spoke to both players and I don't think there's any bad blood between Rocco, Jamie and me.

ROCCO ROMANO:

That whole incident got blown totally out of proportion by that reporter. Doug phoned me and asked if that's exactly what was said and I said, "Not at all." There were some things that were taken out of context.

JOHN HUFNAGEL:

Whether or not the guys were misquoted or whatever, Doug was a great team player and I think sometimes people lose sight of what his talents bring to a team and how he enhances the rest of the team's talents. I thought it was very unfair — and I guess the word is unfortunate — that it came out that way.

DAVE SAPUNJIS:

When the writer interviewed these players, they probably had eight great things to say about Doug and they probably had two borderline things to say about him and the negative stuff was written. And that frustrated Doug. That really threw Doug off. I knew he was hurt by all that. We were great friends, so I would touch base with him in the off-season and he was back in Boston at the time and we talked about the article after it came out. He was disappointed and he also understood about the guy that wrote the article wasn't a classy individual. But, at the same time, there was some validity to the frustration from a few of the players and it hurt Doug and he was frustrated. We both thought the best thing to do was give those guys a call and touch base with them. Those players were very apologetic to Flutie and

explained exactly how those comments came out and also explained
about how there were positive things said about Doug.

It was suggested in the article that I could have done more to promote the league. My only comeback to that is I probably did more to promote the league than anyone else at that time. Of course, I could always have done more, but there's no bad blood between me and any of the Stampeders players — at least not on my part.

I loved my years in Calgary. The city was good to me and my family. The organization was first-class — as far as the way I was treated by the coaches and the administration — other than the Larry Ryckman situation. Even then, Larry treated me well up to a certain point. Looking back on my CFL career right now, Calgary was my home. Calgary was the team with which I made a name for myself. I played four years there and we set records and established standards that I think have changed the way a lot of teams play this game. I never wanted to leave Calgary, but it was time to move on. It would have been nice to have Darren join me in Toronto, but it wasn't to be.

Jack was talking to the Argos and the Eskimos about Darren. Don Matthews said publicly the Argos were committed to making Paul Masotti the team's highest-paid receiver and they thought they had made Darren a fair offer. I wanted Darren to come to Toronto because it was closer to home and he had two kids. I was prepared to make up the difference between what the Argos and the Eskimos were offering and use it as a tax deduction in the U.S., but I also knew Darren needed to feel wanted. Darren honestly felt Edmonton really wanted him and Toronto was kind of indifferent. That was the difference. You have to go where you feel you're wanted.

DARREN FLUTIE:

I thought Toronto was going to be a great option for me — it's a lot closer to home and Doug was on the team and I thought it would be

great to go there — but I wanted to make sure I didn't make a
decision just based on where Doug was going to be or because it was
closer to home. I wanted a team that was sincerely interested in me
and wasn't going to make me less of an offer because they thought
there was other reasons I was going to go there. In the end I just
thought Toronto didn't make the effort because they thought, "Oh,
he's coming here because Doug's here." Or maybe they just didn't
want me as bad as Edmonton. They just didn't make that good of an
offer.

There were high expectations again of coming in and turning around a team. I was very frustrated early on in training
camp. Don told me I would have more fun than ever before playing football and looking back on it he was right. However, it
was kind of frustrating in training camp. Adam Rita was the
offensive coordinator and I think Adam was sitting back waiting for me to take control. I just wanted to go in, learn an offense
and get started. We had only put in a few plays after a couple
days into training camp and I felt like we were losing time. Finally, I went to Adam and asked him if we could do this or do
that and he said, "Anything you want." That kind of opened the
door and opened the lines of communication.

It was just a unique situation for me. I've always had coaches
that had their offense, put it in and said, "Okay, Doug, this is
what we're doing, go get it." Throughout the year you add little
tidbits or things that you do well or alter some things or little
wrinkles. But it was pretty amazing to me that he was basically
sitting back, waiting to see what I wanted to do. And then we'd
do it. I thoroughly enjoyed playing for Adam; there was a lot of
give and take between the two of us throughout the year.

Tie Domi, a popular player with the Toronto Maple Leafs
and a friend of Don's, practiced a bit with us in training camp as
a kicker. Don thought it would create some interest leading up
to the first preseason game in which Tie would be given a chance
to kick an extra point and/or field goal for charity. Tie had played
semipro soccer, but he was known more for his fists than his feet

as one of the Leafs' tough guys. Someone in the media nick-named him "Toe Domi" when he was practising with us.

The week before the preseason game, Tie attempted about a dozen field goals from various distances. He had about a 40-yard range and hit one from 50 yards. It was interesting the day he was practising with us since there was an especially large gathering of the media, which had been notified he would be kicking. On his first attempt he hit the snapper, Jeff Cummins, in the backside. He told the media afterward I ordered him to do it — I was the holder — but really he just mishit it.

It was an easy thing for Tie to step up and kick a field goal — he could do that — but now he was in pads, around football players and on a field rather than on the ice. He was out of his element a little bit and got nervous. I could relate to it. During my college years I went to a Celtics game and had a chance at halftime to attempt a three-quarter court shot from one foul line to the other basket. I went out there in the afternoon, just mess-ing around, and made three out of my first four shots. I threw one, shot one and threw one underhand, testing it out to see which was the best way to make the net. Come game time, the whole atmosphere had changed. The place was packed, there was all this crowd noise, all the guys on the team were jokingly giving me a hard time and I wasn't comfortable. I wound up taking the shot from my hip and the ball only landed at the other foul line, 15 feet short. Nine out of ten times I could have been around the rim or caught a little bit of the backboard, but I threw an airball. I choked. It was just a matter of being comfortable with your surroundings and I wasn't.

That's all it took with Tie. After one or two kicks he was com-fortable with the people around him. Once he got to know some of the guys, it made it a lot easier for him.

The first preseason game was a pretty big deal to me be-cause it was against Hamilton, which had signed Matt Dunigan to a big contract, and people had made such a big deal about the rivalry between Toronto and Hamilton. I think I actually felt anxious about that game because of the new situation and the realization that I would have to earn the respect of the guys on the team and gain the confidence of the fans right away. Don wanted me to be in a position to close out the game, so he started off Marvin Graves. I came in for the start of the second quarter with the score 14-1 for Hamilton. There was a tremendous ovation when they announced I was coming in.

We started off with a field goal on my first series and later I scored a touchdown on a 33-yard run. We put together a drive right at the end to tie it 27-27 and lost the thing 37-27 in the overtime. Because it was preseason, we could just blow it off. The loss bothered me a little bit, primarily because I played almost the whole game. When I play that much — even if it's in preseason — I expect to win. I completed 26 of 51 for 346 yards and ran six times for 87 yards.

Tie Domi kicked a 25-yard field goal and one extra point, raising $3,500 for charity. He kicked the ball great and it was a lot of fun.

We played Ottawa in the last preseason game and won easily. I played most of the game and was spelled in the fourth quarter by Marquel Fleetwood and Marvin Graves.

We opened on the road against Montreal, which was back in the league for the first time since the franchise folded on the eve of the 1987 season. The team had loyal fan support in Baltimore but had to leave and relocate to Montreal when the Cleveland Browns moved to Baltimore.

Don's theme all year was "find a way to win" and a perfect example of that happened in that first regular-season game, which we won 27-24. Down by four with about three and a half minutes to play, we started at our 35-yard line and moved the ball downfield. On second and goal from the six-yard line with less than 30 seconds on the clock, I started left but saw nothing was there and then scrambled around. As I started to turn the corner to the right, I saw Paul Masotti, one of our wideouts, break back to the middle of the field with five yards separating him from his man. Once I saw that, I got myself out in the middle of the field and just tried to step into it from about the 20-yard line. I drilled it to him going across the end zone, but all of a sudden, Jimmy Cunningham, the other wideout, came into the picture.

Jimmy went for the ball and it touched his hands and deflected through to Paul, who made a great catch only a couple yards from the back line of the 20-yard end zone. There was only 14 seconds on the clock.

Some people were saying that I didn't see Paul and I was throwing the ball to Jimmy. That's not true. When it first left my hand, I thought for sure it was a touchdown.

PAUL MASOTTI:

We had already used that play a couple times during the game where I was supposed to come down and do a pick play on the guy defending running back Robert Drummond. He was supposed to break outside, and I was supposed to come in and try to pick his man. What happened was Robert came to the line too quick and his man came too close to him. His man knew he was involved in the play and I knew it was going to be screwed up from the start. Right then and there Doug and I knew it was a broken play. I thought I would scramble across the back of the end zone and he said he saw me the whole way and he just wanted to make sure I cleared the goalposts and then he could set his feet and throw the football. He didn't want to hit the goalposts. Jimmy had a backside pattern and he actually went up for the ball and it went right through his hands. It did change the trajectory of the ball, but it had enough speed to get through.

I think it was a very important win from a couple of respects. Number one, we needed to win early. I was concerned going into the season that we'd be only .500 or a little better through the first half of the season, and as the season went along we'd get better and better. Offensively we had a long way to go yet. To get a win like that just throws one on your side of the ledger that maybe could have gone the other way. We needed to win fans over right away and get some people in the seats. Most importantly, I gained the confidence of my teammates. In a pressure situation we came back and won the game. The team had heard all this stuff and had seen me do it before. It was a great way to start out the season for us and it was a great confidence builder for the entire team.

DON MATTHEWS:

When we got the ball back at that point in the game, everyone felt that he was going to get a touchdown and we were going to win the game. There was just an amazing confidence that came over everybody, emulating from him. He's done that so many times in that situation that you just figure it's going to happen again and it did. It was the Flutie magic that he does whenever he steps on the football field. He just has that ability that when the game's on the line, somehow he finds a way to win.

We opened at home against Hamilton and it was one of our biggest crowds of the season. I thought this was the way things are going to be all year, that the crowds could only get bigger. There was a lot of excitement about that game. I realized it was the rivalry with Hamilton and all that, but I think I underestimated how many people came from Hamilton for that game. Obviously it was Matt and I and when we played against one another there were usually a lot of points scored.

There was definitely that little extra motivation, but there was also a lot of respect for each other. I respected his ability, and I think he respected mine. We did things in completely different ways. Matt liked to go for big plays by throwing the ball deep. He held on to the ball and had a strong arm. He just had a knack for throwing the deep ball. That's the only way I can describe it. He liked to gun the ball in there up the field. I like to be consistent and conservative and careful. You find your spots and take your chances.

That day, Matt was on. People were getting open and he was putting the ball on the money. They were making plays. Matt threw five touchdown passes. The one incident that put us in a tough situation was an interception I threw. It was intended for Paul Masotti on a comeback route. I tried to throw it on time and the defensive back had the play covered, broke on it and made the interception. Late in the game, they caught a big break as well. Their kicker, Paul Osbaldiston, lined up for a punt but dropped the snap. When he picked it up and saw there was no one around, he ran 13 yards for a first down. You would not expect Paul Osbaldiston to be the guy running with the football to make the difference in the game. Hamilton ended up scoring on the series.

We had enough time to put a legitimate drive together, but they were running a three-man rush, dropping people off in coverage and making me throw it way underneath. What I started to do was run some quarterback draws. I was just trying to get eight yards per play to reach field goal range. After looking at the film, I noticed on one of the quarterback draws that I made a bad cut. If I had broken to the right instead of to the left, I would have had a good crease and got about a 10-yard gain. We probably would have wound up in field goal range. Instead, I broke left, got strung out and gained only three or four yards on the play. All this time, the clock continued to run.

There were a couple of plays I wish I had back in that drive, but for the most part we moved the ball and were getting into the edge of field goal range. I still feel like the clock operator ran the clock at the wrong time or something because we lost a handful of seconds somewhere. I thought we had at least two more plays and then I looked up and it was basically our last play. Our kicker, Mike Vanderjagt, tried a 50-yarder but was just short. Don told the media, "If your team has to rely on a 50-yard field goal on the last play of the game, you won't win a lot of games."

Unfortunately, it was the last game I played against Matt. He suffered a career-ending concussion a few weeks later in a game against B.C. Without him and with the loss of others to injuries, Hamilton lost all hope. I felt bad for Matt. I had a serious elbow injury but knew I would return. A head injury is completely different.

We rebounded from the loss to win our next four against Winnipeg, Ottawa, Saskatchewan and Montreal. Next came Edmonton. There was a lot of excitement about the game because it was against Darren. Afterward, Darren and I played a gig with some members of our Flutie Brothers Band at a downtown Toronto club called The Silver Dollar. It was fun because it was a chance for Darren and I to get together and play in the middle of the year for the first time. Some of the guys in the band came in from Boston for the game, so we put together a makeshift band even though we hadn't practiced together in about 10 weeks. There was a lot of media attention.

As far as the game, we won 24-21. Darren banged up his knee late in the match but we played a couple of sets that night as planned. There were players from both teams there and some reporters. We also attracted a decent-sized crowd. Everyone had a good time in a nice atmosphere. We weren't trying to show off or prove anything, we were doing it just for the enjoyment of it.

DARREN FLUTIE:

It was fun, but I don't think we'd ever do it again during the season. It was a little bit of a distraction. Once we made the commitment to do it after the game, we had to follow through on it. I did bang up my knee a little bit, but we had the commitment that we were going to play there, so I just went and did it, even though we had lost and I was hurt. I really wasn't into it, but I had to follow through.

We followed up the Edmonton win with back-to-back victories over Ottawa. I was starting to use Pinball more regularly at this point, as I developed a better feel for how he ran his routes.

We had a little break and then prepared for the Labor Day game against Hamilton. It's as big a game as the Labor Day game between Calgary and Edmonton. Hamilton had lost its last five games after jumping out to a 4-1 start. Marvin Graves, who left our team at the end of training camp rather than accepting a practice roster spot, had surfaced in Hamilton after a brief stay in B.C. and was given the start. We won 38-7.

Next came Saskatchewan and Duane Dmytryshyn, who was playing in only his second game as a starter due to injuries to our Canadian receivers, played the game of his life, catching seven passes for 118 yards and two touchdowns. He was named the league's offensive player of the week. It was quite a month for him. His wife gave birth to their first child and they won $15,000 in a lottery.

We played out in B.C. next and our streak came to an end as we lost 35-11. The thing I remember most about that game was the hour or two before kickoff looking at the Diamondvision scoreboard which was showing the final game between Canada and the U.S. in the World Cup of hockey. The Lions received permission to allow people to come into B.C. Place to watch the game on the big screen, figuring it was a way to draw fans. The Lions were struggling on and off the field and only 15,000 and change showed up anyway. There wasn't a lot of focus or attention directed to the football game. Everyone was paying attention to the World Cup, and when we walked out on to the field it felt like it. We were making a lot of mistakes. It was one day when everybody was going in different directions and it was probably the most frustrating game I've played in a long, long time.

We had Calgary coming up a week later at home and it was billed as The Best versus The West. I was pumped. At our final practice the day before the game, it felt weird talking to Patty Clayton and some of the Stamps equipment staff and realizing I would be in the home team's dressing room instead of with the Stamps.

There was so much talk in Calgary about Jeff replacing me and doing just as good a job. They were a great football team with or without me and I knew that. Paul Masotti said in the locker room that I was jacked up. I had a little extra emotion going that day. I could feel it. I remember thinking to myself — and Huf and I had talked about it — the games that I run the football a little bit, whether it's by design or not, I seem to get into it a little quicker and it causes a lot of headaches for defenses. Calgary had a great defense, so we put a few wrinkles in to let me run the ball early on and it kind of got me into the flow of the game.

It was intense from beginning to end. We were down 13-4 at the half but led 20-13 by the end of the third quarter. Jimmy

Cunningham started things off early in third on a 93-yard punt return and Paul Masotti finished the quarter off on a 97-yard pass-and-run play. It was kind of a fluky thing. I called the play hoping for Paul to run a guy off and hoping to stick it into the hole to Tyrone Williams. I had a shot at getting it to Tyrone, but just as I was ready to release it, I saw the cornerback eyeing him. I just didn't want to take a chance that deep in my own end of trying to gun it in there and getting it picked off or something. At the last second, I held on to it, pulled it back and let it fly deep, throwing it on a wing and a prayer up over the top to Paul because the defensive back was kind of settling a little bit. He got caught a little flatfooted, then wound up misplaying the ball. Paul caught it in stride and took off for the touchdown. That was kind of a bonus.

When Don was asked by the media after the game if he was glad to have me on his side, he said: "Flutie is the best Canadian Football League player I've ever been around. Every day I go home and am thankful he's on my side."

The entire team played extremely well and part of the motivation stemmed from them knowing how important the game was to me. The team really wanted to win it for me. It's really about bragging rights. It's funny how after the game you're not going to sit there and boast about anything or brag to one another, but you feel like you've got one up on the other team. You've got yourself in the driver's seat a little bit.

I think we established ourselves as the best team in the league at that point. On a personal note, I maintained my status as the No. 1 quarterback in the league after the game. Jeff played well in the first half and then when he started struggling a little bit, they pulled him out and put in Danny Barrett. He engineered a touchdown drive in which they scored with 45 seconds remaining.

Throughout the second half of the season, whenever Jeff struggled, they yanked him. I don't know that I really agreed with it all the time. Danny Barrett is an excellent quarterback and when he stepped in, he usually played very well. In fact, in the second Calgary game, he was the one that saved the day for them and won the game.

We beat Winnipeg 28-12 in our next game to clinch first in the East and then headed out west to play Calgary. There was a lot of hype about me going back for my first game there. I really enjoyed being back in Calgary and playing that group of guys again. The first game had more pressure in it because it was a home game and it was the first time we played them. The second time I just felt relaxed and had fun.

The *Calgary Sun* poked fun at my return by creating a charity drive in which readers were asked to donate clothes to keep my hands warm. It was a reminder of the '93 playoff game against Edmonton. Initially, it bothered me that that game had to be drudged up again. I hate people trying to find something wrong or, in this case, something they think I don't do well. The thing everybody was going to cling to was my so-called inability to play in cold weather. I've already talked about that. I'm not going to harp on it anymore, but that was the first thing that hit me: Would these people just get out of my face with that cold weather crap. That was my first reaction and my second reaction was it's an opportunity to collect some warm-weather gear for needy children. I collected some stuff and some of my teammates contributed as well. We brought the clothing — including an Argo jacket I autographed — to Calgary and handed it to Larry Tucker. The *Calgary Sun* ran a front-page picture of it with a caption that read: "Argo QB Doug Flutie may get cold hands, but he showed *Sun* columnist Larry Tucker his warm heart by donating clothes to our Flutie Flannels campaign." In his column, Larry Tucker wrote: "It takes a big man to take a gag at his own expense, but that's just what this four-time CFL most valuable player did."

There was no need to get upset about the attitude of some people, but I take everything personally. I always have. I always will. It's just the way I am. I know I don't go up to people and make snide remarks. I've always been a very sensitive person when it came to things written or said about me. People might say, "They're sports writers, it's their job," but it's not their job to take potshots and criticize. When it's justified, yes, but very rarely has it been justified. A lot of times it's just to stir things up or a writer trying to draw attention to himself or make a name for himself. That's what irritates me about some of the people in the media. You're not looked at as an individual. They think you're an athlete and there's no real personal side to you. You're treated like an object rather than a person.

I had no idea what reaction I would get at McMahon Stadium from the Stampeders' fans when they introduced me, but they were good about it. I was playing the game with a smile on my face. At one point, I threw a pass up too softly and Marvin Coleman broke on it and picked it off. I was right next to him when he got tackled. I shook my head and told him that I ought to know better than to throw the ball near him. It was just a real fun atmosphere.

Danny Barrett came in midway through the second half and really sparked them to the lead. During the last drive of the game, there was no doubt in my mind we were going to tie it up and send it into overtime. Absolutely no doubt. They started running these blitzes that they had run all day, but it was a very unorthodox blitz where they were bringing defensive backs from both sides of the field at the same time and leaving people uncovered. They were putting pressure on me and I couldn't get rid of the ball fast enough. Paul Masotti did a great job all game of reading coverages and getting open and we made some plays. However, I really should have been able to hit Pinball for a couple of big ones. I hit him early on in the flat against that blitz and if I had stuck with some of that stuff, they probably would have gotten out of the blitz. But I think I got away from it. On what should have been our final possession, Anthony McClanahan, a linebacker who was a teammate of mine in Calgary and had been making negative comments about me talking to the media, hit me late and was assessed an unnecessary roughness penalty. That gave us another shot.

We got down close and wound up not sticking it in the end zone. I threw a pass to Paul Masotti around the nine-yard line of Calgary, but the referees ruled it incomplete. Paul thought he had caught it. The biggest factor of that whole play was that double blitz they ran again. I had to get rid of the ball quickly and I should have hit Pinball down the middle of the field. He had a linebacker covering him and he blew by him right down the middle of the field. I had locked onto Paul because I knew I needed a big play on third down and I knew he'd get open. I saw that Pinball was initially locked up with the linebacker, but I wasn't sure whether he'd go over the top or underneath him. I didn't want to have any hesitation. It wound up being the other way around. If I had just looked at Pinball, there would have been no hesitation. He blew right by him on the outside and I should have hit him for the touchdown.

We lost 30-23, but I had a lot of fun. I played my heart out and we lost. However there wasn't a lot riding on the game at the time and it was just a thoroughly enjoyable experience. It was also memorable because I broke the Argo single season passing yardage record held by Condredge Holloway.

We bussed immediately after the game to Red Deer, about an hour and a half away, to prepare for a game in Edmonton six days later. Don did the same routine the year before in Baltimore, figuring it cost about the same as flying back home and returning again. Moreover, you don't lose any practice time. Red Deer is halfway between Calgary and Edmonton, and the town really enjoyed having us there. We practiced each day at a high school and the kids loved it. The first day it snowed early in the practice for a few minutes, but no one seemed to care.

We beat Edmonton 24-17 and closed out the season with a bitter 25-21 win over B.C. in our final home game. Then we hammered Hamilton 47-14. Pinball and Paul both had big games and I thought our effort was close to perfection.

For the fifth straight season I finished on a team with one of the best regular-season records. We threw for a ridiculous amount of yards and had the leading offense, but these were things I had done before in Calgary. The bottom line was we hadn't won the championship the last three years and that was what it was all about for me in 1996: finding a way to win it all.

This was where Don Matthews came into play more than ever before. I think Don was getting uptight about the playoffs and all deep down, but he never let that on to the players. He stayed relaxed and he didn't change the routine in the way we did things, even after we got beat out in B.C. Don had the knack — and he did it all year long — of keeping the atmosphere loose and relaxed. People got their work done and we focused on what we had to do to be prepared. He made it a fun atmosphere. We very rarely wore shoulder pads in practice. We had the bye week after clinching first and were given almost six days off. I continued to throw every other day, to keep sharp while resting my arm. I was biting at the bit to throw every day because I was getting excited about the playoffs. Then I figured, what the heck, let's keep resting it, be careful and keep my arm strong.

When it came down to the Montreal game, we were all anxious, but we just went out and played like it was any other game and executed. We put in a few wrinkles to attack some coverages and I just nickled and dimed them up and down the field. It felt like we could have scored 100 points that day. We were killing them at halftime and we had fumbled twice and had some things happen. We missed some field goals and we were still killing them. Pinball ran the opening kickoff back for a touchdown, which was just unbelievable. It took the pressure off, made everybody loose and relaxed and turned it into a fun, fun game to play.

Robert Drummond just had an amazing game, catching seven passes for 148 yards and rushing eight times for 44 yards. All year long he was the workhorse. He was basically our running back where Pinball was more of a receiver. Robert had to pick up the blitzes and block — and he did a great job of both — as well as become a receiver — which he did for one year in college — getting 798 yards. He also ran for 935 yards. He was so versatile it was remarkable. I thoroughly enjoyed playing with Robert. He gave us a tool that I don't think I've ever had before: a runner and a receiver. What we started to do late in the season was line him up as wide receiver so Paul Masotti could move into the slot a little bit and work on halfbacks and linebackers. Paul reads coverages so well it was like stealing for him. In order to take Paul away, they had to back the corner off Robert outside. Now, all of a sudden, you've got a guy with unbelievable speed out there who can blow by people deep or turn a little hitch into a big play. He just made some great decisions on reading coverages and some great catches.

At the beginning of the year, Robert's athletic ability was blatantly obvious. There was a while during the middle of the season that we got away from him a little bit, although not intentionally. It turned out to be a good thing, because when we needed him most — we leaned on him in the playoffs — he just played great.

Toward the end of the Montreal game, Marquel Fleetwood came in to play and scored a touchdown on a one-yard run. I guess everybody thought we were rubbing it in. I didn't think we should have scored that touchdown. I thought we should have knelt down, since it was in the last 30 seconds or so, but you can't tell that to a kid who has never played in a playoff game before and wants to be out there and wants to do his part. And that led to me trying an extra point for the first time in my pro career.

All year long I was messing around kicking field goals just for fun in practice. Don said, "Keep doing it because if Vanderjagt were to get hurt, we need someone who can go in and kick short field goals anyway." Don kept begging me throughout the season to kick a field goal or an extra point during a game. In the last regular-season game in Hamilton, he had me talked into it, and I almost did it. I went on to the field and then I said, "Nah." I just knelt down and held it for Vanderjagt to kick it through.

I was just having a good time in the Montreal game. The fans were having fun, we were blowing them out and going to the Grey Cup. When I went out and knelt down for that extra point after Marquel's touchdown, Vanderjagt looked down at me and said, "Do you want it?" I said, "Get out of here." I was getting ready to hold and I looked back up. Vanderjagt said, "Come on, come on," and I was thinking, "What the hell, we're just having fun; it's been a fun day, let's do it." I jumped up and he went down and held. Usually Paul Masotti would be the guy holding for me. Vanderjagt held it and I kicked it. I didn't even hit the ball well at all. It went straight down the middle but I just hit the ball way underneath and it went about 20 yards total. It went through and everything went well, but I don't think their players were too excited about that.

The bottom line is, you've got to go out and have fun. On one hand I'm saying we shouldn't stick the ball in the end zone from the one-yard line. That's the way I was thinking at the time. Some people said some things about me kicking the extra point as far as sticking it in their faces, but it's professional football. We're all out there playing and earning a living and if we can't have fun at it as well, it's not worth doing. It's the same reason you run trick plays, fake punts and all that. You're trying to win games, but you're also trying to have fun out there and keep guys loose and relaxed. That's just the way I play football. Some day I believe I'm going to try to drop kick a field goal through.

Showdown in Snowtown

Wally Buono said for some reason there's always more tension getting to the Grey Cup, but the Grey Cup game takes care of itself. Everybody is jacked up and ready to play their hearts out and whatever happens, happens. But it was the playoff games where people had a tendency to get uptight and nervous. Just look at Calgary in '96 and their inability to get past Edmonton. Calgary had a tremendous year, but I knew what it was like to go through that frustration for three years and not win it. I could imagine how it felt for that same group of guys to go through it a fourth time and I was very thankful that I was in a situation where we could win it all.

Losing is the most heartwrenching thing in the world — it's impossible to describe the empty feeling it leaves after a great regular season. People ask, "Would you have been better off to have lost the week before than to have lost in the Grey Cup?" No. Then you get labelled as someone who can't even get there. You go as far as you can go, but there's only going to be one team at the end of the year that's going to be able to relax and enjoy its off-season. I don't think the fans and the public really realize how much it hurts when you lose an important game, or lose a playoff game and get knocked out. I don't think anyone not involved in sports can relate to it. There's just a hollow, empty, sick feeling. It doesn't leave you alone and go away at all. It's there until you win it again. For three years I was very frustrated and finally we won it all. You finally get that off your back. When you win the championship game you can actually relax for six months and enjoy yourself and then the pressure's on to win it again. I would start thinking about the next year two or three weeks after the Grey Cup is over.

Getting to the Grey Cup was important because there were so many expectations placed on us throughout the year because of Don and me coming to Toronto. We felt we should get there, but I think there were expectations that we'd better get there or else. I don't know what the alternative would have been. We were playing Edmonton, a team we had beaten twice, but both games were dead even. They had the best defense in the league by far and I was just very loose and confident all week long that we were going to find a way to win the game. The only thing that scared me was Danny McManus and Darren; that combination had beaten us in Calgary a couple of years ago. I'd seen Danny throw the ball well in big games and Darren always seemed to have his biggest games in the playoffs. They made me nervous as far as our ability to stop them.

Early in the year, their offense was terrible. They didn't move the ball well. But at the end of the year they put in a bunch of five-receiver stuff and they started moving the football. And it got scary.

Everybody wanted to make a big deal out of me versus Darren and to tell you the truth, Darren and I really don't care about that. I think we had fun that week. Darren got sick answering questions about me. I was sick about answering questions about him.

DARREN FLUTIE:

They built it up so much that the brothers were playing against each other. I enjoyed it on one hand, I guess, getting the recognition or the publicity, but then it started to become a little bit of a distraction just because in Edmonton I'm not the quarterback. If I was the guy that got us to the Grey Cup, it would be different. We had a great defense and Danny McManus played very well at the end of the year, so I was afraid it was taking away from the rest of our team a little bit. Overall, it was really positive. It was a good experience. For both of us to play in such a big game like that with the whole season riding on it, that was special.

I was thankful that Edmonton beat Calgary for a couple of reasons: Number one, it got Darren an extra paycheck and got him in the Grey Cup; number two, it kind of helped put to bed the stuff between Jeff and me — about who was the better quarterback. Not that it was Jeff's fault that they lost or anything like that. Fans read into things so much it's ridiculous. Jeff's a great quarterback. Fans are going to have a what-have-you-done-for-me-lately attitude. That's just the way this business works. Darren and I never worry about bragging rights. It's never about bragging rights to us. It's about winning and losing, going out and playing the best football, staying healthy and earning a living as well.

I was sick about answering questions about cold-weather games and everything else. I think I won more cold-weather games than anybody else in the CFL. I've played in cold weather since my high-school days. Every Thanksgiving Day we played in high school and it was always in the snow. And there was that game against Alabama in college. And the games in Chicago. When I played for New England, we played in minus 4 temperatures. I've won more than my share of those games.

Seeing it snow on game day, I remember shaking my head. It was funny. Chris Perez, one of our offensive tackles, was my roommate. I don't think Chris could relate to the cold-weather tag with which I had been labeled. Paul Masotti could though. And I remember talking to Paul about it during the day. Paul was actually sick as a dog. I don't know if it was nerves or he had gotten sick. He was vomiting and laying in bed all day and I kept going in and checking on him to make sure he was all right. I told him he'd better get his butt out of bed and get ready to play. He became dehydrated a lot during the game. I think it was because he'd been sick for the last day and a half.

When I saw it snowing, I thought it was a great opportunity

to win the Grey Cup after not winning it for three years — and then put to rest all the talk about the cold-weather thing. It was cold, but it wasn't frigid, frigid cold and the heaters were working on the sidelines this time unlike that game in 1993. I went ahead and wore glass-cutter gloves that have a rubbery-like covering and an extremely thin lining. I'd been trying to throw with them for three or four years. When I was with Chicago, Jim McMahon used to throw using sweat-absorbent Neumann gloves, normally worn by receivers and running backs. I liked throwing in them, but in order to do that you had to really throw the ball hard. When I threw the ball with touch, I didn't like the way they felt. Also, your hands would freeze in Neumann's. The same would happen with glass-cutter gloves. Your hands freeze in those, but they offered a constant, consistent grip on the football.

My ability to grip the football was always the bottom line for me and I made the decision to go with the gloves. During pregame, I threw with them and they felt very comfortable again. I had done it a handful of times throughout the year. I've always worn gloves, messing around with them about once a week or every other week. During the off-season, I throw with them occasionally, just to find a pair I can throw with. Danny Barrett has a certain glove he likes to throw with. Jim McMahon has a certain glove he can throw with. Danny tried to talk me into these other gloves, but I wasn't comfortable with them.

It wasn't a big deal for me to use the gloves, but it was a big deal on the field because I was running around, pitching the ball and throwing with one hand and running off balance without any concern about my grip. I could hold the ball in one hand. I could throw it sidearm. I could pitch it underhand. The gloves gave me the confidence to do the things I like to do. If I don't have a good grip on the ball — which is the case when it's cold or windy — my delivery becomes a lot more deliberate and a lot slower because I have to make sure of my grip. And, it can cost me. I can't get rid of the ball quite as quickly. I can't put it where I want to put it on time.

The crowd was divided in its support. Even though we were

representing the East, we were still the Argos — the hated Argos — in Hamilton. The city is one of the most loyal in the league in terms of its support and the rivalry between the Argos and Ticats wasn't any less just because the Ticats weren't in the game. The Ticats sold season-ticket packages, giving subscribers the same seat for the Grey Cup game. Consequently, you can understand why, even though it was a national game, it was almost like we were on the road and Edmonton was the home team.

The game didn't start off well for us. In our second series, we called a direct snap and the ball sailed over Robert Drummond's head. I fell on it in the end zone and we gave up a safety. The Eskimos made it 9-0 when Eddie Brown made a hellacious catch off his foot for a touchdown. Two big plays by Edmonton and I was thinking this was going to be a war.

The thing I remember, looking back at the game, was the intensity level. Every possession was vital. Every series seemed like life and death.

I realized early on I was going to have to run with the ball a little bit. Because of the way they ran their coverages — they read a lot of things — you had to give them certain looks and then change them. There were numerous double moves: guys had to start and stop start to cut one way and come back the other way. On a sloppy field, that was very difficult to do. That was something I think we ran into a few years earlier in Calgary against Edmonton in the snow. I had this thing in the back of my mind that every time we played Edmonton I had to run with the ball a little more because of the nature of their coverage and the way they put people out in coverage. In addition, Huf had always told me that when I ran the ball successfully we won the game. Even though the games were always close, competitive and a war, it was always necessary for me to run the ball a little bit against them.

Early on I started trying to take off a little bit and run for first downs and that became a big part of the game as we went along. Finally, at the end of the first quarter, we started moving the football. We kicked a field goal early in the second quarter and made it 9-3. Jimmy Cunningham's punt return for a touchdown, after they were unsuccessful on their next series, was huge. That took the pressure off of us and put it back on them. Jimmy fielded the ball, hit a crease and just took off. I was never so thankful as I was to see him blast off with that ball. After that, we got the ball back again, moved it well and kicked a field goal. It was a back-and-forth game the entire first half.

Edmonton came right back after we kicked that field goal with a touchdown on a long pass to Jim Sandusky, who found a seam in between two of our defenders. Then we marched the ball down the field. Gizmo Williams ran the kickoff back for a touchdown and then we scored another touchdown just before the half. The two teams combined to set a Grey Cup record for total points scored in one quarter. The thing that amazed me was the number of people who told me they were watching the NFL game that night and switched to our game because of that second quarter. They got hooked on the game — and I guess the NFL game that night was boring as well — and we had an extended audience.

In the second half it was more of the same — both sides moving the ball up and down the field — and I started getting nervous that we couldn't stop them. Our defense was starting to struggle a little bit at times. However, we were still in a position to take control of the game. Jimmy Cunningham dropped a sure touchdown and we had to settle for a field goal. He felt sick after that. At the end of the game, a shot was taken of me hugging Jimmy on the sideline. I just came over to him to say how big of a play that punt return was since he was still kind of brooding and frustrated over the dropped touchdown pass. He was thankful we won because he didn't want to have to live with dropping that pass. That's the way it is in those big games. Say we were to have lost it at the end, for the rest of Jimmy's life he'd be sitting there wondering about that dropped touchdown, whether or not that would have made the difference in the game. When you put yourself out there on a limb, you're taking risks. Everybody looks at the glory of it, but what about a guy like Scott Norwood who missed a field goal that could have won a Super Bowl. He was the All-Pro kicker that year; he was in the Pro

Bowl and he had the best efficiency. You miss a kick or throw an interception or misplay a ball at the wrong time — Billy Buckner had a ground ball go through his legs that could have ended a World Series — and you get labeled for the rest of your life for those things. I've been lucky that the one play people will always remember me for was a good one not a bad one. Sometimes you wonder if it's worth the risk to go out on the field.

The Eskimos were in a situation where they weren't going to give up. They came back, marched the ball down the field and stuck it in the end zone. We were up by only a couple of touchdowns at the time. I just remember playing very conservatively. We got into scoring position and I wanted to make sure we came away with at least three points. The key play of the game for us — no doubt about it — was the shovel pass. I got back to the way we had run the shovel pass early in the season. We started running it to the weak side of the field and because of the way they played their linebacker on the weak side so much in coverage, it made it very difficult for them to defend. Plus the fact that Larry Wruck, their veteran linebacker, wasn't playing because of an injury made it much more difficult for them. But, that was the play that bailed us out of many situations and allowed us to get drives going. Robert Drummond was the guy obviously carrying the ball. That and the quarterback draw were our go-to plays.

When they scored a touchdown to cut our lead to three points, there were a few minutes on the clock and I knew this was going to be the drive that would make or break the game. If we didn't move the football, they would have so much momentum that they would score some points. I wanted to eat up the rest of the clock and walk the ball down the field. That's exactly what we started doing. We moved the ball out of our end with a shovel pass to start the drive. We got a few first downs and were eating up the clock.

The dumbest play I made the entire day was a first-and-10, quarterback draw up through the middle. I got about eight yards and I slid down. All day long I had been diving forward or trying to move forward. Here I thought I was close enough to the first down that I would just slide. I was right there. I slid down and that put us about a yard and a half short of the first down rather than just a couple of inches. We ran the ball and got stuffed, and that made it third and inches. But, it was only inches and it should have been an easy first down. If I had just run the ball, put my head down and gone forward, we never would have been in that situation. On third down I ran the quarterback sneak like I would any other time, but just as I tucked the ball under my left arm and started moving forward, I hit my center Mike Kiselak in the butt with my left arm and, boom, lost control of the ball. I dropped to my knees and tried to spin back to just fall on it and as I started to look for the ball I definitely heard the whistles blow. The ball got kicked and squirted far back in the backfield. I heard the whistles going, so I didn't pay attention from then on.

I didn't even pay attention to who recovered the ball or who fell on it or anything like that. I was just hoping the officials stuck to their call because I knew the whistles had blown the play dead and the ball could not be recovered by anybody. It was third and inches and the question would be where they marked the ball. That was the first thing I thought about. The easiest thing in the world for them to have done was to think, "Okay, we missed this call, the ball was loose, we blew the whistle, it was an inadvertent whistle, how do we rectify it?" They could have just marked the ball short of the first down and it would be Edmonton's ball. I thought it would be human nature for them to do that. Instead, they marked the ball legitimately where the official that blew the whistle thought it should be and we wound up with a first down.

DARREN FLUTIE:

I thought it was a fumble. I'm the type of guy that just lives with the call and you go on because there's not much you can do about it. I wasn't sulking, "Oh, geez, he got away with it," nor did I care that it was my brother who did it and feel bad for him. I was upset we didn't get the call our way, but you go on.

It was a big deal, and three plays later we kicked a field goal to go up by six. The thing that bugs me is the impression that if that had been ruled a fumble and they recovered it, they automatically would have won the football game. It seems everyone I talk to thinks we won the game because they ruled it a non-fumble. Really, it had no bearing on the outcome of the game at all because they got the ball back at the 35-yard line after the field goal and the first play they ran was intercepted. Danny McManus threw a pass to Darren, it bounced off his body and Adrion Smith picked it off and ran it in for a touchdown.

Whether they're down by three or down by six, if we intercept the ball and run it in for a touchdown, we're still up by two scores with a minute to go. You can't anticipate what the sequence of events would have been after the fumble. It may not have been the interception, it may have been a big play, but they might have gone down and scored and we might have had time to win it at the end.

DARREN FLUTIE:

I was coming almost across the middle on a little in-route and it was a little bit behind me and as I stopped to get it my feet came out from under me and as I went down and tried to get the ball it glanced high off my shoulder pad. I didn't see what happened after that. I had hurt my right shoulder earlier in the season. I was the third-string emergency quarterback and I couldn't raise my hand over my shoulder any more. I had some trouble, but it wasn't separated. In the second quarter of the Grey Cup, Ed Berry hit me coming me across the middle and I did have a third-degree separation in my left shoulder. At the time I told Danny I separated my shoulder and asked whether or not he wanted me to stay in. He said, "We've got one more half, can't you just suck it up and take some painkillers, you have a long time to heal?" That's kind of what haunts me the most about that game — that I stayed in even though I was hurt. Maybe I wasn't as effective as I should have been and maybe someone else could have done a lot better. That's one regret I have of that game, but I did it and I live with the results.

I've had more than my share of those calls go against me. They had the ball with enough time on the clock to do something with it. They were down by six and we made the play with the interception and ran it in for a touchdown. That's the play that iced the game for us. It was a great feeling of satisfaction to win. When I saw Adrion running to the end zone with the ball, it was just a very comforting feeling. Even then, though, I was eyeing the clock. They marched it right back down and stuck it in the end zone. They had a chance to go for the onside kick. Pinball made the great play to go up and catch the ball, but he took a big-time hit and the ball was jarred loose. Duane Dmytryshyn recovered it.

I knelt for the last kneel-down and Vic Stevenson, our right tackle, wanted the game ball. I handed it to him right there on the field. Throughout all the interviews and the postgame stuff, there was a constant feeling of satisfaction, of getting to where we wanted, and of putting to rest all the doubters.

RON LANCASTER (Edmonton Head Coach):

He's a tough guy to corral. We knew we couldn't stop him. We needed to slow him down a little bit more. We did a fairly good job, but he made some great plays just getting rid of the football on those little shovel passes to Drummond. A couple times we could have just as easily seen the ball on the ground but, hey, that's why he's won the MVP five times. I like to watch him play. I think he's a great guy to watch play. He's worth the price of a ticket to me and I just knew that when the game's close the ball was going to be in his hands.

BOB NICHOLSON:

I always believed, as I said throughout his negotiations, the thing would happen eventually. There was some extenuating circumstances with the receivership in Calgary and things like that that dragged it on, but we always knew Doug was coming [to Toronto]. I don't know if I could have imagined the impact he was going to have — that it was going to be as large as it was — but I always knew

*that he was going to be a big impact guy for us and he was every-
thing and more than his advanced billing. He was the difference.*

It was a great credit to Don and the coaching staff and the
team. Pinball became my go-to guy. He was a guy who, when
we were struggling offensively, I knew no one could cover man-
to-man. I'd just put him on little five- or six-yard routes, let him
bounce off the guy or put on a little spin move and then I'd stick
it in his chest and let him run with the ball. I think I did more of
that with Toronto than I've ever done before. We did wrinkles
and things that I hadn't done before. It was great seeing Pinball
set a team record for receptions in his first season as primarily a
receiver. And how about Drummond racking up all his yards
with receiving and running and leading the league in touchdowns? And what about Jimmy Cunningham leading the league
in all-purpose yardage, Paul Masotti having another 1,000-yard
season, Tyrone Williams playing extremely well in his first full
season in the league and Duane Dmytryshyn stepping in and
doing the job he did?

There were guys that just came in and did a tremendous job.
I always have the offensive guys in mind, but it was an overall
team effort. Mike Vanderjagt kicked five field goals in five attempts in the Grey Cup. It was just an awesome job and we
needed every one of those field goals. Mike had only played
two league games back in 1993 and had struggled to find a job
afterward but proved himself big-time all year.

Looking back at the whole year, it was a fun season. I
wouldn't have changed anything in it for the world. It was the
most relaxed year I think I've ever had as far as trying to enjoy
playing football. Don Matthews created an atmosphere that made
it easy to work. It was a situation where there were a lot of high
expectations. Meeting all the goals was not an easy thing to do.
In my mind, I had a certain impression of Don Matthews being
a cocky, arrogant type of head coach from other teams, but to
actually play for him was thoroughly enjoyable and caused me
to revise my opinion of him.

People just think, "Oh, yeah, they were good, they should

have blown the other teams out," but it's not that way. You don't just walk out on the field and blow people out. Those guys on the other side of the football are getting paid, too. They're professional athletes and they expect to win. Every time you win a football game, it's a great accomplishment. Every week you step on to the field, every down you play, if you don't have everybody going all out and giving 100 percent effort, you don't get things accomplished.

I think a big part of the Argos — and it stemmed down from Don Matthews, who tried to keep everybody loose and relaxed — was the camaraderie between the guys. Pinball did a routine before each game to get the guys loose. We'd gather around him in a circle, and he'd say, "Who's in the house?" And we'd say, "Daddy's in the house." We'd be singing and dancing, and the media always got a big kick out of it. Linebacker Donnie Wilson, who is a real character, was always joking and laughing and dancing and causing a ruckus. Different guys had different little routines they did all year, and at the last practice before the Grey Cup, the best performers did their routines and Mike Kiselak read a poem he had written especially for the game.

It was still just a fun, party-type atmosphere. We'd score touchdowns and guys would come running off the bench to meet Drummond and Adrion Smith in the end zone and they'd all be dancing. It wasn't a matter of trying to stick it in the other teams' faces. It was just a matter of guys having fun on the field and off which also carried over into the locker room and in the way we'd celebrate a win. People don't realize the team has to be close and I think this team was. It was a close-knit group.

The night after the game, the team had a big reception, which was attended by the Argo cheerleaders, fans and players' family members. Pinball got on stage and did his routine. That party went most of the night and I woke up about six in the morning. I don't even think I went to bed that night. I went in and did *Canada AM* — a national TV show — and brought the Grey Cup in. One of the better things about the tradition in Canada is the Grey Cup itself: You get to take it around with you, share it with the public, share it with the city you've won it in, allow the fans to acknowledge it and drink out of it, touch it or whatever.

After *Canada AM*, I took the Cup with me to the Lone Star Cafe and hung out with some of the guys. We put the Cup on the counter so people that came into the restaurant could see it and touch it. Here was a trophy they had grown up with or seen their whole lives on TV but had never been able to actually see in person. It was not like that in the NFL. I don't even know if the players got to see the Vince Lombardi trophy.

The most surprising thing occurred later that day during the parade thrown by the city. I thought it was a great gesture, but I thought it might be a little embarrassing. I didn't really think the people in the city were that fired up about the Argos. I feared that we'd have this parade and nobody would show up. It was really kind of a neat thing. The people lined up in the street and showed their support and I was very pleasantly surprised. The snow was falling lightly and we were driven in open convertibles through the downtown area en route to city hall. I had Alexa riding with me and Don Matthews in a car and I think she got a big kick out of that. I was taken aback by the show of support from the fans that day. It was very nice and left a good feeling. The guys did their celebrating and dancing on the podium.

The parade and reception created a fun atmosphere for us all and it was a nice little reward to be acknowledged in that way.

Going for the Repeat

Our goal was to win the Grey Cup again. No team had won back-to-back championships since Edmonton in 1981–82. And no Argonaut team had done it in 50 years. Not only did many people in the media pick us to win again, but there was talk of us going undefeated.

This time it was a lot easier going into the season, because I wasn't coming into a new situation. I was feeling comfortable now with guys like Pinball Clemons, Robert Drummond, and Paul Masotti. After opening the season with a 38–23 win over Winnipeg, I sat down to watch the game film with Don Matthews. We noticed rookie slotback Derrell Mitchell was getting open all the time on the backside of routes. When you're watching film you watch the back side to see what's going on. I'd call a route to the primary side and throw the ball and there'd be Derrell on the back side, just turning people around on the weak side of routes. So in the following game we started getting Derrell the ball a little more and he became a very explosive weapon for us, finishing with 77 catches for 1,457 yards and winning rookie of the year honors.

In that second game, while trying to break a tackle, I rolled over on my right foot and sprained the big toe. It affected all the toes because of the swelling and made it difficult to run for half to three quarters of the season. That was very frustrating. We lost the third game of the season against Saskatchewan and I think that was directly related to me not being able to move. They did a lot of their zone blitzing and came at us. They put pressure in my face and created some problems because I couldn't move around. But we still should have won. We made a bunch of stupid mistakes late in the game that cost us.

GERRY TOWNEND (Team Athletic Therapist):

The toe was a big concern. He was going to go regardless, he kept telling us. But by all rights if he had said, "This is not getting any better," we would have sat him. He wouldn't have played, but he made the call. I look back and most guys wouldn't have played through it. They'd just shut it down until it was better. Not Doug. He played through it and it got better. Fortunately, he never aggravated it too much. He never made it much worse. But he had a lot of injuries that year, a lot of nagging, little things.

We won our next three games. Then we played in Calgary and lost 45–35. A lot of things happened in that game that went their way. It was a very evenly matched game and I felt great that day as far as my arm strength and mobility and all that stuff. Our middle linebacker, Mike O'Shea, was kicked out early for a hit on Jeff Garcia. I threw a ball up the seam that should have been a touchdown, but it got knocked down in the wind, or I just underthrew it — one or the other. It just cleared the DB's hand and ended up as an interception. It could have gone for six our way; instead, they're sitting on our 20-yard line. I threw an interception in the third quarter that William Hampton ran back 61 yards for a touchdown.

I actually thoroughly enjoyed that game. It was a fun, competitive game. It's always frustrating to lose — it doesn't sit well — but both games I played in Calgary with the Argos were very intense, enjoyable games to play even though I lost both.

After the Calgary game we played at home against the Edmonton Eskimos and won, but I injured my right hamstring. It healed after a couple games but I re-aggravated it three games later against the Winnipeg Blue Bombers, though we won 66–25. We played the Bombers again three games later and Robert Drummond suffered a knee injury in the first half. He didn't play again until the final game of the season. Pinball filled in as running back and was named player of the week twice. Don Matthews set a record for all-time wins by a coach in the CFL, and Pinball set a professional record with 3,840 all-purpose yards, shattering the record of 3,300 he set in 1990.

Our final game of the year came in Montreal. I wanted to win to finish with 16 victories for the first time. Drum returned and you could definitely tell he was a little hesitant. We had some holes there where he'd bust through and get only 12 yards, where he might have taken it and gone all the way. But you could also see the difference with the team. It just made it a lot easier with him back on the field in short yardage situations. All of a sudden we had the whole offense back in. It was fun to see Drum excited about playing.

Also, Paul Masotti played that game with the passion of a 22-year-old. At the very beginning I hit him in a little under route. He hit a crease and took off and got about 40 yards or something. He needed 150 yards to get to 1,000 and you could tell right away that if he didn't get it, it wasn't going to be his fault — it was going to be *my* fault. In fact, late in the game he broke open on an in-route where he would be off and running for a good 30-yard gain and would have gone over that 1,000-yard mark if I could have gotten the ball to him.

It would have also given us an opportunity to win the game. But I got rushed and couldn't wait for him to run out the back side. I tried to squeeze it in the front side of the linebacker and sit him down a little. If I had led Paul perfectly, I would have thrown the ball right to the linebacker. I just had to put it on one side or the other. Paul was all aggravated after that play. Like I said, it would have been my fault if he didn't get to 1,000 yards at that point. He was playing his best game of the year. It was fun to see that fire in his eyes and the chance to make plays.

PAUL MASOTTI:

The game didn't really mean much. The 1,000 yards was on my mind but not the foremost thing. The thing that was on my mind was just getting ready to go into the playoffs. I hadn't caught the ball much near the end of the season, and you don't turn it up at the end, you just want to go into the playoffs on a good note. It felt good to be able to get the ball like that, but it also pissed me off that I could have had games like that all year if I had gotten the ball. Going into the game, Doug wasn't trying to get me the ball to get the 1,000 yards. He said, "If you get a big play or if you have a really good first half, then we'll make an effort." But 150 yards is a long way to go. I ended up having some 100 yards in the first half, so it was pretty academic after that. But that one play early in the game when he hit me for that long gain started it off and kind of set up the whole day.

I thought offensively we played a great game. We made a couple mistakes that cost us a few points, but in general we moved the ball up and down the field and we scored a lot of points. The Als blocked a punt for a touchdown, and for the first time they moved the ball on us and scored some points. They won 43–38. I didn't think there would be any doubt we would be able to move the ball against them come playoff time, but you could tell they were gaining confidence in playing us — their offense against our defense. That was the only thing that concerned me about that loss — it was disappointing to lose the last regular-season game and not go 16–2. I wanted to do that because that would have tied a league record, but 15–3 was a good record for me. Every time I won the Grey Cup we had a 15–3 record.

We had a bye week going into the Eastern final against Montreal, who beat British Columbia. It's amazing how, when your team has a bye, no matter who you play next, they've just won their last game and you haven't played in two weeks, so the other team gains momentum in the media's eyes. That's all the talk was about all week — how Montreal had beat us in the last regular-season game and had won their last game and were on a roll. Of course they're going to be on a roll! They've just won a playoff game and we haven't played yet! We didn't have the opportunity to be on a roll because we hadn't played. That always irritates me going into the playoff game. Every year I've gone into that game as the favorite and won it probably 75 percent of the time, and each time the other team is almost becoming the favorite going into the game. Then you go on to the field and everything takes care of itself.

I was sick as a dog that week. I didn't go to practice two days and didn't go to the dinner for the Eastern nominee player awards (I was the East nominee for the Outstanding Player Award). I felt miserable all week long. The day before the game I was feeling a little bit better, but I was still weak. The medical staff had to get some fluids in me and did it intravenously. I did it again the morning of the game so I wouldn't dehydrate.

GERRY TOWNEND:

We were fortunate that, when [the flu] hit him, at least it gave him enough time to get ready for the game. You knew with Doug that even if he was near his deathbed, he was going to be there regardless. We were ready at any time if we had to take him in during the game to give him more IV, but he didn't even take IV at halftime. He was doing all right.

I think you're always concerned when a guy has the flu because you just never know. He may get drained and hit the wall early. With Doug, you just knew he would have finished it right to the end, the way he was, the attitude he had. You're going to have to drag him off the field literally or go out and pick him up. He was going to leave it all there. But, he was doing really well leading up to the game. In all honesty when I look back on that, Laurie came up Friday night and he did much better when she was there. Any time Laurie was there, he felt much more comfortable. I think that helped him a lot, especially with the flu.

You feel like death walking on to the field, but for some reason when the ball is snapped you concentrate and the adrenaline is pumping so much that you just go. I remember watching Michael Jordan play a playoff game in which he was sick all night, and he just lit it up. Maybe when you're sick your focus gets better or something. You know you have to concentrate that much harder on what you're doing.

Montreal missed a field goal on their second-last series. It wouldn't have bothered me if they had made that field goal because we would have started on the 35-yard line and had a chance. I would have probably played for a field goal to send it to overtime rather than go after the touchdown and make a mistake. When Terry Baker missed the field goal, I thought Pinball was going to just take it and go. In fact, he had a real good shot there around the 15-yard line. He made a stutter step and had an offensive lineman in front of him. If he had gotten around that guy, which I thought he would, he would've had a chance to go up the sidelines quite a ways. But he kind of stumbled and went down around the 16, and that scared me. If we didn't get a first down we were going to be punting the ball; Montreal would gain possession near mid-field with probably 30 seconds left in the game and have a chance to get a field-goal opportunity again.

My first order of business was to try to keep the clock running and make a first down or two, then go after a field goal or whatever to win the game. On first down I called a quarterback draw. There was a nice little crease and I slipped through, but I got tripped up and went down.

Montreal safety Tommy Europe hit me late on the ground. He couldn't tell if I had gotten touched and in his mind he still had a chance to hit me because he thought I had just fallen. He got a 15-yard penalty for it, which got us out of our own end and into a position where we could be more aggressive. It's all part of the offense — where you spread people out. You use the quarterback as a runner and now you can block everybody because you've got the extra man. I called a quarterback counter and there was a nice little crease and got another nine yards. Drummond picked up the first down and now we were out near mid-field. There was still about a minute on the clock.

Now it was time to get aggressive. If we made a mistake or threw an interception, or if we turned the ball over or went two incompletions and punt, we'd still be all right. We would still be safe. That's when I went into the shotgun and threw the ball. Pinball lined up with his man playing him outside-in. Pinball had a crossing route called, so he was going to run away from his man. All I had to do was control the free safety, Tommy Europe.

On my drop back, I looked left, let Pinball cross the field, and threw back into the middle. Tommy Europe didn't even acknowledge my eyes. He was playing Pinball all the way and was starting to close a little bit. So I threw the ball kind of softly and back to the inside to flatten Pinball out across. Because Pinball slowed to catch it, both Als players started to overrun him. Pinball caught it and spun off them, went back inside and walked down the field for a 58-yard touchdown. He iced the game for us with 40 seconds to go.

TRACY HAM (Montreal quarterback):

You've got to keep Doug off the field. We didn't do that down the stretch. For the most part we did a good job. Hey, I'm happy with how we played offensively. I thought we gave ourselves a chance to win it and that's all you can do in these situations. The game was won in the last minute. I tell you what: I'm tired of losing to Doug in the last minute of the game. I've been in games like this before. He's done a great job. He has super talent around him that make plays. You've got to give them their due.

Going into the Grey Cup, Saskatchewan was on a roll. They finished third in the West with a 6–12 record, but beat Edmonton and Calgary to make it to the Cup. The crowd numbered more than 60,000 and it felt like 59,000 were cheering for Saskatchewan. The bottom line is, once you get out on the field, chances are the more talented team is going to win. To me it was a matter of taking care of business — "Let's get this game over with. Let's get out there and play the game and get back home with the Cup."

They bobbled the opening kickoff and it looked like we were going to pin them deep or get a big play right away. All of a sudden they busted it and that's what they needed. They were playing on a lot of emotion early on. The fans were behind them.

We were the bad guys and all that stuff, and here they go, making a big play early. We stuffed them right there and they kicked a field goal. It hit the upright and went through. It was like, "Oh, geez, they're going to get some lucky breaks and keep themselves in that game."

That's just the way it felt. It was like things were going to go their way and this was going to be an uphill battle. Once we got on the field offensively, it felt easy. We walked the ball down the field right away. Then I made a mistake and threw an interception. It was the same play I hit Pinball on for the touchdown against Montreal, but this time the man covering Pinball broke flat underneath him and made a nice interception. It bothered me that we lost a scoring opportunity. In playoff games, that can kill you.

Defensively, we shut them down and got the ball back, then *bang, bang, bang* — down the field we go. It felt from the very beginning of that game we were going to have a big day offensively. We could do just about anything we wanted. We walked the ball up and down the field. Just before the half we came down the field and got a field goal. I wanted us to get in the end zone. We were on the eight-yard line and had one play, then we were going to have to kick the field goal. I wanted to go for the end zone. They zone blitzed us and came flying off the corner. I had to get rid of the ball quickly and I dumped it to Derrell Mitchell. He worked his way down to the five-yard line. The worst mistake in the world would have been to let the clock run out and not be able to kick the field goal. We got the field goal right at the end of the half.

Right at the start of the second half, Adrion (Peewee) Smith returned the kickoff 95 yards for the touchdown on a fake reverse to Pinball. You could just feel the emotion leave Saskatchewan. The bubble just burst. All of a sudden it went from 20–9 to 27–9.

We scored 21 points that quarter and went on to win 47–23. I was named the game's MVP and was awarded a truck, which I gave to Paul Masotti. He was named the top Canadian and awarded two plane tickets to anywhere Canadian Airlines flies.

After I gave Paul the keys to the truck, he gave his tickets to offensive lineman Chris Gioskos. I gave the truck to Paul because I thought Canadian players deserved more recognition. They're never looked at as MVP candidates in the Grey Cup. Since Paul was the top Canadian and he did so much for me, I figured he was deserving of the truck.

PAUL MASOTTI:

I had no idea about what was going on, but apparently Doug had told Mike Vanderjagt and some other guys in warmups that he was going to do that if he won the award. I knew he was up to something when he called me up during the presentation. I thought he was going to go off on one of his tangents. Then it turned out he just wanted to give me the truck. I was totally in shock.

People talk about the troubles of the CFL, but then you look at the support Hamilton, Regina, Edmonton, Calgary, and Winnipeg receive — it's second to none. They have great fan support. Their fans love the game. They love the players. They'll do anything in the world for them. It says a lot for this league.

Take Saskatchewan for example. The thing I love the most about Saskatchewan is the enthusiasm of the fans. I talk about the field in Regina as being kind of dumpy, but the people show unbelievable support for their team, whether they're winning or losing. If you want to draw a parallel to the NFL, I would say that it's the Green Bay of the CFL. No matter what the situation, the fans love their football team and they show that kind of pride.

Edmonton is the same way. They even have the Green Bay colors. As much as I always hated playing the Eskimos when I was in Calgary and it was a big rivalry, there's no doubt that Edmonton and Saskatchewan have the best fans in the league as far as individual team support. Both are first-class organizations. Blue Bombers football is very important to Winnipeg and it's a big deal to them. Calgary, as I said, was where I made a name for myself in the CFL and has loyal supporters.

In the bigger markets especially — Montreal, B.C. and

Toronto — the league struggles because I guess there are other things available. I can't really explain it or put my finger on it, I just know I love this game.

I don't know if the Canadian fan has an insecurity about the CFL because it is purely Canadian. It definitely is something unique. I was always under the impression that if it was accepted in the U.S., the Canadian people would accept it that much more. I think the Canadian people have to step up and realize this is a great game. The people that I talk to who watch a lot of the NFL and CFL don't argue that the CFL is better as far as the rules and the nature of the game. It's more exciting and wide open. They will never argue that issue. It's just the packaging and the production.

There's just a mystique about the NFL that everybody loves, but there's no comparison between the two games: The CFL is a much more exciting game and I think a lot of Americans will admit it

Shuffling off to Buffalo

While Doug put all his efforts into his National Football League comeback, co-author Perry Lefko followed his progress. This is his description of the events leading up to and following Doug's signing with the Buffalo Bills.

No sooner had the 1997 Canadian Football League season ended than the selling of Doug Flutie to the National Football League officially began. Doug's agent, Jack Mula, faxed all 30 NFL teams indicating Doug's impending free agency. Mula had been talking to teams all season to gauge interest in Doug, but now, with Doug's CFL contract set to expire in five weeks, he had the chance to make a deal. The CFL and the NFL had reached an historic accord earlier in the year which, among other things, allowed CFL free agents — whose contracts normally ended the following February — to negotiate with NFL teams as of December 23.

Doug indicated publicly after the Grey Cup he felt he could play for another three years, likely in the CFL, but added, "We'll see how it goes. If we can keep this group together, that would be nice. But we'll take it one year at a time, one game at a time."

The desire to play once more in the NFL in the twilight of his career burned within Doug's competitive soul, but he needed a chance to do it. Only six teams responded to Mula's fax: New Orleans, St. Louis, Philadelphia, Arizona, Oakland, and Buffalo. A.J. Smith, the Bills director of pro personnel, had been scouting

Doug for the last five years. When Bills quarterback Jim Kelly announced his retirement in January 1997, Smith began thinking about Doug as a player who could compete for the job. Smith knew Doug's contract expired in December and began his "tracking process" in October with little fanfare or publicity. He discussed it only with Bills general manager John Butler, although Smith regularly mentioned potential prospects to him.

Smith had watched Doug play live in five games over two years and had analyzed game film of him. At one point, he talked to Mula and told him he needed game film of Doug as far back as high school. By the time Mula collected the film, Smith told him he had already watched everything he could. Smith told Mula the Bills definitely had some interest in Doug, and re-affirmed that on December 23.

Even though Smith hadn't talked to anyone outside of the organization, media outlets in Toronto, Boston and Buffalo pounced on the possibility of Doug joining the Bills. Mula began fielding calls similar to those he had received two years before when it became apparent Doug would be leaving Calgary for Toronto. This time, however, the volume of interest had heightened considerably. Before, it had just been a question of arguably the greatest player in the CFL moving from one team to another; now it involved moving from one league to another or, more specifically, moving back to the league that had given up on Doug eight years before.

Smith telephoned Doug to inform him he believed in his abilities and the Bills might have an interest in him. Smith strongly indicated the Bills would only pay Doug a salary of $250,000, the minimum required by the NFL Players Association based on his previous NFL experience. Doug understood the situation and did not have a problem with it. He only wanted a chance and Smith told him it could possibly happen.

Smith then approached Butler and head coach Marv Levy and "laid it on the line." Smith endorsed the signing of Doug as fervently as he had linebacker Chris Spielman, whom the team had signed as a free agent from Detroit in 1996. Spielman had been an alternate in the Pro Bowl in 1995 and led the Lions in tackles each of his eight seasons. Smith knew endorsing Doug as highly as he did Spielman would gain Butler's attention.

"They looked at me kind of funny," Smith said of the reaction of Levy and, to a lesser extent, Butler. "I think I caught them off guard. I don't think they expected it. I think Marv kind of said, 'How much time does he have left, a year?' I said, 'How about three or four?'"

The situation took a radical twist when Levy announced his retirement on December 31, leaving Doug wondering if his dream had just died. The new coach, whomever that would be, might not have the same interest in him. Smith called Doug on New Year's Day and told him to hold on to his hopes. Smith talked to Bills defensive coordinator Wade Phillips, whom the team planned to hire as Levy's replacement, about his interest in signing Doug. Phillips quickly gave it his blessing.

Smith figured New Orleans would be the only other team pursuing Doug. Saints head coach Mike Ditka liked Doug from their days with Chicago in the 1986 season and expressed an interest in signing him in 1997 when talk of the NFL-CFL accord surfaced. "If I felt he was the key to making it work, I'd go after him in a minute," Ditka told me. "It wouldn't bother me one bit."

The accord did not allow Doug to sign with an NFL team until December 23 at the earliest, and even then he wouldn't being playing south of the border until the 1998 season. The Argos wanted him back in '97 to finish out the final season of his two-year contract. This temporarily stalled Doug's NFL aspirations, but he looked forward to playing again for Toronto and trying to win another Grey Cup.

Even when Doug's contract officially expired, Ditka believed NFL teams still had a prejudice against him because of his size. "They've got the same people with the scouting departments basically, so they're going to judge him on that," Ditka said. "They're going to say it's the size thing, but how many Grey Cups and MVPs has he won now? His records are every bit as good as [Warren] Moon's were up there, aren't they? Even better. Maybe I don't know what I'm talking about, but I would say if Warren Moon could do it, Doug Flutie could do it. As a matter of fact, I know he can do it. I'm that sure he could do it."

Jack Mula headed out to the East-West Shrine Game in Palo Alto, California, on January 10–11 and tracked down Wade Phillips, whom he didn't know. Mula wanted to reassure Doug of the Bills' interest. When Mula introduced himself to Phillips and told him why he had come, the new Bills head coach confirmed he planned to give Doug a shot. Mula believed him and called Doug back with the positive news.

Mula then headed off to Mobile, Alabama, to talk to "anyone and everyone" regarding Doug. Mobile played host to the Senior Bowl and brought together coaches, management types and agents from all factions of the football industry for meetings and potential deals. If Mula hoped to find any interest in Doug beside the Bills', this would be the place to look for it. Mula had already begun discussions with Bills vice-president of administration Jim Miller, who handled Buffalo's contract negotiations. Mula also planned to speak to Argo president Bob Nicholson about Toronto's interest. Nicholson had just returned from a two-week vacation and had not talked to Mula since Christmas, preferring to let he and his client exhaust their NFL opportunities.

Contacted in Mobile, Phillips refused to wade into any conversations about the Bills' interest in Doug. "We're looking for better production at the quarterback position and when we sign one, if it's him, I'll be glad to talk about it, but I'm not going to speculate on all of that," Phillips said. "I've talked to John Butler about that and he said, 'Don't make any statements,' so I'm not."

Argo head coach Don Matthews, who was in Mobile, indicated he did not have a good feel about whether or not Doug would leave the Argos for the Bills. He considered it a 50–50 split.

Sports agent Jerry Vainisi, the 1986 general manager of the Chicago Bears, which had acquired Doug's rights from the Los Angeles Rams just minutes before the trade deadline expired, indicated to me he felt his former quarterback could still play in the NFL.

"I saw him play two games this year in Toronto and I don't think there's any doubt he can still play in the National Football League," Vainisi proclaimed. "He's an exceptional athlete."

Doug stayed free of all the media hype, vacationing in Hawaii as a guest of the Hula Bowl, which brought together former Heisman Trophy winners. It turned into a working vacation for Doug, who talked daily with Mula and also had to fend off the media that desperately tried to track him down for an interview. The messages piled up daily and it became an irritant for Doug and his wife Laurie, who had joined him for the holiday. Ultimately, Doug used an alias, taking the name of his nephew, to fend off the media. Doug did only one interview, speaking to Buffalo's Empire Sports Network, after he picked up the phone thinking it was somebody else and opted not to hang up. He did not say anything in the interview to indicate anything other than he hadn't made a definitive decision.

Mula returned from Mobile on January 14 and indicated Doug's future could be decided in days. First he had to talk with the Argos' Bob Nicholson and the Bills' Jim Miller. Mula did his "due diligence" the morning of the 16th and called Nicholson, who had indicated in an interview on the 15th that he believed Doug would still come back to the Argos. At that point the Argos had not even tabled an offer amid rumors the team planned to slash Doug's annual million-dollar stipend by as much as $500,000 because they didn't have to bid against anybody. Nicholson confirmed the story, but gave no hint of what the team planned to offer Doug, who commanded almost $600,000 more than the next highest-paid player in the league. It all became a moot point when Nicholson talked to Mula and determined Doug planned to sign with Buffalo. The Argos had no plans to engage in a bidding war.

Later that day, Mula issued a press release with comments from Doug stating his desire to return to the NFL but thanking the Argos and the CFL.

Although financial terms were not disclosed, the two-year deal with Buffalo gave Doug a first-year base salary of $250,000, and a $25,000 signing bonus. Mula structured the deal with a myriad of incentives, which collectively could make the overall package worth $6 million. Many of the bonuses kicked in if Doug played in 70 percent of the Bills games. The contract called for a salary of $375,000 in the second year, but the bonus money Doug collected in the first year would become his salary in the second year over and above the base pay.

"He's accomplished, I think, everything he can accomplish here," Nicholson said at the time. "He's a competitive person, he wants new challenges and the NFL offers him those challenges. My feeling is the lure of the NFL is something that's important to him and I'm not going to try to compete against that."

Doug's signing caught Argos head coach Don Matthews by surprise. "I thought he would think it over some more, but I guess he has his own agenda, so we all wish him well."

News of Doug's signing elicited various responses from family members, teammates, opposing teams and critics. "Whether he's 35 or 25, I'm excited for him," Darren Flutie said. "I think it's great. They're getting a player with three times the heart of a normal football player. I've played with him and I know how much it means to him to win. To me he deserves the opportunity."

"It's about proving himself and starting in the NFL, that's all it is," said Argo kicker Mike Vanderjagt, who followed Doug to the NFL a few weeks later by signing with Indianapolis.

John Tory, the CFL's chairman/acting commissioner, praised Doug for his contribution. "He did it in a time when the league was under a lot of other stresses and strains," Tory said. "I think he really helped us in the task of holding the league together during tough times. One can't underestimate the role he has played."

Not everyone in the CFL bemoaned Doug's decision. "He totally eclipsed all the other QBs in the league and he clearly could turn games on his ability alone," Calgary Stampeders owner Sig Gutsche told the *Calgary Sun*. "It had become a problem of equality. It is for the CFL's best interest."

Hamilton Tiger-Cats vice-chairman George Grant said, "Flutie was quite an outstanding player. It's not like he's irreplaceable, but he probably is as good as any player that has played this game in Canada. I think he's been a valuable asset for us as a league. I'm not surprised he has done it, the rumors were ripe that he was going to take this shot and I can understand why he'd want to do it. He would like to prove he can play in the NFL at this point in his career."

Bills administration v.p. Jim Miller told the *Buffalo News* he didn't believe signing Doug had a downside. "You have to compare him to what we have now and that's where the competition will start," Miller said. "I've always believed in giving a guy a chance. Obviously we need to upgrade the position. Doug has put together an excellent record in the CFL. Certainly he deserves a shot to help us win. He is mobile, which is a positive attribute for a quarterback these days."

Miller denied the signing had anything to do with the Bills trying to draw Canadians to home games. The Bills had attendance problems and reportedly drew about 15 percent of their fan base from north of the border. Doug's presence in Toronto only contributed to a 25 percent increase in his first year with the Argos, and the overall figure dropped in his second season despite the prospect of back-to-back Grey Cup championships. What Miller did not know then — and what nobody could have possibly anticipated — was how much Doug could contribute to the Bills on and off the field. Doug became the symbol of not only a resurgent quarterback, but a resurgent franchise, which had flopped the year before with a 6–10 record in the first season without Jim Kelly.

Doug called me a day after the official announcement and explained why he had given up the comfort of the CFL — something he often talked about — to go back to the NFL. It meant proving himself all over again and subjecting himself to criticism about his height, ability and age. Moreover, he did not have any financial guarantees. It seemed like a risky move to me.

"I'm a glutton for punishment," he joked initially. "I always said if the opportunity was right, if there was a situation where I thought I would get a legitimate shot that I would be able to compete for the starting job where it's not etched in stone who the starter is, then I would take a peek at it; then I would take a shot. I'm not in any great awe because it's the NFL or anything like that. I just think it's the right move to make now and I have a legitimate shot. I'm just totally grateful to the Toronto Argonauts for everything they've done and especially Bob Nicholson, Don Matthews and the guys on the team for the relationships I had. It was just a fantastic situation, but right now this is the better opportunity for me and it's what I have to try to do, I think, just to satisfy myself.

"It's a better opportunity for me and that's the only way I can describe it. I have an opportunity that if I were to start and do well and all that, I could make a heck of a lot of money. It just became an intriguing option for me. I'm more or less going on a gut feeling. I think things are going to work out. I've played in that league before. It's nothing special. I know I can play at that level and I would like to prove it."

Doug also talked about handling criticism, which had already begun in earnest in the Buffalo area, both among fans and the media. Vic Carucci, a longtime respected football reporter for the *Buffalo News,* wrote a column a few days earlier stating the huge risk in signing Doug:

> By NFL quarterbacking standards, that is as bargain-basement as it gets. But the issue isn't about money or not having to part with a draft pick. What we're talking about here is something far more valuable — something called credibility. The pursuit of the undersized, overaged Flutie does not inspire confidence that the Bills have their act together in addressing their woeful quarterback situation ... The mere fact the Bills are trying to sign the little guy has generated a tidal wave of conversation, not only throughout Western New York and Southern Ontario, but also throughout the NFL. The phrase I've heard a number of times in the past several days is, "What are those guys thinking?" ... Regardless of the spin the Bills attempt to put on it, a Flutie flop would be perceived as yet another mistake at their most important position. And this move has mistake written all over it.

Chuck Dickerson, the blustery former Bills defensive line coach who had become a talk radio personality in Buffalo, soundly trashed the signing, trotting out Jim McMahon's hoary "midget" comments. He said fans would be inundated with buzz phrases such as "moving pocket" and "turnback protection" in reference to Doug, but derisively laughed them off and chastised the few callers supporting the signing.

Those critics who didn't lambaste the signing as much as Carucci and Dickerson had cautious optimism at best. Forget about the fact had Doug played only two hours south of Buffalo for the last two years; few people in the Queen City truly appreciated his talents. To them he simply did not measure up physically or athletically to NFL standards and had a lot of convincing to do.

Throughout the whole process, Laurie Flutie worried about that kind of criticism. She considered Doug crazy for wanting to subject himself to that again, but he planned to ignore it all by not paying attention to what was said or written about him in the media.

"I realized a long time ago you can't please everybody," he said. "I'm just going to play football and have fun. You just go and play for yourself and the guys on the team, have fun and enjoy it while it lasts because it's not going to last forever. I know the coaches are excited to have me and that's all I care about."

When I contacted Ditka for a reaction and to ask him why he hadn't pursued signing Doug, he told me the Saints had committed themselves to veteran Billy Joe Hobert, whom the Bills had discarded midway through the previous season, and youngster Danny Wuerffel. Ditka wished Doug well. Moreover, he considered the signing an example of destiny.

"It's a great opportunity for him up there," Ditka told me. "They don't have a quarterback in my opinion. What's meant to be, will be. God does things for reasons. He's meant to go to Buffalo. I hope they win a Super Bowl. I really do. I thought we'd win one in Chicago, but we didn't. That's life. It goes on. He shouldn't be anywhere but where he is. I believe that. Things don't happen just because they happen. They happen for rea-

sons. I think he's a winner. I don't think there's any question
about it."

Some of Ditka's comments became prophetic in the months
to come. Jerry Vainisi, meanwhile, figured Doug could be a short-
term solution for Buffalo. "Doug would be perceived as somewhat of a stop-gun type while you're developing your younger
quarterback, but he's a veteran who might buy you some time.
He's a very accurate passer. But the thing with Doug Flutie to
me is if Buffalo decides to commit to him, then they have to make
a full commitment and design an offensive system that moves
the pocket, so it enables him to see the lanes. He'll find the open-
ings and find the receivers as long as he has the opportunity to
move from the pocket and avoid the rush."

Doug returned home to Boston and boarded a flight to Buffalo on January 20 for a physical and to sign his contract.
MetroWest Daily News sports columnist Lenny Megliola, who had
been the paper's sports editor when Doug first started to show-
case his athletic ability as a 13-year-old baseball player, covered
the historic signing. When Megliola did a report on Doug's final
high school game, he thought that would be the last time he'd
need to talk to him for a story. Now, almost 20 years later and
after countless columns, Megliola found himself writing about
Doug again and, coincidentally, sitting across from him in the
same aisle en route to Buffalo. As the plane descended, Megliola
watched Doug, who shook his head and uttered the word "Buffalo" in some disbelief.

"It was a dreamy way of saying it, it was like, 'Here I am in
Buffalo, I'm going to get a chance,'" Megliola said. "It was the
irony that eight, nine years later the opportunity was here. If we
were flying into St. Louis or San Diego I think he would have
said the same thing. He had a pleased look on his face that he
was flying into an NFL city and was going to get a chance."

Dressed in a black sports jacket, an open dress shirt, black
jeans and cowboy boots and sunburned slightly from his stay in
Hawaii, Doug walked from one end of the Ralph Wilson
Fieldhouse — the site of the Bills indoor practice facility — to
the other end while the cameras clicked. Normally the Bills con-

ducted media conferences in the nearby executive building, but they needed this location to accommodate the gathering of journalists from Toronto, Buffalo and Boston. The setting lacked the glitz and glamour of some of Doug's more-celebrated signings, but had more of a continental feel with the various journalists from the two countries.

Doug answered queries about his decision to return to the NFL; his size; the irony of playing for Buffalo, which had a shot to draft him in 1985; playing so close to his last CFL stop; and Bills incumbent starter Todd Collins, whom he had last talked to as a high school star in the Boston area. When asked about those records he still had a chance to eclipse in the CFL, Doug stated there's always "unfinished business," but indicated the business at hand belonged in Buffalo.

A.J. Smith stood in the background watching the proceedings as anonymously as he did watching Doug play. When Doug arrived for his physical, he gave Smith a hug and thanked him for believing in him.

"I believe in the guy, he's a winner, he's got a lot of strong points," Smith told me resolutely. "Is the league too big down here? I can't wait to find out. I really can't wait to see. People say he failed the last time he was here. I totally disagree with that. He wasn't really given an opportunity. He was just there and that's a long time ago and this is a 35-year-old professional football player with 13 years [pro] experience and with a great mind and still some abilities and instincts and so on and so forth, so I think this is a totally different situation. There's been a lot of small players who've made it but you don't know until they get here. Will Doug Flutie be an exception to the rule? We're about to find out because he's going to get his opportunity in the National Football League and I think it will be very exciting."

John Butler defended the move to sign Doug. "We lost a [potential] Hall of Fame quarterback here [Jim Kelly] and a great leader and a winner," Butler said. "To me Doug Flutie's a leader, he's a winner and somebody we want to have on our team. Whether he starts or not, that leadership in the locker room is a great thing to have. I don't really call it an experiment. I think it's a calculated, good, solid move on our part right now. Good things can happen. If it doesn't, we'll sure move on in another way, but I'll take my chances on somebody like Doug Flutie."

Doug used the occasion to donate half of his signing bonus to the Hunter's Hope Foundation, started by Jim Kelly and his wife to create awareness for Krabbes Disease. The degenerative genetic disorder afflicts infants and affects the brain, spinal chord and nerves. Doctors diagnosed the Kellys' three-year-old son Hunter with the terminal and incurable disease at four months of age.

"The situation with Jim's son has really hit home for me," Doug said. "I sometimes feel sorry for myself about my son's situation and I look at Jim and realize things can be 100 times worse. If there is something I can do to help him, it would be a great thing to do."

Doug traveled to San Diego the week after his signing to play in the Jose Cuervo Bowl, a sports celebrity flag football game on the beach. During this time he announced plans to wear jersey No. 11 because "one and one make two." Doug couldn't wear his preferred No. 2 because that belonged to kicker Steve Christie, who offered one scenario to me whereby he'd give up his number to his newest quarterback: "He's going to have to be the quarterback and we're going to have to win the Super Bowl and after that game I'll take my jersey off and give him No. 2 and he can keep it. If he wants it bad enough, that's what he'll have to do."

Christie chuckled when he made the comments, but did not doubt Doug's ability. He had seen him play and respected his talents. "Just let him play," Christie said, reacting to the negative comments directed at Doug in the Buffalo area. "Let him see what he can do. I'm looking forward to it."

During his San Diego sojourn, Doug met the Bills' owner during his annual Super Bowl party. Ralph Wilson shook his hand and said, "So you're our new savior." Wilson's somewhat facetious comment would turn out to be prophetic.

Even with Doug, the Bills planned to add another quarterback, either through the free agent route, the draft or a trade, and hire an offensive coordinator. Ten days after the Bills signed

Doug, they announced the hiring of Joe Pendry as the team's new offensive coordinator. He came from the Carolina Panthers and brought a conservative reputation. He planned to develop a strong running game with two backs lined up behind the quarterback positioned under center. The situation did not bode well for Doug, who for the last six years had played primarily out of the shotgun formation and with his running backs spread out wide. But in the months ahead, as Doug became more prominent in the offense, Pendry adjusted the Bills offense to accommodate his quarterback's strengths and abilities.

Twenty-four days after signing Doug, the Bills completed their quota of quarterbacks when they acquired Rob Johnson from Jacksonville for a first- and fourth-round pick in the upcoming draft. Johnson, a graduate of the University of Southern California, had apprenticed behind Mark Brunell for three years. Despite starting only one game in his professional career, the 6-foot-4, 214-pound Johnson had shown the ability and readiness to start. Even after the Bills acquired Johnson, there had been reports the San Diego Chargers, who needed a quarterback and were prepared to trade to acquire one, wanted the California native.

At the media gathering to introduce his newest quarterback, Phillips declared, "Rob's our No. 1 quarterback. I don't think there's any doubt about that. We've started forward with a new era. It isn't the Marv Levy and Jim Kelly era. Hopefully, it's the Wade Phillips and Rob Johnson era."

Johnson had one year left on his contract paying him a stipend of $400,000, although reports indicated the Bills planned to tear up his existing deal and sign him to a multi-million-dollar, long-term arrangement. The media began speculating that the acquisition of Johnson — and the heavy price the Bills paid for him, with the pivotal first-round pick and the likelihood of the new contract — virtually assured him the starting job. Rumors began to surface of Doug's unhappiness, even though he told an Albany TV station he welcomed the competition. A Canadian Press story quoting anonymous sources suggested Doug could be back with the Argos by training camp in June if he didn't feel the Bills gave him a fair chance in the two mini-camps to compete for the starting job. The story appeared the same day the Argonauts signed Doug's replacement, Kerwin Bell, who had been the backup in Indianapolis the previous two years.

Doug's agent, Jack Mula, dismissed the story, acknowledging the Bills made no secret of their intention to acquire another quarterback after signing Doug. Moreover, Mula suggested that even though the Bills signed Johnson, they did not know how good he was going to be because they had not made a big-money commitment to him.

"It represents a gamble and that's what sports is all about — a chance," Mula told me. "It's simply competition and I think people are reading too much into it. It's an over analysis but you have to hear it from the man."

Doug reiterated he looked forward to going back to the NFL and planned to take full advantage of it, but the perception that the acquisition of Johnson diminished his chances angered him.

"Rob Johnson's a third-year guy going into his fourth season and he's started one football game," Doug told me. "I've played 13 years — why should I be afraid of that? I talked to Wade the day before they got Rob and he told me what they were doing and that it doesn't change anything as far as their viewpoint on me and having a chance to compete. I talked to Joe Pendry and he told me he's going to do whatever it is that I'm comfortable with offensively. I don't see that anything has changed from my standpoint and from what people have been telling me. Whether they've been saying something different publicly or to other people ... it sounds like it, but I don't know that for a fact.

"I plan on going to Buffalo, making a name for myself and being a starter and winning a Super Bowl. That's what I want to do. You play to the best of your ability and let the chips fall where they may. I'm the only one of the four that's been a consistent starter anywhere. I've played more NFL games than these guys and I've played eight years in the CFL as a starter. That's my approach to it."

Doug regretted leaving his family for a 13-week period of

off-season training in Buffalo beginning in mid-March. However, he had to begrudgingly sacrifice his family time for his professional pursuit. After training with his would-be teammates, Doug regularly played basketball at the Buffalo Athletic Club with Eric Moulds, a lanky receiver the Bills drafted in the first round in 1996 but who had yet to become a starter. At times the pickup games became really intense as the two tried to outdo one another. In the process they learned about each other's skills and athleticism. They further cemented their relationship by going out for meals afterwards. It foreshadowed a great alliance that would carry onto the field.

"It helped me out a lot," Moulds said. "We were in somewhat of a similar situation. People were saying they didn't think I was fit for the NFL and they didn't think Doug was fit because of his size. We developed a rapport. He wanted to prove people wrong and I did, too."

During this time, Doug drove about once every two weeks to see his former Argo teammate Paul Masotti, who lived about an hour and a half away from Buffalo. Doug regularly telephoned Masotti, who became "more of a sounding board." Doug talked about how the NFL's procedures differed completely from the CFL's, which for one did not have the financial resources to pay players to train in off-season programs. He also discussed some of the ideas he tried to implement with the coaching staff to simplify things. In a nutshell, Doug talked about how tight the NFL mentality is and how the atmosphere is not as jovial as in the CFL. Doug often told the Canadian media how his two years in Toronto brought back the fun of the game and how he planned to take that with him in his return to the NFL — if given the chance.

In April, Doug and Laurie announced the formation of the Doug Flutie, Jr. Foundation for Autism as part of the Giving Back Fund, a national, non-profit organization that creates and professionally manages charitable foundations for athletes, entertainers and others. Doug and Laurie set up the foundation as a legacy for Dougie and organized charity events in the months to come, including a benefit with the band Aerosmith.

"Our main mission in establishing the Doug Flutie, Jr. Foundation," Doug announced, "was to create a mechanism by which other families across the country with autistic children who do not have the financial resources we do can receive financial assistance for the heavy educational and equipment expenses they constantly face."

MetroWest Daily News sports columnist Lenny Megliola, who attended the media conference for the Foundation, wrote about it the following day and commented to me about Doug's personal growth because of his son's situation.

"Here's a guy that's been healthy all his life and thought he had a healthy son and then all of a sudden came the silence and the remoteness," Megliola said. "It shook him to the core, as it would any parent obviously, but out of that comes personal growth. Some of the things he said was like another person. Well, it was another person in a sense that you find your son is autistic. It's going to change you and it changed Doug quite a bit."

Later that month, the Bills conducted their first mini-camp and the media attention focused primarily on Johnson, whom the club wanted to wear No. 11. Doug switched to No. 7, which proved to be lucky indeed. Johnson took the first snaps, followed by Doug and Collins. Collins' backup the year before, Alex Van Pelt, had an injured shoulder and did not practice, while youngster Jim Ballard played in the developmental NFL Europe. When Johnson threw an interception on a deflected pass in the first full scrimmage, it became the subject of the media keen on seeing the youngster under fire. The majority of the players had only been educated in the team's new offense for an hour or less before the first practice, which primarily featured two-back sets and quarterbacks under center. The two opening sessions featured minimal rollouts.

"Joe Pendry realizes how comfortable I am with the shotgun and all, so in obvious passing situations I'll be able to get back there," Doug said. "If we can get the running game going, which is what I think we'd like to do, the play action becomes part of it."

Asked if he expected the shotgun to evolve into the offense,

Doug replied, "Hopefully — I don't know. It's day one and [they're] throwing everything at us and guys are trying to learn on the fly."

Bills head coach Wade Phillips stressed the importance of Doug re-adjusting to a conventional offense. "It's good for him to start doing that," Phillips said. "You've got to play under center some in our league, especially the running game. There are some good running plays from shotgun, but you can't have your complete running game unless you're under the center. He has to be able to do that for us."

Most of the media questions directed at Doug related to the acquisition of Johnson.

"If Rob becomes the starter and I'm backing up, that's the role I play but I'm going to prepare myself as if I'm taking every snap," Doug responded. He dismissed suggestions the price the Bills paid to acquire Johnson automatically made him the starter: "That makes no sense to me. It's not because of the price, it's because he's a great quarterback. Price has nothing to do with it, and Rob is an excellent quarterback." Doug also said he had no plans to ask the coaching staff who will be the starter. "If I get the answer I don't want then I'll know, so I'll just compete as if I had a shot," he insisted. "It's not really going to change the way I compete, so whatever happens, happens."

The Bills opened the second day of the mini-camp to the public, which also had a chance to participate in a festival of games and view exhibits inside the indoor practice facility. NFL commissioner Paul Tagliabue attended the festival and delivered a rousing pep talk, along with state and local politicians, to help the team in its drive to sell $11 million in luxury seats by December 2. If the team reached the goal, it would renew its lease for at least another five years and receive $63.25 million in state assistance for stadium renovations. At this point, the Bills appeared to need a Hail Mary to have any hope of reaching the financial goal.

The Bills conducted the second of their allotted mini-camps with considerably less fanfare, yet Johnson's contract continued to be the main topic in the media. Just before training camp opened in July, the Bills signed Johnson to a five-year contract totalling $25 million, of which he received $8.5 million in a signing bonus. That seemed to solidify Johnson's stranglehold on the starter's job.

Doug appeared to struggle in the pre-season games, in which he played primarily with the second-stringers. He had problems adjusting to the helmet microphone allowing the offensive coordinator to communicate his play selection to the quarterback. Doug called his own plays the last two years in the CFL and generally ran his own show. He completed only eight of twenty passes in his first two pre-season games, but found success in the third game in Chicago. The day before the game, when the Bills walked into the locker room, Doug received a huge hug from former Bears great Walter Payton, who had become a radio personality in Chicago. The two had became teammates and good friends during Doug's single season in Chicago, which became hostile because of the influence of injured regular quarterback Jim McMahon.

Playing with some of the Bills starters against the Bears, Doug had his best game in the pre-season, connecting on six of seven passes.

"I think he showed tonight when you give him time and some throwing alleys, he'll take advantage of the opportunity," Payton told Mike Zeisberger of the *Toronto Sun*. "I mean, how tall do you have to be to hand off the ball to a running back? And once you get the running game going, it opens everything else up. I would pay to see him on one of those cold days up in Buffalo being chased around on that icy field."

Doug finished the pre-season with 18 completions in 38 attempts for 210 yards. Johnson hit on 28 of 41 for 329 yards, clearly establishing himself as the team's starter and earning high praise from Doug.

"It's the first time I've ever been on a team where I thought another quarterback was as athletic as I was," Doug said. "He thinks like I do — and he's in a 6-foot-4 frame. He has the potential to be a premier quarterback in this league." Van Pelt earned the third-string job, while Collins was released but was promptly picked up by Kansas City.

About this time a Pittsburgh marketing company, PLB Sports, in conjunction with Jasper Foods of Joplin, Missouri, and the Flutie Foundation, prepared for the launch of Flutie Flakes, a frosted corn flakes cereal. PLB, which produces food products with athletes' names, had done a marinara deal for Atlanta Braves' pitcher Tom Glavine, whose marketing company, Woolf Associates, also represents Doug. When PLB president Ty Ballou asked Woolf for its client list and saw Doug's name on it, he thought a cereal box might be a good vehicle to promote the message about the Flutie Foundation, which would benefit from a portion of the proceeds of the sales. There had never been an individual cereal for an athlete — Wheaties features an assortment of stars from various sports — but Ballou felt Doug could be a good person to launch the concept.

Ballou admitted he was "scared as hell" about the initial run of 50,000, wondering if it would even sell out. At the very least, the cereal box had an attractive look. It featured a bright-red front with a head shot of Doug, an action shot, an autograph and the message "Limited Edition Collector's Box" underneath the heading "Flutie Flakes." The back had the same action shot and a T-shirt offer. One side of the box had all the nutritional facts about the cereal, while the other side provided information about the Foundation and another photo.

As it turned out, Ballou had worried for nothing. In no time at all, the Flutie Flakes box became a collector's item. Many people didn't even bother to open it. Moreover, as teammates warmed up to Doug and began to appreciate his talents, they nicknamed him Flakes.

The Bills opened the regular season in San Diego, which featured the Chargers' strapping rookie quarterback Ryan Leaf, the second pick overall in the draft after the team traded with Arizona to move up one place. Doug found himself pressed into action early in the third quarter when Johnson suffered a slight concussion, and a nasty gash to his chin that required nine stitches. Suddenly, the timetable had been accelerated and, after nine years away from the NFL, Doug found himself in a familiar role as a reliever with the score 10–0 for the opposition.

After throwing off his hat and hustling to grab his helmet, Doug ran onto the field and began making plays. When it was over he had completed 12 passes, including two touchdowns, both to veteran wideout Andre Reed, in 20 attempts for 158 yards. Doug put the team into position to win, but kicker Steve Christie missed a 39-yard field goal with three seconds to play. Doug felt more disappointed about the team's loss than excited about his individual performance, which he felt would silence his critics for at least one week.

The Bills took the red-eye home and, after Phillips scrapped the scheduled team meeting, Doug drove to Hamilton to watch a CFL game between the Argos and Tiger-Cats, who had signed his brother Darren in the off-season. Admittedly drained from a lack of sleep, Doug couldn't resist the opportunity to watch the game. He kept close ties with players from both teams and glowingly talked about the league when asked by curious American journalists. Dressed in jeans, a T-shirt, running shoes and his Bills baseball cap, Doug shook hands with former teammates, Argos president Bob Nicholson and people genuinely glad for his accomplishments the day before.

"He was there talking to our guys, but he was there to see Darren and be very supportive," Argo athletic therapist Gerry Townend, who had developed a close working relationship with Doug, said. "It didn't surprise me one bit he was there. We also had an idea. He had told us in training camp that every opportunity he got to be at a game in Hamilton or Toronto, he would be there. He loves the CFL."

Doug did not play in the second game against Miami and threw only two passes when pressed into duty late in the third game against St. Louis after Johnson suffered a mild concussion. The Bills lost 34–33 to St. Louis after squandering an 18-point lead and giving up the go-ahead touchdown in the dying seconds on a quarterback sneak by Tony Banks. Veteran Bills observers classified the loss as one of the most disheartening in franchise history. The players and their anxious fans had to dwell on the defeat for a fortnight due to the bye week which gave the Bills a two-week break between games. The Bills responded next time out with a win against the unbeaten San Francisco, quarterbacked by Johnson.

After practice the following Thursday, Doug boarded an exclusive jet for Boston, where Boston College officially retired his Number 22 jersey at halftime of a game between the Eagles and Virginia Tech. Doug invited linebacker Gabe Northern and defensive end Marcellus Wiley to join him. It proved to be a pivotal move in bonding the team.

"Pop Warner, high school, college ... those kinds of things off the field really help," Wiley told the *Buffalo News'* Vic Carucci. "Flakes wasn't just cordial, he was really open with us. I learned some things about leadership from him, just because of how great a person he is."

The Bills headed to Indianapolis that weekend to play the Colts. The night before the game, Doug convened with his former Argo teammate Mike Vanderjagt, who had won the job as Indianapolis' field goal kicker. They met at the Bills' hotel, where a group of people were huddled with Flutie Flakes. Doug grabbed one of the boxes and flipped it over to Vanderjagt to check out, then they headed over to Planet Hollywood for dinner.

"The funny thing is," Vanderjagt told me, "I'm supposedly one of the stars in Indianapolis, and everybody's coming up to him and asking for his autograph and nobody has any idea who I am."

Before the game, the two had a competition drop-kicking field goals from the 40-50 yard range, something they regularly did in their Argo days. Then Doug held the ball once for Vanderjagt in one of his practice attempts. Both players had prominent roles in the game. Doug found himself pressed into a relief role when Johnson separated his rib cartilage falling on the tip of the football on the third snap of the game. And right away Vanderjagt knew something his teammates didn't.

"I thought we were in trouble," Vanderjagt said. "I thought, that's the last guy we want to have come off the bench. I would much rather go against Rob Johnson than Doug Flutie."

Vanderjagt staked the Colts to a 12–7 halftime lead on four field goals, while the Bills scored a touchdown inside the final three minutes on a seven-yard touchdown strike from Doug to tight end Jay Riemersma.

The Bills broke the game open in the second half, scoring 24 points to win 31–24. Doug finished with 23 completions, two of them for touchdowns, in 28 attempts. Through it all, Vanderjagt just watched his old teammate in amazement, re-creating the magic he demonstrated in two years in Toronto. The two embraced after the game, congratulating one another on their individual performances.

"I wish I was 28 years old right now, which is where I was when I left this league, but I'm not," Doug told the media. "I still have my athleticism, I can still run and throw. Quarterbacking is about making decisions and I'm getting a little smarter in my old age and a lot more comfortable. I always believed I could play. It's a matter of people giving me the opportunity."

"He's a winner," head coach Wade Phillips said, echoing a comment uttered by many of Doug's head coaches at various points in his career. "He made all the plays that needed to be made and I couldn't feel better for Doug, because there's always people who say, 'Well, he couldn't do this and he couldn't do that.' But he can and he did."

"I've always been a fan of Doug Flutie's," said Colts head coach Jim Mora, who had coached against Doug in the USFL. "He's an excellent competitor, he's smart, he's got experience. I've watched his career and it didn't surprise me at all what he did."

Doug received NFL Player of the Week honors for his performance. His 82.14 completion percentage ranked third-highest in team history. His performance prompted the *Buffalo News'* Vic Carucci to humble himself in his column, indicating he erred in his piece back in January.

"Forget everything I said about the Bills jeopardizing their credibility and creating a circus side show by signing Flutie," Carucci wrote. "Forget everything I said about NFL defenses being too, too large and too sophisticated for a 5-foot-9 scrambler and his 35-year-old legs. I believe ... I've learned my lesson. Hand me my membership application to the Doug Flutie Fan

Club and pass me another bowl of Flutie Flakes." Talk show host Chuck Dickerson, who had also been a huge critic, jumped on the bandwagon as well.

Rob Johnson dearly wanted to play in the following game against his former Jacksonville team, which won all its first five games, but the rib injury made it impossible for him to even practice. In fact, doctors told him the injury needed at least three weeks to heal. That provided the opportunity for Doug's first start, a nine-year break since his last one, the longest gap in NFL history.

It would also mark the first professional clash between Doug and Jacksonville head coach Tom Coughlin, his quarterback coach for his first three years at Boston College and the man he affectionately called "Technical Tom." And the game would co-incide with the Bills' annual Canada Day, which included a con-cert — ironically featuring Flutie's friend, Canadian rocker Kim Mitchell — before kickoff in the Ralph Wilson Fieldhouse. John McDermott, a popular Canadian singer whom Doug also knew, sang the Canadian national anthem.

The game dripped with pre-game drama — and Doug gave it a denouement befitting his miraculous career. Down 16–10 in the final two minutes, Doug began a desperation drive he had enacted so many times before. The key play in the 70-yard drive happened with 46 seconds to go on Jacksonville's 39-yard line on a second-and-six with no timeouts. While keeping his atten-tion focused straight downfield, Doug caught a glimpse of Moulds streaking down the left sidelines. At the last second, when the safety drifted away from Moulds, Doug threw the pass blindly to his large wideout, who caught the ball and bounced into the end zone. The crowd erupted deliriously. But the offi-cials negated the touchdown, ruling Moulds' knee touched the one-yard line before crossing the plane of the goal line.

With time ticking away, Doug promptly gathered up the team and spiked the ball on the first play to preserve the precious seconds remaining. Doug attempted passes on the next two plays, but both fell incomplete. That led to the fourth-down play, which will forever be embedded in Bills' history. The play was a series of options but was primarily designed to be a pitch left to running back Thurman Thomas. Due to the thunderous crowd noise, Thomas did not hear his number called and missed the handoff. Doug held on to the ball and bootlegged to his left, untouched all the way into the end zone with 13 seconds to go. He punctuated his play for the ages by spiking the ball into the wall and leaping into the arms of the frenetic fans in the stands. *Toronto Sun* reporter Mike Zeisberger coined it "the Flutie Fling" à la "the Lambeau Leap" in Green Bay. Some of Doug's teammates joined the fans in the group hug. After extricating himself from that celebration, Doug ran back to the sidelines and jumped into the burly arms of a beaming Bruce Smith.

Smith habitually congratulates each member of the offense when they make a big play, but this moment had spontaneity — and history — to it. The two had played against one another in college and with one another in all-star games. The Bills drafted Smith first overall in 1985, a couple months after Doug signed with New Jersey of the United States Football League. Throughout Doug's early trials and tribulations in training camp and pre-season with the Bills, Smith could see his frustrations, wondering if he would receive his chance to play. Smith told Doug to keep his head up because it's a long season. "And that's what he did," Smith said. "The guy's a fighter ... a warrior."

Christie put the Bills ahead with the extra point, ending one of the greatest finishes in Bills history and beginning Doug's true acceptance in Buffalo by his teammates, the fans and the critics. Doug did not have time on the sidelines to soak up the moment, but the emotion hit him in the locker and he became choked up.

"Guys just made plays," Doug said. "It just has a weird way of happening when I'm around."

"I've never seen anything — anything — like it," Thurman Thomas remarked.

"Why can he beat Miami on the last play of the game years ago like he did?" Wade Phillips asked aloud. "Big players make big plays." Now Phillips had to address the ticklish question of who would start the next game. "I'm starting," Phillips said jokingly. "Seriously, I'm not going to comment on that. We just want to enjoy this victory."

"If Rob's healthy, he'll play," Doug said unselfishly. "There's no question about that."

Bills owner Ralph Wilson called the victory one of the top three or four in the 38 years he owned the team. It coincided with his 80th birthday, which prompted him to say, "Who needs cakes and candles. This beats it all."

In the losers' locker room, Tom Coughlin brushed off the suggestion Doug scored on a broken play. "Everybody knows it's a naked [bootleg]," Coughlin spat.

Linebacker Tom McManus added, "We just gave it away. It's really discouraging for that to happen, especially with Doug Flutie — that little guy."

Doug's performance caused the *Buffalo News'* longtime sports editor Larry Felser to write, "A genie wearing No. 7 emerged to create the most dramatic, last-minute victory ever for the Bills. All right, maybe I can think of a more dramatic ending, but that will have to wait until I stop vibrating. But, what I, along with 77,635 spectators saw was Doug Flutie winning the Heisman Trophy again, this time for the Bills ... This man is truly magic. I believe it ... The great thing is that Magic Flutie's Kingdom is now located on the Niagara Frontier."

Felser recanted some of the critical comments he had directed at Doug before the season began: "The undersized quarterback most everyone, including me, said belonged back in the Canadian league did his magic act."

And Buffalo resident Bob Orrange, who led a campaign to pressure the Bills into drafting Doug in 1985 on the basis of his Hail Mary pass, proudly proclaimed his support 13 years later for his favorite quarterback in an interview with the *Buffalo News'* Mark Gaughan.

"When he completed that pass to Eric Moulds, I thought 'Oh, my God, he did it again,'" Orrange said, referring to the Hail Mary pass. "I felt for so long that I had gone from being the Draft Doug Flutie Association to the Defend Doug Flutie Association. Now I don't have to defend the guy anymore."

After the Jacksonville game, the players and their families and friends convened for the usual post-game gathering. When

Doug walked in, Andre Reed gave him a huge hug. Paul Masotti, who attended the game with Argo teammates Duane Dmytryshyn and Brendan Rogers, talked to Doug, who meticulously described to him the big pass to Moulds. Two years before, Masotti had caught a game-winning touchdown pass from Doug in the closing seconds of their first regular-season game.

The front pages of various North American newspapers the following day featured photos of Doug jumping into the stands and leaving the field proudly displaying the winning touchdown ball. In some ways, Doug re-created the hoopla of the Hail Mary pass 14 years before, but this time he did it with his legs instead of his arm. The *Buffalo News'* Mark Gaughan called it the "Blessed Bootleg."

Masotti commented to me a few days later that Doug appeared drained from the stress of the entire week leading up to the game. "There was a lot of pressure on him. I had talked to him about four days before the game and it was like talking to somebody who wasn't there. He knew it was a big game. All the eyes of the States were going to be on him and he was really excited to perform."

Masotti, who clearly missed his daily relationship on and off the field with Doug, did not seem the least bit surprised by his former teammate's game-winning heroics. "Who would you rather have the football with a minute and a half to go and you need a touchdown to score? Obviously it's Doug Flutie. It was just exciting to see and I think a lot of fans that were around me had a lot of faith in him."

Darren, who also attended the game, remarked that his brother had played within himself. "He didn't light up the scoreboard, that's for sure. He played okay, but the bottom line is, they won. That's all that counts. It reminded me of a couple games he played in college where they do nothing the whole game and then all of a sudden, with two minutes left, *bang* — they move the ball and stick it in the end zone and win. Doing it at the right time is the most important thing."

The heroics, following up on his relief appearance the previous week, combined to create what would become known as

"Flutiemania." Sales of merchandise with Doug's number sky-
rocketed, as did the Flutie Flakes. Doug's success had buyers
literally and figuratively gobbling up the flakes, doubling sales
to 100,000 in the first two weeks. The cereal boxes became hats
for some fans who wore them on their heads to the Jacksonville
game. Some fans even starting dressing in full-length facsimiles
of the Flutie Flakes. Such was the euphoria created by Doug,
whom some zealous New Yorkers now wanted to elect gover-
nor.

Bills director of media relations Scott Berchtold, who had been
with the team for 10 years and through its four consecutive Super Bowl appearances in the '90s, was besieged with media requests for Doug. Berchtold said it didn't quite match Super Bowl
standards, but added, "Super Bowls are a little extraordinary
because there's a lot of media guys focusing on only two teams,
but for an individual during the regular season it's as much as
I've ever seen."

When the team reconvened for the first time three days after
the victory, Doug did a conference call, which resulted in na-
tionwide stories focusing on his NFL renaissance following his
eight years in Canada, his son's disorder, and the interrelation
between the two. Clearly, Doug became the feel-good story of
the year: the little quarterback who could do it in the big NFL,
which finally gave him the chance.

Doug's success in Buffalo made him an even bigger star in
Toronto, which had largely ignored his talents in the two years
he played there. He may have been the Wayne Gretzky of the
CFL, but Toronto's taste had outgrown the Canadian game years
ago and craved for the NFL. Paul Godfrey, the publisher of the
Toronto Sun, had been lobbying the NFL for years to bring a team
to Toronto. He even supported the Bills in their drive, buying
500 club seats on behalf of the Sun Media Corporation. In the
absence of its own NFL team, Toronto continued to adopt the
Bills, more so because of the connection to their quarterback,
who still had ties to the Canadian city.

Doug celebrated his 36th birthday four days after his historic victory by attending a game at SkyDome between the Argos

and Tiger-Cats. Along with Mike Vanderjagt, whose Indianapolis team had a two-week break between games, Doug stood near the Argo bench for most of the game. The crowd roared in approval when the camera focused on him, shown larger than life on the Jumbotron, which for two years had provided game footage of what became known as Flutieball. After the game, Doug and Darren, who missed the game with a knee injury, had dinner together.

ESPN televised the Bills game against the Panthers three nights later in Carolina. The Bills won easily as Doug completed 18 of 22 passes for 282 yards. He clicked with Moulds on an 82-yard touchdown, the longest of Doug's NFL career, and had a whopping quarterback efficiency rating of 130.1. ESPN commentator Joe Theismann, whose pro football career began in Toronto in the early '70s, marveled at Doug's ability, saying he was "truly magical."

"People keep waiting for the short fellow to fall flat on his face," Ralph Wilson remarked. He added Doug created an inferno among Bills followers. "I wouldn't want to light any matches in Buffalo this week."

The quarterback controversy continued, much to the chagrin of Phillips, who begged off making any hasty answers on his starter, while Doug kept insisting the job belonged to Johnson. Next came a home game against the Miami Dolphins. With Johnson still unable to play, Doug received the start. It was his first against Dolphins head coach Jimmy Johnson, who had coached the University of Miami in the Hail Mary game back in 1984. The Bills beat the Dolphins 30–24, the key play a 48-yard touchdown pass from Doug to Moulds at 3:14 of the fourth period with the Jets leading 24–14. Buffalo followed up on the major with three field goals by Steve Christie.

One of Doug's friends, John (Cheese) Goodwin, told me he was beginning to wonder if some mystical force had been behind the latest Flutie phenomenon.

"There's always that doubt about Doug Flutie playing in the NFL — there's always going to be questions — but for some reason it's almost like this happened for a reason," Goodwin said. "No one wants to see a player get hurt, but at the same time it happened. It's hard to explain, but it's really the way it works for him."

The victory over Miami extended the Bills' winning streak to five and gave them a tie for the division lead with a record of 5–3 at the halfway point of the season. At this juncture, Flutiemania reached epidemic proportions. Supermarkets couldn't stock the Flutie Flakes fast enough and had to limit customers to one purchase. A story circulated of how a Bills employee extricated himself out of a fine for illegally parking at the Buffalo Airport when the police officer writing up the ticket agreed to forget about the whole thing in exchange for a couple boxes of the flakes.

The Flutie craze extended to other sports. During NBC's coverage of the Breeders' Cup, a commentator referred to pint-sized Buck's Boy as the "Doug Flutie of horse racing." Appropriately, the horse won his race.

Sports Illustrated, which had displayed Doug twice on its cover during his college career, featured him on the front page again. "How apt in this season of mega-millionaire free-agent flops," *SI*'s senior football writer Peter King wrote, "that it's the ultimate blue-light special who has electrified a team, a city and a league ... For all the money spent in the off-season, the 39th-highest paid player on the Bills has paid off in more ways than four of the league's most expensive free agents combined."

Professionally things were going well for Doug, but privately he suffered an emotional heartache in his family life when Laurie suffered a miscarriage after only three months of pregnancy. Doug revealed this exclusively to *Sports Illustrated*'s Rick Reilly. "What was weird was that [Doug] and Laurie knew this pregnancy was going to be worrisome," Reilly wrote. "When you have a severely autistic six-year-old who has to be watched 18 hours a day, non-stop, you think hard before you have another child."

Doug told Reilly, "We were going to watch that kid like a hawk until he was 21. I guess all the worrying started six months early."

The story was picked up by many newspapers in Canada and the U.S. When Doug's former teammate Mike Vanderjagt read about it, he contacted Doug and offered his condolences. The Bills had literally reached a pivotal point in the season. Doug had been playing at a Pro Bowl caliber and had captured the attention of the team, while Rob Johnson still remained injured. As general manager John Butler told me, a decision had to be made about the starting quarterback. In his words, "You couldn't have your team teetering." Phillips decided to make Doug the starter but, as is the case with many personnel decisions, discussed it with Butler and Wilson, and then the two players involved. Phillips did not consider it a monumental decision, but figured he had to say something to Johnson and the team.

"It's a business, but there's people's emotions and feelings involved," he said. "It wasn't Rob's fault. He didn't do anything wrong. He played well when he played, but he'd been hurt for a long time. It wasn't easy for him and I wanted Doug to feel I had confidence in him that he could keep going with it."

Wilson made it official to the media. He said Doug is like "Mighty Mouse. He came in to save the day. He's a hero. He deserves to play."

"It's satisfying that the front office and the entire organization feels confident that they can put the fate of their team in my hands," Doug said. "I've played four games so far. If you had told me in training camp that I would play four games by the midway point of the season, I gladly would have taken it. I had hoped to have the opportunity to be the No. 1 guy, but who is to say I won't get banged up in a couple of weeks, leaving Rob as the guy again. Rob and I talked this afternoon. He seems to be handling it well. It's an awkward situation, sure, but it's a nice problem to have. Rob Johnson has shown he can get the job done."

The Bills had a key matchup next against the New York Jets, who played at the Meadowlands, a stadium in which Doug had never lost in college and the pros. The New York media hyped up the game, but Doug played down the contest in comparison to his family life.

"Ten years from now no one is going to care who won this football game," Doug said, "but 10 years from now I am going to have a 16-year-old son that is autistic, that is going to be dependent on me, that can't dress himself, who needs his hair brushed, his teeth brushed and to be taken care of. That is what is important. This is only a game."

Jets quarterback Vinny Testaverde had been the loser in the Hail Mary game back in 1984. His professional career had been marred by struggling seasons in Tampa Bay, Cleveland, and Baltimore. But he had re-discovered himself in New York, and he led the Jets to a 34–12 victory over the Bills. Doug completed only 12 of 30 passes and threw two interceptions, both in the Jets end zone. He described it afterward as his worst game in five years, but pointed out he had not lost two games in a row in a long time, and didn't intend to start that streak now.

"It must have been the *Sports Illustrated* cover jinx, it certainly wasn't the *Shout!* cover jinx," wrote Larry Bump, editor of *Shout!*, the weekly newspaper devoted to the Buffalo Bills. "Or maybe, just maybe, Doug Flutie is a mere mortal after all. Not really Mighty Mouse. Not really the Magic Flutie. Not really the savior of the franchise — yet. Actually, even Joe Montana lost a game every now and then."

Following the Jets loss, Doug prepared for a home game against the New England Patriots, although he took time out to appear on the *David Letterman Show* — 14 years after he had been scheduled to do it. Letterman joked about the CFL, but Doug did his best to defend it while still adding some humor. Doug did the segment a few days in advance of the show, which featured Donald Trump as one of the guests. Trump had signed Doug to a record contract with the New Jersey Generals of the United States Football League back in 1985 and always maintained he would do well in the professional ranks.

The stories leading up to the New England game concentrated on Doug playing his home town team, but he downplayed it, saying he expected the game there to be more special. Doug's family and some friends attended the game, which the Bills won. Doug addressed the media in one of the CFL's Radically Canadian sweatshirts. At one point he looked up at the TV monitor, showing an NFL game, and asked aloud if the media realized there was a CFL playoff game being played that day and televised on another channel. He asked to switch the station and had his request promptly served.

"The press conference basically stopped and then we hung around there and watched a bit of [the game]," said Argo athletic therapist Gerry Townend, who attended the game.

The Bills played their next game at home against Indianapolis, and once again Doug and Mike Vanderjagt drop-kicked some field goals in warmups. The Bills crushed the Colts, and Doug quickly addressed the media so he could head back to his residence and watch the Grey Cup game with some family and friends. Along the way, Colts kick returner Keith Elias asked Vanderjagt to introduce to him to Doug. He was Elias' idol growing up on the East Coast, so Vanderjagt grabbed Doug, who was being mobbed by fans, and introduced Elias to his idol, whom he addressed as Mr. Flutie.

The Grey Cup pitted Hamilton and Calgary, providing Doug with mixed emotions. His brother played for the Tiger-Cats, but several of his former teammates and friends played for the Stampeders. In the end, Doug rooted for his sibling's squad. The Tiger-Cats, who had finished last in the league the year before with a 2–16 record, appeared headed for a Cinderella victory in their first year with new head coach Ron Lancaster. But they lost on the final play on a 35-year field goal by Mark McLoughlin. Jeff Garcia, Doug's understudy in Calgary, engineered the field goal by leading his team on a dramatic two-minute drill.

And Doug predicted the finish. "The guy's telepathic," laughed Doug's friend, John Goodwin, who visited him that weekend. "He called the way the game was going to end. With like five minutes left he had a feeling they were going to lose because of how it was going. He was so disappointed, too. That was a big deal."

Buffalo's next game came on the road against New England, which marked Doug's first game back at Foxboro Stadium, where he had never lost in 10 contests as a collegian and a pro. The

Patriots had beaten Miami 26–23 the previous Monday on a 25-yard touchdown pass from Drew Bledsoe to Shawn Jefferson with 29 seconds on the clock. Bledsoe fractured his right index finger on the play and his status going into the Bills game commanded as much attention as Doug's homecoming.

Buffalo TV station WIVB regularly did live telecasts on the road the night before Bills away games, but decided to add some color to this show by doing it from Natick. Casey's Diner, an institution in Natick renowned for its boiled hot dogs, became the site of the telecast after the locals told reporter Paul Peck it was the hot spot in town. Owner Fred Casey generously agreed to open his diner late Saturday night to accommodate the sportscast and alerted several of Doug's longtime friends to come by. Rumors of Doug's attendance prompted a large crowd which overflowed into the parking lot. Laurie and Alexa showed up for the gathering — Casey generously donated money from food and beverage sales to the Flutie Foundation — while Doug and his teammates stayed in a hotel an hour away. Laurie mentioned how the game had special meaning for the Flutie family because it fell on Dougie's seventh birthday and Doug's jersey number is seven.

"It was a lot of fun, one of the cooler things we've done through the course of the year," Peck said. "Normally you don't have such a built-in story like that when you go on the road. The people were just great. You could just tell why Flutie never left this town. It was pretty neat."

After procuring some 35 seats in a section for family and friends, Doug had his own cheering squad, including his 11-year-old nephew Billy, a highly rated football talent competing in a punt, pass and kick contest. He proudly wore his uncle's No. 7 jersey. The pro-Flutie supporters cheered when the youngster won his age group competition and earned a trip to the nationals during the Super Bowl game.

Some fans from Doug's New England days dressed in his Patriots No. 2 jersey, including one woman who held up a sign that read, "We love Flutie." Another placard read: "Flutie For President." Yet the majority of the crowd could not separate their strong support for the Patriots. One sign said it best: "Doug, Best of Luck But Not Today." The introduction of the Bills starting lineup produced a standing ovation for Doug. The majority of the crowd cheered, but some jeered.

"I was in the stands and you didn't hear a lot of hecklers [toward Flutie], but you heard a lot of heckling toward Buffalo," Goodwin said. "It was more or less, 'Welcome back, here's your reception, now go out and win this game.' It was a warm welcome, but it was one of those things where, 'Yeah, you're from Natick, but you are on the Buffalo Bills,' and there's always been that rivalry."

Doug later described the overall reaction as "lukewarm," adding, "They're rooting for the hometown and that's the way it is. I understand that. People were receptive overall."

One fan, Mario Ramos, told the *Boston Herald*, "We like Flutie, but the Patriots are our team and Bledsoe is our quarterback. We want Bledsoe. That's home-field advantage. I love Flutie and I hope he wins the rest of his games, but we were against him." Another Pats fan, Cisco Herrara, said, "Doug Flutie is a great quarterback but you don't root against a whole team for one individual."

Bledsoe, who received a thunderous applause when announced as the starter, had a splint on his fractured finger. The game knitted together an unbelievable quilt of emotions for both teams and their fans. *Boston Herald* writer Karen Guregian summed it up perfectly: "Without a doubt, Flutie's return will go down in the books as one of the weirdest, wackiest, most controversial and thoroughly entertaining games in history."

The Bills owned the clock for almost 12 minutes in the first quarter, but failed to translate that to points. They found themselves down 14–6 at halftime, as Bledsoe connected on two touchdown passes in the second quarter, while Buffalo managed their points on two Christie field goals. The Bills cut the lead to 14–12 at 4:03 of the third period, when Doug and Moulds connected on a touchdown pass that had highlight reel written all over it. Running between two Patriot defenders, Moulds reached out with his right hand and grabbed the ball without slowing, scampering a total of 84 yards. It eclipsed Doug's longest NFL TD pass of 80 yards back in 1988 at, coincidentally, Foxboro Stadium. The Bills missed the two-point conversion, but added a field goal later in the quarter which, coupled with a New England field goal, had the Patriots leading 17–15 heading into the final quarter.

What happened in the final 15 minutes will go down in NFL infamy, marred by questionable calls and a two-point conversion that the Bills did not even bother to defend. Buffalo scored the go-ahead touchdown at 8:46 when Doug and Reed connected on a four-yard pass, followed by the second failed two-point convert of the game. Buffalo seemingly had the game won, but stalled on a critical third-and-eight play when Doug attempted a quarterback sneak, but gained only two yards, forcing the Bills to punt.

The Patriots took possession at their own 18 with 1:52 remaining and no timeouts on the clock. The Bills could only watch and wait, hoping their defense would do the job. Bledsoe methodically moved his team, but ran into a critical fourth down play at Buffalo's 36-yard line, needing nine yards with only 11 seconds to go. He threw a sideline pass near the Bills bench to Jefferson, who stretched to catch the ball.

While officials huddled to discuss the play, television replays clearly indicated Jefferson had caught the ball out of bounds. Moreover, he failed to reach the first-down marker. The Bills could not believe it when the officials convened and ruled it a completion and a first down. In the Bills' minds, the officials should have given them possession and the opportunity to run out the clock and claim victory.

The contentious call foreshadowed an even bigger play, which Ralph Wilson predicted, sitting in the Bills' owner's box. Wilson figured Bledsoe would heave a Hail Mary pass in the end zone and the Bills would be flagged for pass interference. It happened just like that. Bledsoe's bomb bounced off receiver Terry Glenn in the end zone, but the official closest to the play ruled that safety Henry Jones bumped into him ahead of the ball. The infraction gave New England one more chance, because a game cannot end on a defensive penalty, and placed the ball on the one-yard line. The Patriots responded with a touchdown pass from Bledsoe to his favorite receiver, tight end Ben Coates, deep in the end zone behind coverage.

Hoping to avoid the on-field frenzy, the Bills headed to the locker room angry. When none of the officials called the Bills to come out to defend the two-point conversion, New England head coach Pete Carroll had kicker Adam Vinatieri saunter into the end zone for the deuce. The play proved particularly heartbreaking for a hardluck bettor who had a chance to collect $16,000 on a 10-team parlay costing $2 if the Patriots failed to cover the 3 1/2-point spread.

"We cannot leave this game in the hands of the officials with a couple minutes to go or you take a very big chance of getting beat," Wilson spat. "It's the worst officiating and I'll take the fine [from the league for criticizing the refereeing]. We got robbed."

"I'll start you out with a quote from one official to the other on fourth down and on the sidelines — 'Just give it to 'em,'" Doug began. "One guy was ready to rule it out of bounds, the other guy wasn't sure and gave him that look like it might be in bounds, it might be out of bounds, and the deciding factor was 'Just give it to 'em.' Four guys heard him say that."

Among them was Reed. "Me and Quinn Early were sitting right there going, 'You gotta be kidding!'"

Phillips said the play was definitely out of bounds. "I was standing right there and neither one of [the officials] knew if he was or wasn't and they didn't make a call. We should have made the play, that's first, but they've got to make the play, too. They've got to make the right call, and it wasn't even close." Phillips had an even greater disliking for the end zone penalty. "It's a shame for our team because they played their hearts out, they fought back from behind ... and that's all I can say."

"We now have evidence if we don't quit, if we don't give up, there's always a chance we can come back and win the ball game at the end, so that's a positive for us," Bledsoe remarked about the team's last two games.

"We played with just as much heart," Doug said. "The officials had way too much control of that game ... It's a shame for two teams to fight like we did and it gets determined by the officiating. Am I going to get fined for saying that?"

In the midst of all the locker talk, the officials hastily prepared a release explaining the reason for the final penalty, explaining Jones "just went through the receiver. He was not playing the ball and made contact."

In his column the following day, the *Buffalo News'* Larry Felser wrote, "I began covering pro football before Bill Clinton reached the age of puberty. Sunday I witnessed a first — a penalty called on a Hail Mary pass. I surveyed veteran reporters from both Boston papers, from the *Providence Journal* and ESPN. None of them had ever heard of such a penalty. Calling a penalty on a Hail Mary pass is like standing 100 yards past the start of a marathon and deciding who is in 102nd place as the runners stampede by you ... It's a group grope. An official could throw a flag on every Hail Mary pass ever attempted. As far as I know, it never happened before [referee Walt Coleman's] guys blazoned this questionable trail."

The blown calls caused a torrent of criticism aimed at the officials, who had already come under attack for a foolhardy coin toss three days before in Detroit in a game between the Lions and Detroit. After the teams tied following regulation time, referee Phil Luckett flipped a coin to determine who would receive the ball first in overtime. Pittsburgh running back Jerome Bettis called tails, but Luckett ruled Bettis called heads. When the coin came up tails, the Lions received the ball and scored a winning field goal on their first possession. The whole episode became known as "Coingate."

The Bills returned home and the focus shifted away from the loss to the luxury seat drive, which saw the team reach its $11-million deal on the Tuesday deadline. A day later, the story shifted back to the Patriots game when league president Paul Tagliabue slapped Ralph Wilson with a $50,000 fine for his refereeing remarks, which he deemed had "destructive and corrosive effects on the game." Seven months earlier, Tagliabue had come to Buffalo to convince the people to literally buy into the team's future. Now he was hitting the owner in the pocketbook. Wilson responded by chastising Tagliabue in a press release issued by the team.

"The Commissioner lecturing me as if I were a novice, instead of one who has been involved in football infinitely longer than he has, contends that criticizing a call has 'destructive and corrosive effects on the game.'

"What is more destructive and corrosive — errant calls in front of millions of viewers or my statements of opinion? People all over the country registered shock at the way the officials, however honorable their purpose, took the game away from us. Even the league has admitted to us that the calls near the conclusion of the game were incorrect.

"I have yet to decide whether I will challenge the fine, but at 80 I do know I don't need pompous lectures from the Commissioner and I feel that the $50,000 is not only unwarranted but punitive in nature. The next time he may ask me to sit in the corner."

The Bills rebounded from the loss by beating the hapless Cincinnati Bengals 33–20. Buffalo started off strongly as Doug connected with Moulds on a 55-yard completion on the opening play of the game. The Bills scored a touchdown on that series and added a field goal on their next series. What appeared to be a blowout quickly turned into a close game when the Bengals took advantage of some Bills mistakes to lead 13–10 after one-third of the second quarter.

The Bills rebounded inside the final two minutes when Doug and Moulds connected on a 70-yard pass-and-run play for a touchdown. Doug threw a short slant pass to the area where the Bengals were blitzing and Moulds took the ball and turned on his afterburners, breaking free from three defenders who seemingly had him stopped. The Bills added three points just before the end of the half on a Christie field goal and never looked back. Doug clicked with a wide-open Moulds on a 30-yard TD early in the fourth quarter, punctuating a personal best for the young receiver, who finished with 196 yards on six catches. Coupled with the 177 yards from the previous game, Moulds set a team record for total yardage in back-to-back games, eclipsing the old standard set by Glenn Bass, who had 372 in 1964.

After the game, Doug sat in an area outside of the locker room, listening to the final moments of the Jets game, while Laurie described it to him on a cellular phone. The Jets beat Seattle 32–31 on a disputed five-yard touchdown run by Testaverde, who clearly fell short of the goal line. The officials discussed the contentious play, while Laurie described it.

"Are they sure or not [it's a touchdown]?" Flutie asked Laurie, while television cameras filmed the moment.

"They're talking about it," Flutie said incredulously to the media.

The play stood, and for the third time in 10 days critics of instant replays cried foul. In fact, the league began discussing the possibility of implementing instant replays for the playoffs. Wilson, who had repeatedly shot down the idea when it came to a vote, indicated he might be in favor of casting his ballot for its re-installment.

By this time, Flutiemania had grown even bigger. Doug did a national television spot for MCI endorsing a long distance telephone service promoted by famous entertainers and athletes. He also did a humorous commercial endorsing a submarine for Wegmans, a Buffalo-area supermarket, tying in the fact he started out as a sub. In both cases, the Doug Flutie, Jr. Foundation benefited.

Companies besieged Doug's marketing representative Kristen Kuliga of Woolf Associates with as many as six endorsement offers a day. Clearly, Doug had captured the public's fancy, something which completely surprised him. He discussed it at one point with A.J. Smith, the Bills director of pro personnel, who told him the football world had changed in his eight years playing in Canada. "This is the way they treat NFL stars," Smith said.

Doug wanted to focus primarily on football, while allowing all the ancillary things to wait until after the season ended. As Doug's friend, John Goodwin, said to me, "He knows a lot of it will benefit Dougie, but at the same time, his main concern is football. He does not want anything to get in the way of what he can do out on the field. For a week he wanted to call me and he said he sat down on the couch and he'd open the [playbook] and he'd never pick up the phone to call me. That's how focused he is."

To clinch a playoff spot, the Bills needed to beat Oakland the following Sunday, combined with victories by Jacksonville over Tennessee and Tampa Bay over Pittsburgh. The Bills handled Oakland 44–21 in a game featuring an outstanding punt return by Kevin Williams and great plays overall by the defense, which contributed two touchdowns on an interception and a fumble recovery.

"Flutie Magic vs. Raiders Mystique was no contest [for] the Buffalo Bills ... their most complete victory yet in this incomprehensible season," wrote Leo Roth of the *Rochester Democrat and Chronicle*. "Quarterback Doug Flutie toyed with Oakland's banged-up-defense, reading blitzes faster than Evelyn Wood reading books."

While Tampa Bay stopped Pittsburgh, Tennessee defeated Jacksonville on a field goal with four seconds left on the clock, temporarily delaying the Bills playoff hopes. The Bills immediately set their sights on the Jets, who beat Miami a few hours later. That set the stage for arguably the most important game of the Bills season. Doug said he wanted to win the game more to prove the Bills belonged with the division-leading Jets than to personally avenge his performance the first time the teams met.

The day after the Oakland game, Doug received the award as Man of the Year, selected by the fans, touching off a week of individual honors. Two days later, he received an invitation to the Pro Bowl as one of two backups — New York Jets' Vinny Testaverde being the other — to starter John Elway of Denver. Five of Doug's teammates — Eric Moulds, Bruce Smith, guard Ruben Brown, fullback Sam Gash and nose tackle Ted Washington — also earned trips to the all-star game in Honolulu in February. Ironically, it represented Doug's first all-star game as a professional because the CFL does not have an all-star game. In fact, the last time Doug participated in an all-star game was in college in Honolulu for the Hula Bowl. Coincidentally, it was while in Hawaii for the Hula Bowl 11 months earlier that Flutie made the decision to return to the NFL.

Doug received word of the invitation from Bruce Smith, who received his 11th selection in his stellar career. "To be honest with you, they couldn't deny him," Smith said. "It went beyond the call of duty, what he's done. How he's come through adversity, what he's done — it goes far beyond my imagination and I'm sure beyond his imagination."

Doug called Laurie with the news on the cell phone and caught her in a meeting with some of Dougie's teachers. Laurie relayed the news to the crowd, which celebrated with hearty applause.

"This is definitely a signature of an NFL quarterback now or that I'm definitely an NFL quarterback and not just a toy or a point of interest," Doug told the media. "It's people taking you for real."

The same week of the Pro Bowl news, sales of the Flutie Flakes reached the 1 million mark. The historic box was pulled from the assembly line to be auctioned off, with all the proceeds going to the Flutie Foundation. PLB Sports president Ty Ballou indicated plans for a second version of the Flutie Flakes, featuring a new action shot of Doug and a family photo, to be sold early in 1999.

"It's laughable how far we've gone beyond that [original run]," Ballou told me. "The numbers that Doug's done so far are off the charts. We could add up the sales of all our athletes' [products] and they would not equal what the Flutie Flakes have done in 10 weeks."

Boxes had been mailed across the U.S. and to every continent except Antarctica. An Associated Press story quoted a marketing analyst who called the quick success of Flutie Flakes unprecedented.

"Not only is the cold cereal market a mature market dominated by a handful of very large companies, there's also been a general decline in sales of ready-to-eat cereals," remarked Tom

Vierhile, general manager of Marketing Intelligence Service Ltd.

A Flutie Flakes Chocolate Bar, licensed by PLB Sports but produced by the Buffalo-area company Fowler's, surpassed its initial run of 150,000 in the first week, and there were plans to go to the 500,000 mark.

Heading into the Jets game, a newspaper story indicated Doug's on-field success had helped him achieve $2 million in bonuses and the likelihood of a new long-term contract before the start of the following season.

Playing in front of a capacity crowd at the newly named Ralph Wilson Stadium, the Bills and their fans had high hopes against the Jets. The game was played on a historic day in American history, with the U.S. House of Representatives voting on whether or not to impeach U.S. President Bill Clinton for lying to the grand jury about his affair with Monica Lewinsky. One Jets fan held up a sign that read "Impeach Flutie."

It turned out to be a losing day for both Bill and the Bills. Clinton lost out to the partisan Republicans, while the Bills lost 17–10, squandering several opportunities and becoming victim again of another blown call by the officials. This time they gave the Jets an interception when replays showed Victor Green dropped the ball. Doug completed only 14 of 38 passes in his toughest outing of the season, both mentally and physically. He limped off the field at the end of the game after injuring his left leg just below the knee on the final play, scrambling all over the field before throwing a Hail Mary pass that fell incomplete. Doug lamented the lost opportunity and wished for a chance to meet the Jets in the playoffs. There was, however, something to sweeten the loss personally for Doug: Jets coach Bill Parcells personally gave him a $5,000 check for the Flutie Foundation.

A day after the Jets loss, Green Bay defeated Tennessee to give Buffalo a wild berth in the playoffs. The Bills became only the fourth team in NFL history to qualify for post-season play after losing their first three games.

The Bills announced the following Wednesday that Doug didn't practice that day because of the injury. As a precautionary move, the Bills rested Doug for the entire game. Rob Johnson started his first game in eight weeks and guided the Bills to an easy victory. Johnson threw three touchdown passes and ran for another.

Leading up to the game, Saints head coach Mike Ditka talked glowingly about Doug and explained the circumstances that led to his 1987 departure from the Bears. What many people didn't realize is that the person who played a major role in Doug Flutie coming to play in Canada stood next to Ditka on the sidelines. Lary Kuharich, who first met Doug in 1989 and coached him the following year with the CFL's B.C. Lions, had been hired as the Saints running backs coach in 1998.

While the Bills finished deadlocked with Miami at 10–6, the Dolphins received the home-field advantage in the wild-card game based on a tie-breaking formula. The oddsmakers made Miami the favorites by anywhere from two to four points, largely based on their 7–1 home record, their only loss administered by the division-leading Jets.

"To me it's just like lining up and playing Montreal," Doug said three days before the game. "It's the playoffs and the loser goes home." He played down wanting to win to add another chapter in his comeback season. Doug simply wanted the victory so that he could achieve his goal of playing in the Super Bowl.

He also found himself embroiled in a controversy over comments he made two days before, accusing the Dolphins cornerbacks of holding tactics. Doug wanted to send a message to the officials, but his comments found their way onto the Dolphins bulletin board.

Early in the Bills practice, which the media could only watch for the first 15 minutes, the team worked on a streak play in which the quarterback throws a high arcing deep ball to the receiver. That play portended a specific strategy the team planned to employ.

In the first play from scrimmage, Doug threw a deep ball to Eric Moulds, who beat cornerback Terrell Buckley and caught the pass in stride. Unfortunately, the 65-yard pass-and-run play turned into a turnover when Buckley punched the ball out of

Moulds' right hand. It typified off the top the many twists and turns in the roller-coaster game.

After Miami led 6–0 on two Olindo Mare field goals, Dolphins head coach Jimmy Johnson called for an onside kick, but the Bills recovered it. On the ensuing series, Thurman Thomas scored on a one-yard run and Steve Christie kicked the convert to give Buffalo the lead. The Bills had a chance to increase their lead late in the first half, but Miami picked off a pass Doug threw to Andre Reed near the goal line. Miami put itself in a position to score on its final possession, but missed on a field-goal attempt that hit the upright.

Miami took the lead midway in the third quarter on a touchdown and a two-point convert, but the Bills tied it on a 32-yard touchdown pass from Doug to Moulds, followed by Christie's convert. That set up the pivotal fourth quarter, which had all kinds of drama. Mare gave the Dolphins the lead again on a 23-yard field goal, but the Bills appeared headed for some points of their own on a pass from Doug to Reed. It ended in a turnover, however, when Reed lost control of the ball attempting to stretch out his reception with Dolphin defenders draped all over him. Miami took it in for a touchdown on the ensuing series, which appeared to end Buffalo's hopes.

Characteristic of the determination that saw the team regroup from a 0–3 start, the Bills rebounded with a long drive and appeared to score a touchdown when Reed hauled in a 10-yard pass and lunged forward over the goal line. However, field judge Steve Zimmer ruled Reed's knee hit the ground before the ball crossed the goal line, sparking the latest in a series of official controversies that plagued the Bills all season. An infuriated Reed rose to his feet and inadvertently bumped into Zimmer, who promptly flagged him for unsportsmanlike conduct, which cost him an ejection and the team a 15-yard penalty. The Bills tried valiantly, but could only settle for a field goal by Christie from 33 yards with 93 seconds remaining.

The Bills tried an on-side kick and recovered it at Miami's 31-yard line, giving Buffalo one more opportunity. Immediately people began to ponder the possibility of Doug engineering another Miracle in Miami, more than 14 years after the Hail Mary game at the nearby Orange Bowl. The Bills worked their way downfield on a series of passes, including one to Moulds who set a NFL playoff record with 240 yards on nine catches. On the penultimate play of the game Doug did a quarterback sneak, taking the ball to the five-yard line. Buried under a pile of players, he signaled time out with one arm, stopping the clock at 17 seconds. The Bills' ensuing play called for a slant pass, but Doug couldn't locate his target. While attempting to recoil and throw away the ball to stop the clock, he found himself sacked from the blindside by defensive end Trace Armstrong, who jarred the ball loose. The Dolphins recovered at the three-yard line with nine seconds remaining. Dolphins quarterback Dan Marino kneeled down on his team's first possession, ending the game and the Bills miraculous season in a 24–17 defeat.

"I thought I was going to have a slant route and it wasn't there,"Doug said. "I held on to it, turned to look over the middle, and was just going to throw it over Jay Riersma's head out of the end zone. And as I recoiled, I got hit. It's a three-step drop, it's not a great protection, and the ball should have been out earlier. I wished we'd had the touchdown earlier when we got on the one-inch line there with Andre, and then we could have played for the tie. We fought, we clawed, but we turned over the ball too many times."

In the Dolphins' locker room, head coach Jimmy Johnson opened up a box of Flutie Flakes and dumped the contents on the floor. He then stomped all over them and was followed by his players. "It's just all in fun," Doug said initially. However, when he had a chance to further consider Johnson's actions, Doug did not find the matter humorous. "As far as I'm concerned, that's like stepping on my son."

A couple days later, Johnson issued a press release indicating he planned to send a letter to Doug apologizing for his behavior. "Jimmy certainly meant no disrespect," a Dolphins spokesperson said in a statement released to the media. "It was simply from a football perspective and not meant as disrespect for anything Doug has done off the field."

Perhaps Johnson finally found a way to stamp out the demons eating away at him after Doug beat him in the famous Hail Mary game and in the 1998 regular season. Linebacker Zach Thomas put a more objective summation on the game when he said, "It was so nervewracking at the end with Flutie because he's always the Comeback King. You always see the last-second plays he's made, even against Jacksonville this year. He's a great quarterback, he's a competitor and they gave it their best shot but we came out to win today."

The Bills could take consolation in a courageous comeback, which typified their season following their slow start, while Doug proved he could play in the NFL if given the chance. Doug became football's version of astronaut John Glenn, re-creating his fame while overcoming criticism from others. Moreover, he used his celebrity status to create awareness and help raise money for autism.

"He's an extraordinary, enduring American story, there's no question about it," *MetroWest Daily News* sports columnist Lenny Megliola told me. "I still have to pinch myself to think he's a Pro Bowler. What odds could you have gotten in August when they were in training camp that all this would have happened and he'd get a chance to start because Johnson got hurt and he'd absolutely maintain the job on merit, to the point where he'd be picked for the Pro Bowl. I just think it's a great story. I think it's been a boost for the league."

Wade Phillips echoed those comments when he added, "He's the story of the year without a doubt. Testaverde has done well for the Jets, but he was in the Pro Bowl two years ago for a different team. Nobody said he couldn't play or that he wasn't a good player, but when Doug came in they said he couldn't even play. That's what's been so exciting about it. This guy's not only proven he can play, but he's in the Pro Bowl. I think it's been really great for not only our team, but the National Football League itself."

Appendix:
Quotes and Anecdotes

BILL FLUTIE (DOUG'S OLDER BROTHER):

"The thing that Doug did the best back in Pop Warner football was stripping the ball from the ballcarrier to the point where the referees almost never knew what to call. He would take the ball away from the runner on almost every play and start running the other way. Most of the time they wouldn't give us the ball — they'd say, 'That's not quite right' or something, and they'd give it back to the other team — but occasionally they'd say, 'Yeah, that's legal, you can do it' and that's a touchdown for us. He wasn't a tough tackler, but he'd always get the guy down or make the play."

BARRY GALLUP (DOUG'S BOSTON COLLEGE ASSISTANT
COACH ON NAMING HIS FIRST CHILD):

"My wife liked the name Darren better than Doug, so I said let's name him Darren Douglas. I said it's a special time in our life. It will be a special thing that my son will always remember that he was named after the two Flutie brothers. Doug's dad was the photographer at our wedding. We're just very close. It was just a special time. The night my wife gave birth, I had to speak at Darren's high-school banquet. My wife had the baby about 6:15 and I was at the banquet by 7:30 and that was the first public announcement of my son's name."

JACK BICKNELL (DOUG'S BOSTON COLLEGE COACH):

"He's a special kid, he's never been out of shape in his life. He always wants to compete in whatever sport. I remember one day he came into my office and said, 'Coach, could I talk to you?' I said, 'Yeah, sure.' He said, 'Do you mind if I shut the door?' I said, 'No.' I'm saying, 'Oh my God, what happened?' He said, "Coach I've been asked to play in all these golf tournaments and I really don't know how to play golf. I'm sort of embarrassed I'll go out there and make a fool of myself. Will you take me out?' So we went out and played golf and I tried to give him little tips. Here I thought he was having a problem. All he was worried about was not embarrassing himself on the golf course. That's the kind of kid he was."

GERARD PHELAN (COLLEGE TEAMMATE) ON THE REENACTMENT OF THE FAMOUS HAIL MARY PLAY AT A BLACK-TIE CHARITY AFFAIR HONORING DOUG IN 1993:

"The wife of the chairman of the charity had this notion it would be fun for Doug to throw the ball across the banquet hall, which sat more than 600-700, to me on the other end. It was probably 55 yards. There were enormous chandeliers made out of glass. There were balloons extended from all of the tables, which had 12 seats around them. They were that big. There was very little room to walk between the pushed-out chairs back to back against the tables.

"I remember walking into the room and thinking, 'These people are crazy. We're not going to pull this thing off. We can do it now when it's empty, but when there's hundreds of people in here this can be a catastrophe.'

"They brought us in prior to everybody coming in and we did a little practise, and Doug warmed up and threw it to me 10 yards away, then 15, then 20, then 25 and I would throw it back. When I got to about 30 yards or so, I threw it back — and I'm no quarterback — and it hit one of the balloons, bounced of the table and broke a few of the glasses. At that point I gave the ball to someone to run back to Doug as we moved further and further apart. It gave Doug a chance to see what would happen if he didn't throw it on the mark. I could tell he got a little nervous about it. I definitely got a little nervous about it because if he doesn't throw it on the mark, I've got to make a diving catch across the tables.

"The night built up and Doug did a good job with his speech as did a number of other people and they decided they were going to announce us doing this. I went to one end and Doug went to the other and we both took our jackets off. They actually started us out about 20 yards apart and then the MC said, 'Move further, move further.' Then the crowd got into it, 'Further, further,' to the point where Doug was standing against one wall and I was standing almost against the other across the hall. We were 40 or 50 yards away, I would imagine.

"He threw the ball across and I took about two or three steps back and I caught it. The place went crazy. They thought it was great."

GERARD PHELAN ON THE FORD COMMERCIAL HE DID
WITH DOUG IN 1985:

"The guy gave Doug his lines. He did all the lines. I had one line. He did a really good job with it. He's a very bright, articulate guy; he's got a good presence. And they made him do it over and over again to the point where he almost got silly about it. I guess that's the personality they were trying to get out of him. At that time it seemed to be more of a nuisance, but these people knew what they were doing.

"They had the van parked and Doug was walking around it, selling the van about how tough the truck was, about the rack and pinion steering, about the brakes, the weight of the truck, the bumper, the length of the truck, etcetera. He had little sound bites that he would have to say while walking through different places around the van. After he was done talking about it I was in the truck and he had a football in his hand and his line to me was, 'Go long.'

"I drove the truck down the field about 15 yards or so and he had to throw the football through an open window on the passenger side as I cut across the field driving the truck. That was the theme of the thing. I was supposed to lean out the window and say something like, 'Hey, Doug, try to do that again' and his line is: 'What do you want, another miracle?'

"It was really kind of funny because it had snowed at various times during the shoot and they didn't want it to be a snowy thing. They wanted it to be a summer-fall type thing, so they would have to stop and do it over and over again. It was kind of a windy, nasty, cold day and the very first time that I took the truck down the field and drove across it, he took three steps back and threw it in the window 20 yards down the field, which I thought was pretty damn impressive. He wasn't using a real football, but a Nerf football because they didn't want to damage the truck. It could have been a steel football and it wouldn't have made a difference because he threw it right through the window.

"Similar to making him do his lines over and over, they made him continue to try and do this thing. He threw the first one in and then it took him about 15 chances after that to throw the second one in. I just thought it ironic that with Doug you just do it on the first take. He does it right the first time. That's just the way he's always been about sports or about anything. As we're getting to know the business of what comes out of football, the business people were getting to know what Doug was all about: He just does it right the first time, does a good job and moves on."

FORMER B.C. LIONS PUBLICIST ROGER KELLY ON FLUTIE
DINING WITH THE 0-LINE:

"A Calgary radio station wanted him to do the morning show or something like that and they offered him a dinner at a nice little Italian place for him and whoever he wanted. I talked to him about it and he said, 'Yeah, Roger, tell them I'll do it, but I want the entire offensive line for dinner with me.' Of course, that's going to cost the Stampeders a ton of money. But, that was Doug. He wanted the O-line with him. He was real loyal to those guys.

"There's Doug in the corner with all these 6-foot-5, 270-pound, 280-pound O-linemen polishing off every morsel of food they can in the entire restaurant — and it's a fancy restaurant — and Kevin Gallant, the Stampeders publicity director, is turning green and I ended up having to pay for my dinner because the Stampeders are already paying for the Lions team."

LARY KUHARICH ON RECRUITING DOUG TO THE B.C. LIONS:

"It's kind of ironic Doug went to Calgary and had some great years there when we tried to get him there in the beginning. That staff, Wally Buono and John Hufnagel, released him from their negotiation list and that's how we were able to bring him into the league. As poetic justice would have, he goes back there and does a great job for them. Strange things happen."

ARGOS HEAD COACH DON MATTHEWS ON THE ORIGIN OF FLUTIEBALL:

"Somebody in the media asked before one of our games, 'How do you get Flutie prepared? What do you do to coach him?' I explained what we do. We put a menu of different football plays together and practise those during the week. From that menu, Doug Flutie selects a short list. It's his selection, things he feels comfortable with — things that he understands and feels good about — that he will call and then we just go out and play Flutieball. That just came out. Flutieball is his selection of his plays and his ad-libs. That's what I was referring to. Flutieball is his selections of short lists and when those things break down, he ad-libs to make it a positive play. To me it was just a descriptive term of how he plays the game."

DAVE SAPUNJIS (CALGARY TEAMMATE):

"In 1992, the first year we were together, our team went to Toronto for a football game, but it was postponed a day because of the World Series and Doug and I were like kids at the SkyDome. We were running around beforehand talking to some of the players on Atlanta.

"It was fun to see the baseball players who recognized Flutie and would talk to him, and here they are getting ready for their game in about three hours. Doug and I were running around the stadium collecting extra balls and saving them. It was like two kids having fun at their first baseball game.

"That kind of really highlights what Doug is all about: He loves sports so much and he knows how to have fun with sports. He will go out there and be like a kid on the football field. He'll go out to watch a baseball game or a hockey game and he'll watch it with the excitement of a seven-year-old watching his stars on the TV. That's something I really have never seen in other players I have played with. He loves sports, that's his life and he certainly knows how to have fun with it."

FROM DOUG:

ON BOB WOOLF DYING:

"When he passed away, it was a shock more than anything else because he was in great shape. He was playing tennis all the time. He liked to play pickup basketball and just fool around doing that stuff. It was kind of weird because I was up in Calgary at the time and as long as you're removed from the situation, it doesn't really hit home. It didn't really hit me until I got back in the Boston area and he wasn't there. To see his wife as upset as she was and the people around him, that's when it hit me. For me it was the loss of a friend, a confidant, someone I could complain to about things or ask advice. He was someone I could always turn to for appropriate advice on certain situations. I always looked at him as a father figure."

SUPERSTARS COMPETITIONS:

"Those were fun for me primarily because I was in the CFL and I had a chance to compete against NFL athletes. In the two years I did it, I finished ahead of all the NFL athletes. To them it probably wasn't a big deal. They were out there having fun and messing around. I always feel like I have something to prove. I'm always trying to outdo the guy next to me. I was happy that I got selected to compete in those competitions because it's a great honor and I was glad I fared well winning the basketball segment and finishing second in the cycling. To me, that's a big deal. I really enjoy that. It was a chance to go to Hawaii to spend a few days and compete and have fun. If I was there on vacation, that's what I'd want to be doing: playing basketball and competing against somebody else or having a race or doing whatever. I get very bored being on vacation and sitting around on the beach. It's not exactly my idea of a good time. My idea of a good time is competing. To be in that atmosphere — whether it's Hawaii or Cancún or whatever — makes it nicer."

MEETING CHRISTIE BRINKLEY:

"Laurie always idolized Christie Brinkley because she was attractive and was classy and wanted to be a mother. She named her daughter Alexa and Laurie really liked the name and decided if she had a girl she would name her Alexa. Christie's girl's name is Alexa Rae and ours is Alexa Dawn.

"We were at the Super Bowl game in Miami where the 49ers played Cincinnati. After the game I went into the locker room and was talking to Joe Montana, whose agent was also Bob Woolf, and Bill Romanowski, my former college teammate. I turned around and there was Huey Lewis in the room. We were all talking and I wasn't really looking up when a football was presented to me. Then this woman asked if I would sign it.

"I didn't really look up, I just started to sign it and then I noticed it was a Super Bowl football with the 49ers players signatures. I said, 'You don't want me to sign this. This is all 49ers guys.' She said, 'No, I really want you to sign it.' Then I did the double take and noticed it was Christie giving me the ball. I said, 'You're Christie Brinkley, aren't you?' She said 'yes.' I asked, 'are you sure you want me to sign this?' She replied, 'Yes.' I signed it and then asked her if she was going to be around a little while — Billy Joel, her husband at the time, had sung the national anthem. I ran out of the locker room to the concourse and got Laurie and pulled her right past security into the locker room. I don't think she'd ever been in a players' locker room before.

"There was kind of an entrance area where you didn't quite go into the locker room and Laurie met Christie and they talked for quite a while about their daughters and the names and all that stuff."

KNOWING JON BON JOVI:

"I got to know Scott McGhee, who was a wide receiver with the Houston Gamblers, when we merged with them. Scott's older brother Doc managed Bon Jovi. The first time I spent any time with Jon Bon Jovi was in Chicago with the Bears. He came to do a show, I gave him a jersey and he wore it on stage. After the show, I was hanging out with him and the guys, and we all played pickup basketball till about two or three in the morning in a hotel.

"We have gone to a prize fight at the Trump Plaza and have done a couple things together. Whenever I played a game where he was in the same city for a show, he'd come to the games. Whenever he's playing somewhere where I am, I make an effort to get to his gigs. It's kind of a mutual respect type of thing.

"In Boston they did a benefit show a couple years ago and I ended up playing with the band on stage. I usually call the day of the gig or the day before to let them know I'm coming and to put my name on the list. I called Margaret, his secretary, and she said, 'The guys have been waiting for you. Why don't you make it down to sound check around three-thirty, four o'clock?' I said, 'Okay, I'll meet them there around four o'clock.' I had the kids that day and couldn't get to the sound check, so I go there about half an hour before the show. As I walk in, Tico, the drummer, says, 'Doug, where were you earlier? We could have done something.' I said, 'Yeah, right, quit B.S.ing me.' I said hi to the other guys, and they were kind of teasing me the same way.

"I hadn't seen Jon and just before he went on stage, he said, "Where were you? We could have done something.' As he's walking on stage, he turns around and says, 'Got the guts to go cold turkey?' I just shook my head in disbelief. They started the show and about two or three songs into it I'm sitting on the side of the stage and Jon's doing a song, 'Keep The Faith,' where there's a guitar solo going on. He's got this maraca thing going and he looks over at me, takes the maracas, throws them to me and points to the microphone. I walk up and start doing the maraca thing. I figure this is pretty cool, I'm on stage with Bon

Jovi. But, I think this was my test to see what kind of rhythm I had. I kind of did my thing and it was cool. I had a blast and flipped them back to him.

"About four or five songs later in the middle of the show, Jon gets up to the mike and says, 'Why is it every jock wants to be a rock 'n' roll star and every rock 'n' roll star wants to be a jock? Please welcome Doug Flutie on drums.' I'm like, 'Oh my Lord.' I've got cowboy boots on and I don't like playing with them, so I'm pulling them off and throwing them down. I get on the drums and Tico's standing there and I say: 'Tico, don't go too far. Hang tight.'

"We did a Rolling Stones cover of 'Let It Bleed.' It was straight ahead, easy and not too complicated. I had trouble hearing what was going on, but that was probably the biggest rush I've ever had. In fact, the father of Richie Sanbora, the group's guitarist, was there with a home video camera. He got most of it on video and they sent me the tape, which I have at home.

"A lot of times entertainers will have an alias when they stay at hotels. They don't want to leave their legal names, obviously, because people will be calling them all the time. Jon used Jarvis Redwine, a one-time player from Nebraska, as his alias. I always liked the name, so whenever I need to use an alias, that's what I've used."